current

nursing

practice

Plastic Surgical and Burns Nursing

Plastic Surgical and Burns Nursing

J.V. Harvey Kemble MA(Cantab), FRCS(Eng)

Consultant Plastic Surgeon
St Bartholomew's Hospital, London, and
North East Thames Regional Plastic Surgery
and Burns Centre, St Andrew's Hospital
Billericay, Essex

Brenda E. Lamb SRN, ONC, DN(Lond)

Director of Nursing Services
St Andrew's and Mayflower Hospitals
Billericay, Essex

Baillière Tindall London Philadelphia Toronto
Mexico City Rio de Janeiro Sydney Tokyo Hong Kong

Baillière Tindall   1 St Anne's Road
Eastbourne, East Sussex BN21 3UN, England

West Washington Square
Philadelphia, PA 19105, U.S.A.

1 Goldthorne Avenue
Toronto, Ontario M8Z 5T9, Canada

Apartado 26370—Cedro 512
Mexico 4, D.F., Mexico

Rua Evaristo da Veiga, 55–20° andar
Rio de Janeiro — RJ, Brazil

ABP Australia Ltd, 44 Waterloo Road
North Ryde, N.S.W. 2064, Australia

Ichibancho Central Building, 22–1 Ichibancho
Chiyoda–Ku, Tokyo 102, Japan

Second Floor Unit 2, East Asia Commercial Centre
36–60 Texaco Road, Tsuen Wan N.T., Hong Kong

First published 1984

Typeset by Alan Sutton Publishing Ltd, Gloucester
Printed and bound in Great Britain by Wm Clowes Ltd, Beccles

British Library Cataloguing in Publication Data

Kemble, J.V. Harvey
  Plastic surgical and burns nursing.—(Current
  nursing practice)
  1. Surgery, Plastic   2. Nursing
  I. Title   II. Lamb, B.   III. Series
  617'.95   RD118

  ISBN 0-7020-1029-4

Contents

*Education is what survives when what
has been learned has been forgotten.*

B.F. Skinner, 'New Scientist', 21 May 1964

*Education never ends, Watson.
It is a series of lessons, with the greatest
for the last.*

Sir Arthur Conan Doyle (1859–1930)
'Adventures of the Red Circle'

Foreword

As explained in the first chapter of this book, Plastic Surgery developed into a specialty mainly from the experience gained in the Second World War. The progress in this field since then has been quite remarkable, and many techniques in reconstructive surgery have far exceeded those thought possible at that time, partly due to the introduction of microsurgery and also to the research programmes carried out to perfect the various types of flap repair.

As a result of this rapid growth few nursing books have been able to keep up with the specialty and many are now outdated. Miss Lamb and Mr Harvey Kemble have given a very clear description of the Plastic Surgery patient, the different needs of such patients and the difficult role that the nurse needs to play in order to get the best results from this type of surgery.

The authors' knowledge of new developments and techniques is great and they clearly express their understanding of the subject. This is enhanced by the book being planned in such a way that the nursing care can easily be extracted from the surgical procedure. I must congratulate Miss Lamb and Mr Harvey Kemble on their clarity, and it gives me great pleasure to recommend a book written by a surgeon and a nurse who have combined their wide experience to produce a teaching manual which will benefit not only those nurses specialising in Plastic Surgery but also nursing and medical students in training.

Joyce Harvey SRN, SCM
The British Association of Plastic Surgery Nurses

Preface

'To study the phenomena of disease without books is to sail an uncharted sea, while to study books without patients is not to go to sea at all.'

Sir William Osler's[1] quotation is particularly relevant for the thinking practising nurse.

The enormous interest in Plastic and Reconstructive Surgery in the last 20 years, as evidenced by the increase in the number of post-basic courses, the success and enthusiasm of professional medical and nursing associations and the frequent reporting by the media of Plastic Surgical procedures, has placed a considerable burden on teachers trying to keep pace with the rapid advances in the specialty.

The nursing techniques developed for Plastic and Reconstructive Surgery are now recognised as being relevant also to most other surgical disciplines, so that the 'generalist nurse' has much to gain by studying these procedures.

This book aims to satisfy two objectives. Firstly, it seeks to give the generalist nurse in a district hospital a means by which she can provide more than adequate care for her patients when faced with a problem she may not have met before, whether she is working in the Casualty Department, an orthopaedic ward or a general surgical ward. Secondly, for the nurse already well practised in the specialty of Plastic, Reconstructive and Burns Surgery and for the post-registration student on a Plastic Surgical course, it aims to provide an explanation and a rationale for her nursing skills to satisfy her search for further education.

[1] William Osler, 1849–1919. 'Father of American Medicine'. Physician, Baltimore, USA and Oxford.

Acknowledgements

We are indebted to many people who have in one way or another contributed to this book.

The Departments of Medical Illustration of St Bartholomew's Hospital and Basildon and Thurrock District have reproduced the photographs with care and expertise. The drawings are the handiwork of Mr Kevin Marks, who has gone to considerable trouble to portray the essential points. Our colleagues, including Miss Queenie Jackson, have, unknowingly, inevitably influenced for the better the way in which the book has been presented.

Miss Janina Morris, BSc, DipLib, and the staff of St Bartholomew's Hospital Medical Library have unearthed details about our medical forbears whose names have become part of our daily vocabulary.

Brenda Camper, Jean Green, Sandra Nunn and Joan Saunders have toiled to type the manuscript into intelligibility.

We wish also to thank Rosemary Long, Nursing Editor of Baillière Tindall, for her valuable advice and assistance.

The patients we have treated will know whether or not their treatment has been successful, but individually and collectively they have influenced us in whether to persist with or to modify a technique, or even to discard it in favour of another. The distillation of these influences we present in this book in the hope that it will be of help to our readers in caring for those patients who trustingly put themselves into our hands.

J.V. Harvey Kemble   *April 1983*
Brenda E. Lamb

1 Plastic Surgical Nursing

The Plastic Surgery specialty first received wide publicity during and immediately after the Second World War. This came about largely as a result of the high number of burn injuries sustained by airmen. With the advent of both blood transfusion and penicillin at this time, many men survived despite severe injuries. These were mostly young, otherwise fit men, whose most severe burn injuries were to their faces and hands, the rest of their bodies having been fairly well protected by their flying suits. Therefore many of these young men required very extensive reconstructive surgery. This helped to establish the need for Plastic Surgery specialists. The fact that so many young men were left disfigured, even after prolonged surgery, attracted considerable publicity.

The Plastic Surgery specialty became a part of the National Health Service at its inception in 1948. The word 'plastic' is derived from the Greek 'plastikos', meaning 'mould' or 'contour', so the term 'Plastic Surgery' means the reconstruction of contour. This can be the reconstruction of skin, muscle, tendon, nerve or bone in any part of the body.

Misconceptions about Plastic Surgery

Unfortunately the word 'plastic' can lead to misunderstandings. Some patients still arrive in Plastic Surgical Units believing their wounds will be 'magically' healed by some sort of plastic skin. Permanent closure of any skin defect can be achieved only by using the patient's own skin. Wound closure by Plastic Surgical techniques involves the use of either grafts or flaps.

Another common misunderstanding is that Plastic Surgery can remove scars. Wherever there has been an injury or surgery to the skin, there will be residual scarring. Plastic Surgery may improve or camouflage scars, but cannot remove them. The nurse will more effectively reassure the patient who has recently sustained an injury which results in unsightly scars by telling him that the scars can be *improved* (though not removed) by Plastic Surgery.

Explaining the limitations of Plastic Surgical techniques is time-consuming and sometimes difficult, as the general public tend to confuse fact with fiction where Plastic Surgery is concerned. There are many factors which restrict the amount of improvement or change which can be achieved in a person's appearance. For example, when a large segment of the face has been destroyed, reconstructive surgery can provide only a repair, which will not have an appearance equal to the original.

Attitudes towards disfigurement

The attitudes of the nurse, the patient, his family, and the general public all play an important part in the eventual rehabilitation of the disfigured patient.

Facial disfigurement is so obviously a great social handicap that much attention is given to this aspect of Plastic Surgery. However, it is almost as difficult to hide the hands as it is to hide the face. Severe scarring on any part of the body can be very distressing to the patient and his family. The Plastic Surgical nurse learns to be no less sympathetic just because the scarring can be covered by clothing.

To most people their 'body image' is psychologically important. Teaching the patient and his family to live with his disfigurement is an important part of Plastic Surgical nursing. The Plastic Surgical nurse learns to accept the severely disfigured patient, and to see him as a person with a future which holds an acceptable quality of life. She learns how to help the patient to retain his identity, his role in the family, and his social status. The very nature of the nurse's work tends to make her become so orientated to treating the patient's body or mind that she may need to make a conscious effort to regard the patient as a whole person.

Disfigurement may cause the patient to be socially disabled, but scars alone do not make the person physically disabled. In fact the person with a severely scarred face is less disabled than someone with an artificial limb; however, such patients often have more difficulty in finding suitable employment. It is an important part of the nurse's role to educate the general public about disfigurement and to try to modify their adverse reaction to disfigured people.

At the first meeting, a patient who is facially disfigured will become self-conscious if the nurse looks away from the disfigurement. A common complaint from such patients is 'Why do people look, then look away, trying to pretend it isn't there?' The patient knows he is an oddity and it is aggravating when this fact is not acknowledged. Once the nurse looks at the disfigured face, and satisfies her own curiosity, she finds within a few minutes she can continue a normal conversation with the person. Initially the nurse can ask the patient what happened to his face and as the conversation progresses she discovers that she no longer notices the disfigurement but is merely looking for facial expressions. One subconsciously seeks facial expression in day to day contact with people. If no facial expression is possible, then the nurse seeks expression in the voice, or by watching the hands and other 'body language'.

The Plastic Surgical patient

Loss of body image often results in loss of identity. The first step towards teaching the patient a sense of identity is for the nurse to show that she sees him as a person with his own attitudes, characteristics and expectations. The nurse stimulates him to express his personality by encouraging him to state his views on any subject he cares to discuss. The nurse similarly expresses her own views in order to establish a common understanding between herself and the patient. The patient's situation within his family is an important part of his identity, so by encouraging him to talk about his family, the nurse will help him to identify himself as a son, husband or father.

A person's first name is one of the earliest facts committed to memory and it therefore becomes an important part of his identity. Use of first names by both the patient and the nurse may help in re-establishing his identity. First names are commonly used in the Plastic Surgery Unit, but this is by mutual consent, and not automatic assumption.

The clothing a person chooses to wear is a reflection of his personality. Therefore, encouraging the patient to wear his own clothing as soon as possible is an important part of rehabilitation. The fact that the patient cannot get out of bed does not prevent him from wearing his normal clothing. The convalescent patient is encouraged to lie on top of his bed fully clothed during the day-time. Patients who do this often remark that it is pleasant to get into a 'fresh' bed at night.

As soon as the patient is able, he is encouraged to go out into the hospital grounds, preferably with a relative or friend, so that he may first meet the general public whilst remaining in the sheltered atmosphere of the hospital. When the patient returns to the ward the nurse gives him the opportunity to discuss his reactions to meeting the public. It is not wise to suggest to the patient that he needs counselling, as to do so may encourage him to assume that he should, whether the need is there or not. If the patient finds it difficult to discuss his feelings, the nurse learns to ask the right question at the appropriate moment. This means that she does not rush into a counselling session when she first recognises the need for counselling, but waits for the right psychological moment. This may take many days or weeks.

Before his discharge from hospital the patient is encouraged to go out of the hospital for a few hours, accompanied by a relative or another patient. This enables him to experience the reactions he will encounter when he goes home. Many different reasons can be found for the patient to make a visit outside the hospital; the favourite amongst male patients is a visit to the local pub. After such visits the patient is given an opportunity to discuss his feelings.

Patients who have suffered severe disfigurement often undergo a period of grieving for their lost body image, passing through all the stages of grief that follow a bereavement. Some of this psychological trauma may not become evident until he has been discharged from hospital. Therefore, before his discharge the patient and his family are instructed to come to the hospital or telephone the ward for advice if necessary.

At what point the patient is allowed to see his injuries is a controversial subject; generally the earlier he sees all, the better he will accept his problems. If the patient sees his wound at its worst, when he sees the final scarring he tends to see only improvement. It is surprising how often a patient will look at terrible scarring and merely remark on how much it has improved.

Many Plastic Surgical procedures are carried out on children. For the general care of the child in hospital the reader is referred to *Paediatric Nursing* (sixth edition) in the Nurses' Aids Series by B.F. Weller & S. Barlow (Baillière Tindall, 1983).

The Plastic Surgical nurse

To recognise and understand the personality of her patient and his reaction to the attitudes of other people, the nurse must first understand her own personality and her attitude towards her patients.

The nurse may become so accustomed to wearing a uniform and enacting a role which fits the public image of a nurse that, when she is on duty, she tends to lose sight of her own personality. When a nurse starts to work in mufti she finds herself in a similar, although much less disturbing, situation to that of the patient who discovers he no longer occupies the body image he has grown accustomed to. As the nurse gains experience in caring for the disfigured patient, she learns to project her own personality despite the fact that she is wearing a uniform. This provides an example to the patient of how he can project his personality despite his appearance. Nurses working in Plastic Surgical and Burns Units are often thought to have strong personalities. Whilst it may be true that such people find it easier to adapt to the specialty, this generalisation has arisen largely because Plastic Surgical nurses learn to show their personalities. Patients represent every type of personality, so to provide a nurse able to relate to each patient requires many different types of personality among the nurses.

In order to establish a working relationship between herself and the patient the nurse must talk to the patient, as well as listen to him. By taking an interest in his family and establishing a working relationship with them, the nurse learns to recognise the patient's identity within his family.

When there is difficulty in helping the patient to see that it is personality that matters, rather than the image one presents, it may be helpful for the patient to see the nurses wearing mufti. Therefore when staff social functions are taking place at the hospital, the nurses visit the ward before attending the function. This is done tactfully by making the ward the meeting point for a group of nurses. Patients often comment that such visits encourage them to see 'people' rather than 'nurses'. This provides the nurse with a cue to talk to the patient about body image.

PLANNED PATIENT CARE

Many admissions to Plastic Surgical wards are planned, so it is possible to pre-arrange the nursing team that will undertake the patient's care.

Plastic Surgical patients often have to spend long spells in hospital, and many more have to return for repeated short admissions over the course of many years. Continuity of care is very important for such patients, but is difficult to achieve because of the time span between admissions. When it is known that a patient previously related very well to a particular nurse, she is notified of his impending re-admission, even if she no longer works on that ward, so she can visit the patient and help to introduce him to the new staff.

When a patient is to be admitted for major surgery requiring intensive nursing care, those nurses who will 'special' him will, if possible, be called to see him in the Out-Patients Department at his first attendance. If this is not possible the nurses concerned will be involved in his care from the moment he is admitted to hospital.

If a patient is due to have surgery which will leave him disfigured, it is important to learn as much as possible about the patient's personality, family and social background before he undergoes surgery. The patient's appearance after surgery is carefully explained to the patient and his family before his operation. If the patient or his relatives are very apprehensive about the outcome of his surgery, it may be helpful to ask an ex-patient who has undergone similar surgery, and who is emotionally stable, to visit the patient or his relatives before his operation.

The patient's discharge is planned from the moment he is admitted to hospital, so any adaptions to his home, or to the attitude of his family and friends, can be arranged during the course of his admission.

Visiting times for Plastic Surgical wards

'Open' visiting is ideal for the Plastic Surgical ward, and generally presents no problems to the smooth running of the ward.

Since Plastic Surgical Centres serve a large area, the patient's visitors often have a long journey to the hospital. This may mean their visits are infrequent but prolonged. If a patient is unfit for lengthy visits, his relatives are advised to leave him for periods of rest, so that he may enjoy a number of short visits during the course of the day. The high cost of travelling to the hospital may mean that several visitors may travel in one car, and this should not be discouraged.

There are seldom large numbers of visitors on the ward at any one time, so it is usually unnecessary to restrict the number of visitors allowed to each patient.

Child visitors

Patients may worry about the reactions of children to their disfigurement. In fact, very young children cope with the situation better than adults. Children who are too young to have learned tact usually go straight up to such people and stare, or even ask outright what happened to them. Once they have satisfied their curiosity, children quickly lose interest in the peculiarity and then behave normally towards the patient. This is a great morale booster to a very self-conscious patient. For this reason child visitors to a Plastic Surgical ward are not discouraged.

The patient should be prepared for such reactions from children, and the parents counselled before the visit. If the child is old enough, the nurse explains, in terms that he can understand, that he will not see anything frightening.

Management of the Plastic Surgical ward

The working environment on a Plastic Surgical ward is carefully contrived to appear friendly and easy going. This provides the best atmosphere for encouraging close nurse–patient relationships, which will enable the patient to receive the counselling he may require. Patients, relatives or ex-patients may telephone or arrive for counselling at any time. It is important to make them feel welcome, no matter how inconvenient the timing of their visit may be. Maintaining discipline and a high professional standard and generally managing a ward with this apparently free and easy atmosphere requires stronger leadership and firmer control than on a ward where there are set rules and a clear-cut definition of the nurse's role.

Close liaison between the surgeon and the nurse in charge of the ward is essential if each patient is to receive adequately planned nursing care. The optimum time for some Plastic Surgical patients to be admitted to hospital may depend as much on the nursing time available as on his condition, the surgeon's time and the operating time available. When working out the nurses' off-duty rota, the Ward Sister needs to take into account the impending admissions to the ward and the planned date for their surgery. This enables her to plan the nursing team when special requirements are known to her prior to the patient's admission.

The position of the patient's bed within the ward requires careful consideration, taking into account his appearance and the company of other patients around him. Those patients who need frequent observations or treatment (for example to a graft or flap) are positioned so they can be seen clearly from the nursing station. It should be remembered that it is as important for the night staff as it is for the day staff that the patient's wound can be easily seen. Mirrors are strategically placed on the ward so that the patient may see his injuries at an early stage in his treatment.

Many of the patients who are admitted to a Plastic Surgical ward have infected wounds. The nurse in charge of the ward must understand which infections require barrier nursing; for example, infection with some groups of β-haemolytic *Streptococcus* may destroy skin grafts. To prevent cross-infection, wounds should be dressed in a dressing room which has positive pressure ventilation and a doorway wide enough to permit easy access for patients who are confined to bed. Beds should be of the type that wheel easily from the ward to the dressing room, and which can be adjusted to a variable height to enable the nurse to stand or sit comfortably when she is carrying out wound care.

Wound care in Plastic Surgery may take from a few minutes to a few hours. It is important to take a patient to the dressing room for his wound toilet, whether the procedure takes a few minutes or much longer. When carrying out a lengthy dressing procedure the nurse sits comfortably, with her arms supported, so that fatigue does not cause her to hurry or become clumsy. When the nurse becomes aware she is suffering from fatigue she should request a colleague to take over until she can continue. There is often a tendency for the nurse to want to complete the task she has started, but this is not in the patient's best interest. All staff working on the ward must be aware of the delicate nature of some wound care, so that they do not accidentally disturb a nurse who is carrying out a delicate procedure. This is particularly important when the nurse is behind curtains or screens.

Long periods spent on wound care present very good opportunities for counselling the patient. All staff should be aware of this and try not to interrupt when counselling is taking place.

All the nurses on the ward must learn that inter-personal relationships are very complex, and the fact that a patient chooses to talk over his problems with one particular nurse is not a reflection on the counselling ability of the other nurses. Providing a patient with emotional support is very tiring, and the nurse herself will often require emotional support from her colleagues.

2 Wound healing and infection

'I dressed him, but God healed him.'
Ambroise Paré, 1517–1590. French Surgeon.

Wound care should both aid the natural healing process and prevent further tissue damage, for example by infection. Wound healing time may be considerably reduced by careful wound care. In order to assist wound healing, the nurse must clearly understand the healing processes at each stage of wound repair.

WOUND REPAIR

Injury to living tissue triggers a series of biological reactions which usually result eventually in wound healing. Although the process is a continuous one, it can conveniently be divided into phases, while remembering that the phases overlap and may be occurring simultaneously in different parts of the wound. From the moment of injury in clean wounds, closed without delay, healing by first intention occurs.

Healing by first intention

1. There is initially an outpouring into the injured area of plasma, polymorphonuclear leucocytes, lymphocytes, macrophages and enzymes. Dead and injured cells and foreign material such as bacteria are engulfed by the macrophages and polymorphs. Lymphocytes react with foreign material antigens which leads to the synthesis of antibodies and excretion of a protein known as lymphokine. This protein attracts the scavenging cells. Under the control of enzymes, the plasma proteins undergo changes providing a network of fibrin in which the repair process begins.

2. *Regeneration*. Within 24 hours of wounding, the cells surrounding the wound begin to close it by:

(a) *Migration*. Epithelial cells become flatter in shape and slide one over the next towards the centre of the wound.

(b) *Proliferation*. Epithelial cells divide and reform the layers of the skin. Such regeneration of epithelium occurs more quickly in a moist environment with high oxygen tension than in a dry wound. Cells of the walls of capillaries adjacent to the wound migrate and proliferate to form new 'vascular sprouts'; these develop a central lumen and begin to conduct blood. Lymph channels form in the same way, but do not connect with the blood capillaries.

3. *Repair.* Within 4 or 5 days after wounding, fibroblast cells derived from the dermis and around blood vessels begin to produce fibres of reticulin, which are later converted into scar collagen. These collagen fibres give strength to the wound, which reaches pre-wound levels by about 14 to 28 days. The cleaner the wound and the more closely the edges are approximated, the smaller the amount of scar collagen formed.

NURSING CARE

- Since one of the first natural processes is the removal of all foreign material and dead tissue, the primary treatment of the wound will be aimed at the total removal of such debris. This reduces the time taken by the white blood cells to 'clean' the wound.

- Within 24 hours, epithelial cells begin migrating towards the centre of the wound and cells of the skin, blood vessels and lymph vessels divide to reform the damaged tissues (proliferation). Dressings must be removed carefully and the wound cleaned gently so that these delicate cells are not damaged.

- The shearing effect of dressings moving over the wound damages new cells. Dressings should either be totally non-adherent or firmly adherent and held in place by firm bandaging. If the wound is so positioned that this is difficult to achieve, it may be preferable to leave the wound exposed.

- If the wound is left exposed, the patient is instructed to keep the wound clean by washing with a bland soap and water.

- It takes 14 to 28 days for scar collagen to strengthen the wound to pre-wound levels. During this period the wound may be supported with a firm bandage or Steristrip.

- Whenever practical, oedema of the injured area can be prevented by elevation of the wound above the level of the heart. Oedema interferes with the microcirculation and may increase the quantity of scar tissue.

Healing by second intention

Healing of an open wound in which there is a large area of tissue loss, or of a wound which is significantly infected, occurs by the formation of granulation tissue. Granulation tissue consists of fibrous tissue and small blood vessels, and continues to develop until covered by epithelial cells. If this cover is delayed by infection or the large size of the wound, it may become heaped up or 'over-granulated'.

Healing by second intention differs from that by first intention in the greater quantity of vascular sprouts and collagen growing from the bed at the base of the wound. These capillary sprouts provide a surface onto which epithelial cells from the edges of the wound, and from the sebaceous glands deep in the dermis of the skin, can spread over the wound.

Wounds healing by second intention undergo contraction, in part due to myofibroblast cells in the granulation tissue which actively shorten, pulling in the wound edges. This contraction is reduced if the wound is skin grafted, but wound contraction works to assist the surgeon by making a defect smaller. Small wounds may eventually close completely by wound contraction.

Granulating wounds which fail to gain an epithelial cell cover over many years may become sites of squamous cell or basal cell carcinoma in the wound edges (Marjolin's[1] ulcer).

NURSING CARE
- Wound care is aimed at promoting the growth of healthy granulation tissue. All foreign material and dead tissue must be removed before this can be achieved.
- For wounds in which the areas of dead tissue (slough) are initially not clearly defined, daily debridement will be necessary until all sloughing has ceased.
- Debridement of a wound can be carried out without anaesthesia. Since the tissue being removed is dead, and therefore contains no viable nerve endings, it can be cut without pain. However, it may be painful if lifting and cutting the slough pulls on the healthy surrounding tissues. Nitrous oxide, administered as 'gas and air' (Entonox), is an effective analgesic for

[1] Jean Marjolin, 1780–1850. Surgeon, Paris.

this type of procedure. When the appearance of the wound is frightening for the patient 'gas and air' will also help reduce his anxiety. The fact that the patient remains conscious and able to see the wound assists him to become accustomed to its appearance. The patient can tell the nurse when he feels discomfort, and this can be used as an indication of which areas of the wound are not dead, and should not be removed.

- Prevention of infection by good basic hygiene and aseptic technique is an essential part of any wound care.
- Frequent and careful observation of the wound and dressings enables early detection of infection, allowing treatment to be initiated before serious damage has occurred.
- Certain types of infection prevent or retard the production of healthy granulation tissue, for example *Streptococcus haemolyticus* or *Pseudomonas aeruginosa*. Wound swabs are sent for culture every few days to ensure prompt identification and treatment of significant infection.
- Over-granulation is prevented either by trimming off the excess granulation with scissors, or by use of topical applications such as silver nitrate or steroids.
- When healthy granulations cover the wound surface, the wound may be closed by skin grafting.
- The natural healing process of wound contraction considerably reduces the size of a wound. Provided contraction does not interfere with function, it may be desirable to encourage contraction before attempting surgical closure. This may be aided by leaving the wound exposed for periods of a few hours each day.
- If the wound constitutes a cavity which requires 'packing' with dressings, the packing is applied loosely. This allows free drainage of exudate from the base of the wound. Direct pressure on the wound retards the growth of granulation tissue.
- Since bone cell nourishment relies on an intact periosteum, exposed periosteum must be kept moist and free from infection or chemicals liable to cause necrosis. Chlorhexidine tulle (Bactigras) covered with saline soaks is a suitable dressing for periosteum.
- Where periosteum is damaged so that bare bone is exposed, bone necrosis can only be prevented by surgical intervention

to cover the bone with healthy tissue.

- If bone cover cannot be achieved, wound care must be directed towards keeping necrosis to a minimum by elimination of infection. Cortical bone cells will support granulation tissue, so one way of producing cover for bare cortical bone is to drill burr holes into the medulla, which allows the cancellous bone cells to produce granulation tissue. Over the course of a few months, this protrudes through the burr holes and 'mushrooms' out over the cortical bone. Eventually these sprouts of granulation tissue meet, giving a complete cover of granulation over the bone. The granulation tissue can then be covered with split skin grafts to produce wound closure. During the waiting period, all sequestra must be removed as they form, and daily dressings with Eusol (Edinburgh University Solution Of Lime) and paraffin assist in debridement and keeping the wound 'clean'. Sequestrum acts as a foreign body, and the wound will not close completely until all sequestra have been removed.

WOUND CARE

The management of wounds differs to some extent according to the mechanism by which injury was sustained. Wound injuries may be divided as follows:

1. Clean incised wounds, such as those made by a scalpel or knife.

2. Crush injuries, for example under a power press.

3. Avulsion and degloving injuries, for example degloving of skin under the tyre of a moving vehicle or avulsion of the skin of a finger when a ring gets caught in moving machinery.

4. Sustained pressure injuries, such as pressure sores.

Clean incised wounds

Clean incised wounds require exploration to ensure there is no buried foreign body, and early suture with an appropriate material before the wound becomes infected. This is 'primary suture' and should take place within 12 hours of the injury. Longer delay is likely to permit entry of infection. It is important to ensure that blood clot is removed and that there is no 'dead space' in the bottom of the wound where infection or clot could remain. To this end, deep sutures of an absorbable material are inserted, but the number of such sutures is kept to a minimum as, by their nature, they produce a slight inflammatory reaction.

Sutures in the skin are made of non-absorbable material, such as silk or nylon, on a cutting needle. They are inserted under minimal tension and removed as soon as the wound edges are sound. This occurs within 2 to 5 days in the face and about 7 to 10 days in the abdomen and limbs. On the back, or where poor healing is anticipated, sutures remain for 12 to 14 days. Suturing under tension and prolonged delay in stitch removal lead to 'stitch marks' in the skin alongside the scar (Fig. 1).

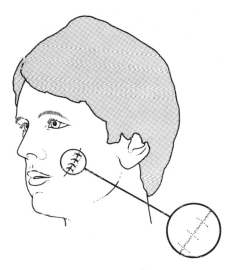

Fig. 1. *Sutures inserted under tension or not removed early leave permanent cross-striations in the scar.*

When it is necessary to leave stitches in the skin for longer periods because of the likelihood of slow healing, a continuous intradermal suture may be used, which leaves no marks.

Suture removal

For this procedure good light and fine instruments are necessary.

The patient's confidence is gained by unhurried purposeful movements and reassurance. The nurse's wrist and forearm are supported on the bed or the patient's body.

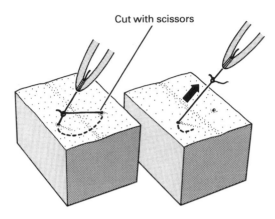

Cut with scissors

Fig. 2. *Removing an interrupted suture.*

Technique for interrupted sutures (Fig. 2):

(a) The wound is cleaned with cetrimide to remove old blood clot and skin debris.

(b) The knot is picked up with toothed metal Gillies'[2] forceps.

(c) The suture on the side of the wound opposite to the knot is cut with fine pointed scissors, or a suture-removing blade, flush with the skin.

(d) The knot is moved over to the side of the wound on which the suture was cut, pulling the suture out of the skin in the process.

Technique for continuous intradermal sutures (Fig. 3):

(a) The wound is cleaned with cetrimide to remove old blood clot and skin debris.

(b) The suture is cut with scissors at one end of the wound, leaving about 2.5 cm (1 in) showing above the skin. (Any of the

---

[2] Sir Harold Gillies, 1882–1960. Plastic Surgeon, Roehampton, London. He set up the first Plastic Surgery Unit in England in 1917 at Sidcup, Kent, for casualties of the First World War.

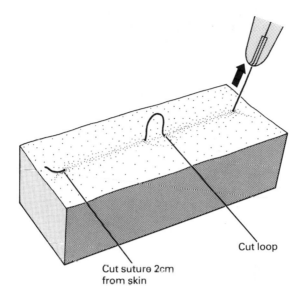

Fig. 3. *Removing a continuous intradermal suture, in two parts.*

suture which has been brought out as a loop onto the surface part-way along the wound is also cut.)

(c) A Spencer Wells[3] artery forceps is clamped to the long end of the suture at the end of the wound.

(d) Firm continuous traction is applied by pulling on the forceps for a period of a half to one minute, in the long axis of the wound. The suture will be felt to 'give', and can then be pulled out.

NURSING CARE

- The type of dressing applied should be appropriate to the individual wound.
- Epithelium regenerates most efficiently in a moist warm atmosphere. Therefore, for superficial skin wounds, saline soaks on paraffin gauze dressings aid the natural healing process.
- For deeper wounds, healthy granulation tissue is required to

[3] Sir T. Spencer Wells, 1818–1897. Gynaecologist, London.

fill the defect. This process is retarded by the presence of necrotic tissue and infection. Daily debridement and dressing with an antiseptic and de-sloughing agent such as Eusol and paraffin speeds the elimination of dead tissue and infection, and therefore allows rapid formation of the granulation tissue required.

- The warm moist atmosphere provided by the dressing encourages bacterial growth as well as new cell growth. Dead tissue or stale blood are ideal media for bacteria to grow on.

- If a dressing is left intact for a few days it should be inspected daily for signs of infection. If the patient is treated as an out-patient, teach him to inspect the dressings himself, and ensure that he understands the importance of reporting for a change of dressing at the first sign of infection.

- The topical use of antibiotics such as neomycin or fusidic acid impregnated in paraffin gauze (Sofra-Tulle and Fucidin Tulle) can be very useful, but must be used with caution since skin sensitivity and rashes often occur.

- Antibiotic-resistant bacteria are an ever-increasing problem. The indiscriminate use of antibiotics in hospitals, especially their topical use, produces multi-resistant bacteria, particularly in the staphylococci group. Therefore, topical antibiotics should only be used prophylactically in exceptional circumstances. Otherwise their use is confined to specific infections in which the wound swab culture has proved the presence of bacteria which are sensitive to the particular antibiotic used.

Crush injuries

Crush injuries produce a significant amount of tissue death. It is necessary to excise all dead and dying tissue by debridement and to trim the wound edge to well-vascularised skin which can then be sutured. In all road accident wounds it is important to remove all road dirt before suturing, as this becomes extremely difficult to remove once the wound has healed.

In severe, dirty crush injuries, and with high-velocity bullet wounds, it may be preferable to leave the wound unsutured and to apply a dressing of tulle gras impregnated with an antiseptic such as chlorhexidine (Bactigras tulle), changing this until the wound is clean enough to permit a 'secondary suture'.

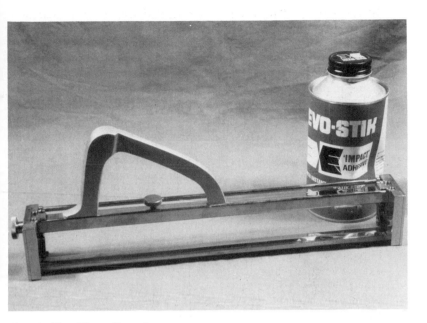

Fig. 4. *The Gibson–Ross dermatome.*

Avulsion and degloving injuries (see page 179)

When skin is rolled off a leg by a skidding tyre, it is usually not viable because of loss of its blood supply. However, it may be possible to use the degloved skin as a partial-thickness skin graft, applied to a carefully debrided fat, fascia or muscle bed. The graft is taken from the degloved skin using a Gibson–Ross[4] dermatome (Fig. 4). Avulsed digits are not usually suitable for microvascular replantation because of the severity of the tissue damage.

INTERFERENCE WITH HEALING

The process of healing is compromised by both internal and external factors:

[4] Tom Gibson, Plastic Surgeon, Glasgow; D.S. Ross, Bioengineer, Glasgow.

Internal factors

1. *Infection*, particularly *Streptococcus haemolyticus*, which lyses migrating epithelium.

2. *Poor vascularisation*, for example due to arteriosclerosis or diabetes mellitus.

3. *Poor nutrition*, especially vitamin C deficiency and low protein states, as in extensive burn injuries.

4. *Genetic factors*. Patients with an inherited disease, xeroderma pigmentosum, cannot repair skin damage from solar radiation and so develop multiple skin cancers.

5. *Corticosteroid therapy* reduces the inflammatory response and delays the formation of collagen.

External factors

1. *Excessive mobility*. While a small degree of movement between bone ends appears to enhance healing, an excessive amount prevents callus formation. Similarly, shearing of new capillaries growing into a skin graft from its bed will prevent grafts from being revascularised.

2. *Interposition of substance between the healing parts*. The presence of blood clot between a skin graft and its bed may prevent capillaries from the bed reaching the graft before it dies. However, blood clot between bone ends, each of which is individually vascularised, provides the scaffolding into which callus can extend. Muscle interposed between bone ends results in delayed union or non-union of a fracture.

3. *Irradiation* reduces the ability of cells to multiply, and produces thrombosis of blood vessels. The resultant scars therefore have poor blood supplies, tend to ulcerate and are slow to heal.

INFECTION

The presence of organisms in a wound does not necessarily lead to a delay in healing, but the degree of inflammation, swelling and wound exudate, and consequently of scar, increases in the presence of organisms.

Whereas staphylococcal infections tend to be localised, producing pus in abscesses, streptococci release an enzyme – hyaluronidase – which permits them to permeate easily through tissue, setting up the widespread pink flush of cellulitis and lymphangitis. Fortunately, most streptococci are penicillin-sensitive. Staphylococci are harboured asymptomatically in the noses and throats of carriers, and are spread from them to wounds. Streptococci reside in the mouth, intestinal tract and perineum, where they are normally asymptomatic.

Pseudomonas aeruginosa has a low capacity to invade tissue, but produces copious amounts of pus, often green, which is responsible for disrupting wounds and lifting off skin grafts. *Pseudomonas* is often carried as a harmless commensal organism in the bowel, so that a patient may infect himself from his faeces.

Anaerobes, organisms which flourish in poorly-oxygenated tissue such as necrotic debris, blood clot or devascularised muscle or skin, produce a characteristic fetid odour and will not be expunged until the involved tissue has been removed. Clostridia are foremost in this group, although some staphylococci act together to produce such anaerobic infection. Since these organisms do not multiply in the presence of oxygen, suspicion of their presence is reported to the microbiologist so that the culture plates can be incubated oxygen-free.

NURSING CARE

- Early detection and treatment of infection can only be achieved by frequent and careful observation of the wound. Experience in detecting the normal appearance of the various tissues of the body when they are damaged or exposed enables early recognition of abnormal appearances which indicate infection. As experience grows, the specific signs of different types of infection may be detected.

- The typical appearance of *Pseudomonas aeruginosa* infection, the copious exudate it creates, the greenish staining of the dressings by the pus it produces, and the characteristic smell make it very easy to recognise.

- A wound infected with *Streptococcus haemolyticus* also has a typical appearance, but one which is less obvious and therefore often missed. The wound appears slightly more pink or reddish, almost flushed. In the early stages the granulation tissue looks very clean and there is no characteristic smell. In a wound which has previously looked 'dirty', this appearance may initially be mistaken for improvement of the wound. One way of checking visually for this type of infection is to dry the wound thoroughly with a blow-dryer. A wound infected with *Streptococcus haemolyticus* dries with a 'glaze' over it, rather like the appearance of dried egg white. As the infection progresses, the damage caused to the surrounding epithelium becomes more obvious, and the size of the defect increases.

- Staphylococcal infection produces pus, which is usually yellowish in appearance and has a characteristic smell. The appearance of the wound is less significant. Initially there may only be a lack of improvement, and only when the infection is well established will evidence of further tissue damage become noticeable.

- Gas gangrene (*Clostridium welchii*[5]) is very readily detected by the strong and very typical smell, and the obvious necrosis occurring in the wound.

- Wound swabs are sent for culture and sensitivity whenever infection is suspected, so that an antibiotic to which the infective organism is sensitive can be prescribed.

- Whilst waiting for wound swab results, treatment is begun by applying a dressing suitable to the type of infection suspected. Flamazine, for example, will kill many bacteria.

- *Pseudomonas aeruginosa* cannot live without moisture so the most effective treatment for this kind of infection is dehydration, i.e. by drying the wound with a blow-dryer. If possible, the wound is left exposed and the blow-drying repeated as often as is necessary to keep it completely dry. Continuing this treatment for 24 to 48 hours will usually clear a wound of even a heavy contamination of *Pseudomonas*. If exposure is impossible, dressings soaked in 0.5% acetic acid are effective, although this will take longer to clear the wound of infection than simple dehydration.

- Bactigras is very effective against staphylococcus infection.

- Gas gangrene requires treatment to excise all dead tissue, by amputation if necessary. (See also 'Hyperbaric oxygen' in Glossary.)

[5] William Welch, 1850–1934. Professor of Pathology, Baltimore, USA.

- If the infection is liable to cause very serious damage, such as osteomyelitis, or is life-threatening, as when accompanied by septicaemia, then an antibiotic will be prescribed immediately, without waiting for swab results. The antibiotic prescribed depends on the type of infection suggested by the appearance of the wound.

- *Streptococcus haemolyticus* is usually sensitive to penicillin and erythromycin. *Staphylococcus* is usually insensitive to penicillin but sensitive to cloxacillin, erythromycin and fusidic acid. *Pseudomonas aeruginosa* is usually sensitive to gentamicin. Gas gangrene is usually sensitive to penicillin, which will be given in large doses immediately this type of infection is suspected.

- Some infected wounds may be little affected by the administration of systemic antibiotics. In a leg ulcer which has occurred because of poor circulation, the lack of an adequate blood supply to the wound results in very little of the antibiotic actually reaching the infected area, so that even when given in high doses, systemic antibiotic therapy is ineffective. This type of wound infection can only be eradicated by dressings.

Spread of infection

Organisms are passed from one individual to another by:

1. *Physical contact*: infected hands or finger nails on open wounds.
2. *Fomites*: clothing, eating utensils, ward baths.
3. *Air*: water droplets sneezed or breathed out, dust from infected hair shaken over a wound or inhaled by a susceptible patient.
4. *Food*: for example dysentery.
5. *Insects*: carriers such as flies and mosquitos.

Barriers to invasion of the body by organisms are provided by:

1. *Mechanical factors*: intact keratin layers of the skin and mucosa of the mouth, nose and throat. Ulceration therefore provides a portal of entry for organisms.
2. *Glandular secretions*: the acidity of sweat and the fatty acids from sebaceous glands are bactericidal.
3. *Flow of secretions*: the flow of mucus upwards from the

bronchioles to the trachea under the action of specialised cells with hairy cilia, or of urine down the urethra from the bladder, helps to keep organisms away from internal organs. Interference with this flow, such as influenza (which paralyses the cilia) or a urethral catheter, puts this defence mechanism at risk.

4. *Bacterial commensals*: the skin, nose, mouth and bowel contain organisms which under normal conditions are non-pathogenic and prevent the establishment of other, pathogenic organisms. If, however, these commensals are reduced, for example by 'prophylactic' antibiotics, pathogenic organisms may replace them.

Septicaemia

The exposure of capillaries and lymphatics to infection (such as occurs in any large open wound) may lead to the circulation of actively dividing organisms in the blood stream.

This usually produces systemic signs such as a fever, tachycardia and rigors when caused by staphylococci or streptococci. However, *Pseudomonas* (and other organisms such as *E. coli* or *Klebsiella*) often produces much less dramatic effects: a normal or even reduced temperature, lethargy and clouding of awareness, pallor and a cold sweaty skin. Unless the staff are aware of the possibility of a septicaemia, the diagnosis may be missed until a brain abscess, jaundice or renal failure occur.

On suspicion of septacaemia, therefore, blood cultures are taken and intravenous antibiotic therapy is commenced; this may be altered if necessary when the organism and sensitivities are known.

Toxaemia

Many of the symptoms produced by infection are the result of toxic proteins derived from the organism. Exotoxins are secreted by organisms such as streptococci and staphylococci; some kill white blood cells, others haemolyse red cells, others interfere with nerve conduction. Endotoxins are released from organisms when they are killed, and it is these endotoxins which are responsible for pyrexia and shock. As the liberated toxins diffuse easily through the tissues and into the blood stream, their effects are felt far from the site of the originating organism, even though the organisms themselves are being contained locally.

THE POORLY VASCULARISED WOUND

Poor vascularisation may be the result of arteriosclerosis, diabetes mellitus, severe trauma or irradiation.

NURSING CARE

- Early awareness of the potential problem of poor blood supply may prevent failure of wound healing.
- Some areas of the body naturally have a less adequate blood supply than others. A wound in the lower third of the leg, for example, takes longer to heal, and suffers more complications, than an identical wound in the upper third of the leg.
- If a patient with arteriosclerosis has a leg wound, failure to heal may be prevented by rest, either in bed or in a wheelchair, with the leg elevated on a suitable support, such as a leg board and Braun's splint.
- If a patient with diabetes has any kind of wound, his diabetes must be controlled very carefully if delay in healing is to be prevented. The injured area will be kept at rest and elevated until soundly healed.

THE WOUND IN THE UNDERNOURISHED

Poor nutrition (especially vitamin C deficiency) and low protein states (such as in extensive burn injuries or the chronically undernourished) inhibit wound healing.

NURSING CARE

- Nutrition is a subject often neglected by the modern nurse, especially since the introduction of the ganymede system for providing meals for patients in hospital. While this system may be very efficient in providing the meal service, it should not remove the need to see what the patient's meal consists of. The meal tray is often removed by ancillary staff and therefore the nurse may be unaware of the patient's intake.
- The natural healing processes require protein, vitamins and certain mineral elements.

- Any large wound leaks protein in the form of serum. This wound exudate constitutes a continuous drain of protein from the body which must be made up by an increased intake.
- Explain this loss of protein to the patient and the need for a high protein diet. Tell him what foods are rich in protein.
- Vitamin supplements may be used if the wound is large, or the patient's general nutritional state is poor.
- If the wound is very large, then supplementary feeding with products such as Clinifeed and Ensure Plus may be required in order to maintain a normal serum protein level.

STEROIDS AND WOUND HEALING

Corticosteroid therapy reduces the inflammatory response and delays the formation of collagen.

NURSING CARE
- Explain to patients who have had long-standing steroid treatment that wound healing may take longer than normal. The injured part is kept elevated and rested, by rest in bed if necessary.
- Infection may be harder to detect because of the reduced inflammatory response. Therefore, wound swabs will be sent for culture and sensitivity every 2 days in order to minimise the risk of untreated infection.

THE IRRADIATED WOUND

Irradiation alters the ability of cells to multiply and produces thrombosis of blood vessels. The resultant scars therefore have poor blood supplies, tend to ulcerate and are slow to heal.

NURSING CARE
- Irradiation damage will delay healing of a wound even 20 or 30 years after radiotherapy. Uninjured irradiated skin may look normal and the potential problem of healing will only be discovered by taking the previous history from the patient.
- Explain to the patient that healing may be delayed and that the resulting scar may be of poor quality.
- Wounds over irradiated tissue usually appear to be healing

satisfactorily for the first 7 to 10 days, but may then become very inflamed and tense, giving an appearance resembling cellulitis. This appears to be part of the normal response of irradiated tissue to injury and will resolve over the next 2 to 3 weeks.

● This inflammatory response makes it more difficult to detect true cellulitis, and therefore wound swabs are sent for culture every 2 days in order to detect infection and commence treatment as soon as possible.

● The poor quality of the scar is not confined to the appearance. The scar tissue may be unstable and liable to break down at the least provocation.

● Explain to the patient the need to take special care of any scar overlying irradiated tissue, protecting it from injury and applying a bland ointment, such as hydrous ointment, if the scar becomes very dry and prone to form fissures.

● These scars have a tendency to ulcerate, even many years after healing. Explain this and make suitable follow-up arrangements for the patient.

REMODELLING OF SCARS

The young scar, once healed, gradually flattens and loses its vascularity (and hence its redness). Nerves grow into the scar over the ensuing weeks. It may take up to about 18 months for a scar to mature fully. During this time scars may shorten which, if gross, produces contractures. Scars usually shorten most along lines of skin tension. Because skin crease lines run at right-angles to lines of maximal tension, it follows that scars running at right-angles to the crease lines are under most tension and contract most. This has two clinical implications:

1. Scars running parallel to skin creases heal better than those running across creases.

2. Scars running at right-angles to skin creases tend to hypertrophic change (see below), which may be corrected by altering the direction of the scar (Fig. 14).

NURSING CARE

● Explain to the patient that scars will continue to improve in appearance for up to 18 months, that they will contract, and

that return of sensation will take several months.
- If scar contracture is likely to interfere with function, explain this to the patient and ensure that he understands the need for the use of splints to prevent contracture and the importance of careful follow-up.

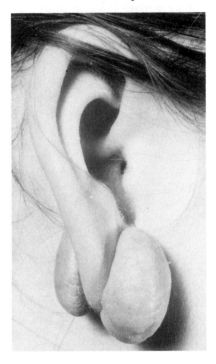

Fig. 5. *Keloid scar following ear piercing.*

HYPERTROPHIC SCARS AND KELOIDS

Following injury to skin, which may be as innocuous as an insect bite or result from lacerations or burns, some people have a tendency to develop excessive quantities of fibrous tissue in scars (Fig. 5). The scar, instead of flattening, becomes raised, red and itchy. Though histologically similar under the microscope, both consisting of large amounts of fibrous tissue (collagen), hypertrophic scars behave differently from keloids (Table 1). It appears that tension within a scar may encourage hypertrophy or keloid formation, so scars may be improved by redistributing the tension by:

1. *Compression*: elastic garments worn over the scar for several months (Fig. 6).

2. *Surgical release*: realigning the scar so that it runs in a line of least tension, i.e. parallel to the skin creases.

The activity of fibroblasts in producing scar collagen may be curtailed by injection of steroid into the scar. Intralesional steroid therapy is more likely to be effective if used early in the formation of the keloid or hypertrophic scar, before mature collagen has been laid down. Triamcinolone (25 units/ml) may be injected using a 2 ml syringe and 25G needle, or using a needleless injector gun such as Panjet (see 'Intralesional therapy', Chapter 21).

Surgery has little part to play in hypertrophic scars but can occasionally be used for keloids. When excising a keloid, it is usual to carry out the incision within the boundary of the scar so as not to damage normal surrounding skin, where further keloids might form.

Superficial irradiation of refractory keloids has been used in the past, but the recognition that a few patients have developed carcinoma in the scar many years later has thrown doubt on the place of this form of therapy.

Table 1. *A comparison of hypertrophic and keloid scars*

	Hypertrophic scars	Keloids
Incidence	Low in blondes	High in Negroid skins
Extent	Confined to site of injury	Extend into surrounding uninjured skin
Outcome	Tend to flatten after a year or two	Persist for many years
Recurrence	Some tendency to recur after excision	High tendency to recur after excision
Sites	Earlobes, front of chest, face and neck	

NURSING CARE

- Use of compression garments may be very distressing for the patient, especially if the garment cannot be hidden by clothing, for example a face mask. Explain the need for this treatment and what will happen to the scars if the garment is not worn.

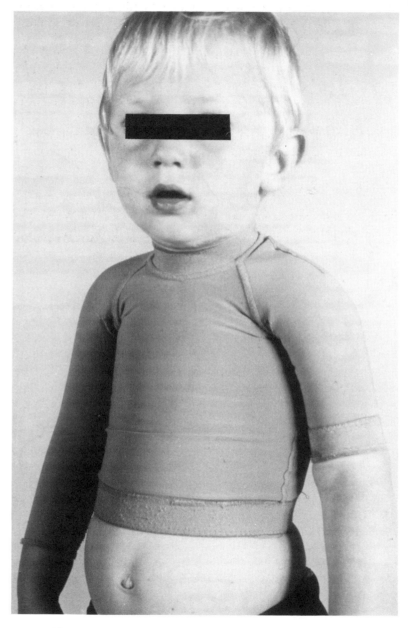

Fig. 6. *Elastic compression garment for hypertrophic scars after burn injury.*

- Sympathise with the patient and his family at the embarrassment he will feel, but stress that the use of the garment is only temporary, whilst unnecessarily severe scarring is permanent.
- Offer emotional support to the patient and his family during the period that he is becoming accustomed to wearing a pressure garment.
- Ensure that the garment fits well, and is as comfortable as possible.
- In growing children, frequent follow-up is required to ensure that the garment continues to be a good fit.

FURTHER READING

Anderson, J.R. (Ed.) (1980) *Muir's textbook of pathology*, 11th edn. London: Edward Arnold.
Peacock, E.E. & van Winkle, W. (1976) *Wound repair*, 2nd edn. Philadelphia: W.B. Saunders.

3 Grafts and flaps

'Skin is the best dressing.'
Lord Joseph Lister, 1827–1912. Professor of Surgery, Glasgow, Edinburgh and King's College Hospital, London. Instituted antisepsis in surgery in 1867.

The replacement of malformed, deformed or congenitally unformed tissue by surgery is fundamental to reconstruction. The use of grafts and flaps is a means by which this can be achieved.

GRAFTS

A graft is biological tissue which is removed from an animal, and then applied to another part of the same or to a different animal.

With the exception of some particular grafts (such as corneal and heart valve grafts), the graft must acquire an adequate blood supply from the new 'bed' (recipient site) if it is to survive. This is achieved in three ways:

1. *By imbibition.* Within a few hours of applying a graft, there is significant bonding with the recipient surface, probably by fibrin and elastin 'glue'. The cells survive by absorption of nutrient fluids and oxygen from the bed and the atmosphere, and can survive thus for several hours.

2. *By inosculation.* A primitive blood and lymph circulation in the graft is detectable within three days. By chance, some capillaries of the bed are lined up opposite capillary vessels in the graft, allowing some exchange of nutrients.

3. *By capillary ingrowth.* The definitive blood and lymph circulation is established by five days by new capillaries growing actively from the bed into the graft (Fig. 7).

Therefore, the thinner and smaller the graft, the more likely it is to survive.

Skin grafts will not be revascularised with a blood supply adequate to keep them alive if placed on bare cortical bone, bare cartilage or bare tendon, though they will 'take' on periosteum, perichondrium and paratenon.

Skin graft

a   b

The 'bed'

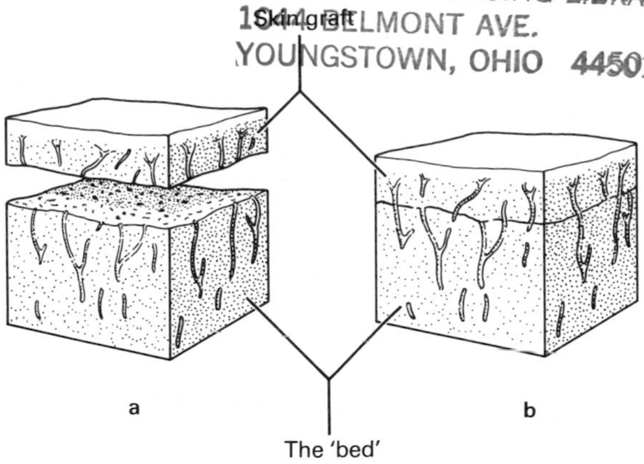

Fig. 7. *Stages in the 'take' of a skin graft. (a) Graft applied to the bed. (b) Capillary ingrowth into the graft.*

PARTIAL-THICKNESS (OR SPLIT) SKIN GRAFTS

Partial-thickness grafts (Thiersch[1] grafts) consist of the epidermis and upper layers of the dermis of the skin (Fig. 8). The method by which such grafts are taken is described on page 365. Their properties are listed below.

1. They are revascularised ('take') readily and therefore are used extensively for covering full-thickness large area burns.

2. They contract in surface area, and are therefore unsuitable for use in areas such as the eyelids, where contracture would result in ectropion.

3. They may be expanded to cover larger areas by cutting them into a mesh with multiple slits (Fig. 9).

4. They tend to break down and ulcerate if subjected to repeated trauma. Thin partial-thickness skin grafts may, therefore, be unsuitable for the fingers of a heavy manual labourer.

5. They acquire, by ingrowth of nerves from the edge, a moderate return of sensation (as would be necessary in the fingers of a violinist).

6. They leave enough dermis in the donor area for it to heal

---

[1] Karl Thiersch, 1822–1895. Professor of Surgery, Leipzig, Germany. First to apply grafts to a varicose ulcer.

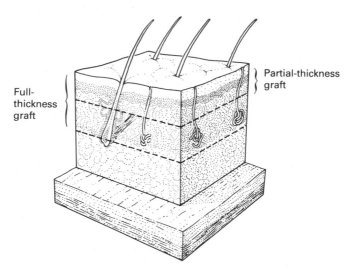

Fig. 8. *Planes of section of partial- and full-thickness skin grafts.*

Fig. 9. *'Meshed' skin (on the left) is produced by passing skin (on the right) under a drum of sharp knives.*

within about 10 days. The donor area can be re-used as the source of partial-thickness grafts.

NURSING CARE

- Pre-operative preparation of the graft 'bed' must be directed towards ensuring an adequate blood supply, removal of slough (or dead tissue) and elimination of infection by organisms liable to inhibit graft take, such as *Streptococcus haemolyticus* or *Pseudomonas aeruginosa*.

- Ensure that the patient understands the operative procedure, and explain that the donor site will be more painful post-operatively than the grafted area.

- On the day of operation the donor site is carefully shaved, ensuring that no razor cuts are made on the skin. When a limb is to be used as the donor site, the entire circumference of the limb is shaved (not just part of it) since, when applying sterile towels in the operating theatre, the whole circumference of the limb will be exposed to the operating field.

- Grafts should be kept elevated above the level of the heart at all times during the post-operative period. This prevents oedema, which may inhibit the microcirculation by pressure. Elevation also reduces the leakage of blood and serum from the wound which may collect beneath the graft, preventing ingrowth of blood vessels. Elevation should be maintained until graft 'take' has been achieved in 5 to 10 days. Special care should be taken to maintain elevation whilst transferring the patient from the bed to the wheelchair.

- If displacement of the graft is observed during the first few hours before bonding has occurred, the graft should be realigned and correct apposition maintained, either by altering the patient's position or by tethering the graft with Steristrip. If any part of the graft has sheared off the wound after initial bonding has taken place, that part of the graft which is lying outside the wound should be trimmed off with scissors and reapplied to the defect. If the reapplied skin fails to bond, losing its pink colour and turning white, it should be discarded and skin which has been stored in the refrigerator applied (if available).

- Any blisters appearing in the graft should be carefully snipped, and the fluid gently expressed by direct pressure using a roll of gauze. During this procedure, care must be taken not to move the graft over its bed. Blisters may reform very quickly on any wound which is oozing copiously, so very frequent observation and treatment may be necessary for the first 24 to 48 hours.

- Observe the wound carefully for signs of infection. Send wound swabs for culture immediately infection is suspected.
- Graft take is usually clearly detectable by a pink or red appearance of the graft after 4 days. All areas of overlap, and any areas of failed graft, should be excised after 4 days and stored skin applied to the defects. When necessary, the graft 'bed' should be reprepared by use of 0.25% Eusol and paraffin dressing. If such dressings are to be applied adjacent to newly grafted skin, these grafts should be protected from the Eusol with paraffin gauze dressings.
- After 7 to 10 days the graft should be stable enough for the patient to commence gentle mobilisation. Grafts on legs are supported by elastic bandages over the graft dressings.
- Grafts may be exposed at night to encourage them to harden (keratinise) providing a bed cradle prevents them being rubbed off by the bedclothes.
- The patient (or a relative) is taught to apply the graft dressings and elastic bandages. Stress the importance of applying the bandages *before* the patient gets out of bed, so that the graft is not hung downwards whilst unsupported.
- When dressings are no longer required (usually 3 to 4 weeks), the graft is gently massaged with hydrous cream 2 or 3 times daily until no signs of dryness or scaling are present.

Skin graft storage

When skin grafts are taken, some may be applied to the defect immediately. The remaining skin is laid shiny-side up (i.e. dermis-side up) onto a layer of paraffin tulle. The skin will stick lightly to the paraffin tulle, making it easier to handle. It is then spread out gently, smoothing out any creases, so that the epidermis side of the skin is entirely in contact with the paraffin tulle. The tulle is then placed onto a piece of gauze soaked in normal saline. All three layers, i.e. skin, paraffin tulle and gauze, are then rolled up together into a tube shape, placed in a sterile container, and stored at 4°C. Skin can be preserved in this way for about 2 weeks.

The repeated warming and recooling of grafts, by taking them out and then returning unused grafts to the refrigerator, shortens the length of time that they remain viable.

Grafts may remain alive for up to 6 months when stored in liquid nitrogen. They must be pre-treated with glycerol, slowly frozen and rapidly thawed.

Grafts may also be freeze-dried, sterilised and stored at room temperature ready for use. Soaking in normal saline reconstitutes the grafts prior to application but, because skin grafts preserved in this way are non-viable, they serve only as a dressing.

Application of grafts

Skin taken at operation and stored in the refrigerator is removed, with a sterile no-touch technique, from the container and unrolled on a sterile board with its paraffin tulle backing still applied to it. The tulle-backed skin is cut to the size of the defect to be covered before application.

A second larger layer of paraffin tulle is carefully laid over the first, and covered with gauze and cotton wool. The whole dressing is held firmly in place (immobilised) with a bandage or large adhesive tape, taking care not to displace the graft during application.

'Delayed' skin grafting

If the 'bed' to which the skin graft is to be applied is bleeding significantly at the time of operation, it is likely that the graft will fail to 'take' because of haematomas forming repeatedly beneath it. In such an instance, the skin may be stored for 24 to 48 hours in the refrigerator, and then applied on the ward to the now dry bed. The main disadvantages of 'delayed' skin grafting are:

1. It may be difficult to immobilise the graft properly in a way that would be possible (for example with sutures) in the anaesthetised patient.

2. Some tissues (such as periosteum) may dry out in the period after the operation if not grafted immediately, rendering them unsuitable to revascularise the graft at a later time.

3. The bed may become infected before or at the application of the graft.

Graft dressing removal

On about the fourth post-graft day, the bandages are removed. Using an aseptic technique, the layers of gauze are peeled off, leaving the two layers of tulle gras. With forceps, the outer layer of tulle gras is peeled off, moistening the wound with sterile saline if blood clot has made the tulle adherent to the wound.

The innermost layer of tulle gras is removed in the same way, exposing the skin graft beneath. Any sutures which have been placed around the edge of the graft are snipped with fine-pointed scissors.

Exposure of grafts

Provided that the graft can be adequately immobilised on its bed and can be prevented from being rubbed off, it may be left exposed with no overlying dressings. This permits frequent inspection to detect the formation of haematoma or infection. A comparison of the advantages of exposured and dressed wounds is given in Table 2.

Table 2. *A comparison of the advantages of exposed and dressed wounds*

Exposed	Dressed
Easily observed	Patient more mobile
Easy access	Reduce nursing time
Slippage and blistering treated early	Pressure on dressing reduces blistering
Less liable to infection	Protected from damage
Stabilise early	Appearance acceptable to patient

CARE OF THE DONOR SITE
● The donor site heals by regeneration of the dermis and

epidermis from those dermal cells left when the partial-thickness graft is removed (Fig. 8). The usual dressing is one layer of paraffin tulle, then gauze, well padded with cotton wool. Crepe or similar elasticated bandages are used in order to apply the dressing firmly. A loose dressing slips about over the wound, causing pain, and absorbs fluid less well than a firm one.

- The dressing is left intact for 10 days, unless there is evidence of infection. If it is removed too soon then the new epithelial cells forming are liable to be destroyed.

- If exudate from the donor site soaks through the original dressing, only the outer bandage and top layer of cotton wool are removed. The dressing is then repacked with cotton wool and firmly re-bandaged.

- Inspect the dressing daily for any signs of sepsis. If infection is suspected, the dressing is carefully removed so as not to damage new cells. Wound swabs are sent for culture. If *Pseudomonas aeruginosa* is suspected, the wound is dried thoroughly with a blow-dryer. The wound is exposed if possible, or redressed with 0.5% acetic acid. If the organism is not known, redress with an antiseptic cream such as silver sulphadiazine.

- After 10 days the donor site is usually healed. The dressing is often stiff with dried blood and firmly adherent to the wound. This is soaked off with saline in a bath.

- After the donor site is healed, hydrous cream is massaged into the area 2 or 3 times a day until no signs of dryness or scaling are present.

- If possible, the donor site is kept elevated until healed. This will not be practical for patients for whom early mobilisation is important for their general health. Failure to elevate the donor site may delay healing.

- An alternative dressing to paraffin gauze is adhesive polyurethane film (Op-Site). The healing time is similar. Patients may dislike the appearance of the fluid which collects beneath the polyurethane film. This fluid, however, is bactericidal, and may be aspirated using a needle and syringe.

FULL-THICKNESS SKIN GRAFTS

Full-thickness skin grafts (Wolfe[2] grafts) contain the full thickness of epidermis and dermis (Fig. 8). Their properties are listed below:

1. They 'take' less readily than partial-thickness grafts.

2. They initially contract, but re-expand within a few days, so are the grafts of choice for eyelids.

3. They regain less sensation than partial-thickness grafts.

4. They require the donor area either to be partial-thickness skin grafted or, if small enough, to be sutured directly.

5. They have a better 'normal skin' texture and colour than partial-thickness grafts, and are therefore superior for grafts on the face. Grafts most closely approximating to facial skin are obtained from behind the ear or above the clavicle.

NURSING CARE

● 'Tie-over' dressings consisting of a foam pad or flavine wool (see page 371) over a layer of tulle gras are usually used to cover full-thickness grafts (Fig. 10). Check the dressing daily for signs of infection.

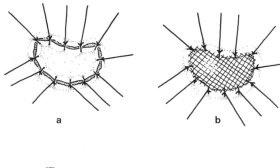

Fig. 10. *The 'tie-over' dressing. (a) Skin graft sutured, (b) covered with paraffin gauze, and (c) in turn covered with proflavine wool immobilised with the sutures tied over the top.*

---

[2] John Wolfe, 1824–1904. Ophthalmologist, Glasgow.

- Check the surrounding skin for signs of cellulitis, and clean around edges of the tie-over dressing daily.
- After 4 to 5 days, remove the 'tie-over' dressing by snipping the sutures over the foam pad or flavine wool. Trim away any graft which has failed to 'take' and has turned white or, later, black.
- Leave the graft exposed when possible. However, if the graft is liable to be damaged, a paraffin tulle and gauze dressing is applied for protection.
- When dressings are no longer required, hydrous cream is applied 2 or 3 times daily until no signs of dryness or scaling are present.

CARE OF THE DONOR SITE

- The donor site will be closed by direct suture or split skin graft.
- Clean the wound daily and apply Steristrips between the sutures to give additional support.
- Remove sutures after 5 to 10 days.
- If the donor site has been split skin grafted, treat appropriately (see above).

COMPOSITE GRAFTS

Composite grafts consist of multiple types of tissue such as skin and cartilage, or nasal mucosa and septal cartilage. Composite skin–cartilage grafts are used to fill in defects of the tip of the nose, and mucosa–septal cartilage grafts for the lower eyelid when conjunctiva and tarsal plate are missing. As they are slow to vascularise, only small amounts of tissue can be grafted in this way. Larger amounts, even if initially successfully grafted, tend to be reabsorbed after a few weeks.

NURSING CARE

- Because they are slow to vascularise, composite grafts are liable to fail in extremes of heat or cold. Explain this carefully to the patient pre-operatively, and arrange for him to be nursed in a bed position which is free from draughts or excess heat.
- Composite grafts usually appear cyanosed for the first few

days. Explain this to the patient pre-operatively, and reassure him that this does not indicate graft failure.

- Composite grafts are most commonly used on the nose and eyelids. Instruct the patient to sleep with his head on a high pillow, and not to stoop or bend head down for 10 to 14 days post-operatively.
- Instruct the patient not to touch the graft for 10 to 14 days.
- Observe the graft frequently for signs of infection. Send wound swabs immediately if infection is suspected.
- Clean the graft very gently as often as is necessary to remove blood and exudate, using sterile saline and cotton wool.

CARE OF THE DONOR SITE

- The donor site will usually be closed by direct suture. Observe the wound for tension and infection, and clean daily. Remove sutures after 4 to 10 days.

REASONS FOR GRAFT FAILURE

1. An inadequately vascularised 'bed', such as a fibrous ulcer, will not support a skin graft.

2. Movement of the graft (i.e. 'shearing' over the wound) prevents the initial bonding (imbibition) and the primary linking up of the microvascular and lymphatic circulations (inosculation). New capillaries attempting to grow into the graft will be damaged, so the graft will fail to establish a new blood supply.

3. Any collection of fluid beneath the graft will prevent the graft from lying adjacent to the wound surface, making it impossible for that area of the graft to link up any of its capillaries with the 'bed'. This fluid may be blood, serum or pus, and will appear as a blister or as a dark blue area.

4. Infection. *Streptococcus haemolyticus* lyses skin grafts and destroys migrating epithelium. *Pseudomonas aeruginosa* produces a large quantity of exudate which lifts the graft off its 'bed'.

5. Graft 'take' is dependent on revasculisation. Any reduction in blood supply to the graft 'bed' will cause delay in the graft acquiring a new circulation.

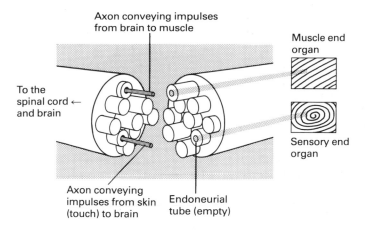

Fig. 11. *To be effective the axon must enter an endoneurial tube appropriate to its function.*

NERVE GRAFTS

Nerve grafts are used to bridge gaps in nerves which have been caused by trauma or neoplasm. A non-essential nerve such as the sural nerve of the calf or the lateral cutaneous nerve of the thigh is removed and sutured into the gap. The graft provides only a skeleton of endoneurial tubes, since the graft's nerve fibres (axons) do not survive. New axons grow from the proximal end of the damaged nerve down the endoneurial tubes of the nerve graft (Fig. 11). Regenerating axons grow at about 1 mm per day. If they escape from the endoneurial tube they tend to grow haphazardly into coils of nerve tissue – neuromas – which are acutely tender.

NURSING CARE

- Pre-operatively, explain to the patient that the donor nerve is non-essential and, therefore, will not be missed.
- Ensure that the patient understands that the return of sensation after nerve grafting is a slow process.
- Post-operatively, maintain splintage or fixation where applicable.
- Keep the wound elevated for 10 to 14 days to reduce oedema.
- Leave dressings intact for 5 to 10 days, but inspect them daily for signs of infection.

- Remove skin sutures after 5 to 10 days, and leave the wound exposed if possible.
- Instruct the patient carefully about movement and physiotherapy.

TENDON GRAFTS

Tendon grafts, usually the plantaris tendon of the calf or the palmaris longus tendon of the forearm, are used:

1. To repair gaps in damaged tendons.

2. When direct repair of a tendon would result in the suture line lying where it might adhere to surrounding tissue, so that the tendon would not glide (for example in the palm and fingers). In such a situation it is preferable to excise a length of the damaged tendon; this gap is filled with a tendon graft, keeping the suture repair well away from adhering tissues. Because of the poor blood supply of tendon, grafts are rarely used at the time of injury but at a later, elective operation.

3. In partly paralysed hands, when it is necessary to lengthen the tendon of an active muscle, so it can exert its pull in a direction which compensates for a paralysed muscle.

4. In facial palsy, when the tendon graft is attached to the angle of the mouth and to the temporalis muscle in the forehead, to give some support and movement to the mouth.

NURSING CARE

- Pre-operatively, explain the operative procedure to the patient. Stress the importance of not *actively* moving the joint (see 'Active' in Glossary) controlled by the newly grafted tendon until the graft is soundly healed. This is usually after 3 to 4 weeks.
- Explain to the patient what is meant by 'passive movement' (see Glossary). If special splints, such as dynamic traction, are to be used, familiarise the patient with the appliance.
- Post-operatively, observe dressings daily for signs of infection and ensure prompt treatment if sepsis is suspected.
- Maintain elevation for 3 to 4 weeks.
- Check splintage or fixation at least once daily.
- Encourage the patient to carry out prescribed physiotherapy conscientiously.

- Remove the skin sutures when the wound is healed, usually after 7 to 10 days.

CARTILAGE AND BONE GRAFTS

Cartilage and bone grafts probably act as a skeleton into which fibrous tissue grows, and later chondrifies or ossifies. Perichondrial grafts from the vascular lining around cartilage are capable of forming new cartilage, and have been used to reline finger-joint surfaces.

NURSING CARE
- Nursing care for cartilage grafts is as for composite grafts.
- Nursing care for bone grafts is as for fractures.

TYPES OF GRAFT

1. *Autografts* are grafts taken from one individual and reapplied to the same individual. They can be expected to 'take', and survive indefinitely.

2. *Isografts* are grafts between identical twins. They, too, can be expected to survive, and behave as autografts.

3. *Homografts* and *heterografts* are used when the extent of the skin damage is too great to be covered by autografts. They are used to reduce loss of protein and fluid from the damaged surface, to decrease pain, and to reduce infection.

Homografts

Homografts (allografts) are grafts from an individual of one species applied to another of the same species. They are taken either from living donors (such as relatives or unrelated donors) or from cadaver donors.

The nearer the relationship, and the closer the histocompatibility of genes, between donor and recipient, the longer the graft can be expected to survive. In the absence of immunosuppressive drugs, however, rejection takes place after 3 weeks to 3 months. Some homografts survive for several months in severely burned patients whose immune mechanisms are suppressed by the burn injury (see 'Immunity' in Glossary).

NURSING CARE

- Treat exactly as autografts but, after grafts have apparently taken, observe daily for signs of rejection, such as fever, malaise, disruption of the graft.
- Once rejection is evident, homografts should be removed and replaced by autografts.
- If an autograft is not available then a further homograft or paraffin tulle may be applied.

Heterografts

Heterografts (xenografts) are tissues from one species (such as the pig) applied to an individual of another species (such as man). They are rejected early and, to avoid the rejection response, should be changed every 3 or 4 days.

Rejection occurs when the patient is exposed to the immunoproteins of the foreign graft. The patient responds by mobilising lymphocytes in the lymph nodes, and develops a fever. A number of cells including lymphocytes, plasma cells and macrophages infiltrate around and into the graft, disrupting and ingesting the graft cells.

NURSING CARE

- For the first 2 to 3 days treat as autografts.
- Some initial bonding will usually be seen after 4 to 12 hours.
- After 24 hours some adhesion should be evident, i.e. when the edge of the graft is lifted, it should feel at least slightly tacky.
- Every fourth day, or sooner if the graft appears to have been rejected, remove all traces of old graft and replace with fresh heterograft.

SKIN FLAPS

Skin flaps differ from grafts in that they retain an attachment and a blood supply throughout their transfer from one site of the body to another. They consist, therefore, of at least skin and underlying fat, but may also contain underlying fascia (fasciocutaneous flap), muscle or bone. The blood supply is maintained through the neck or pedicle of the flap.

REASONS FOR USING SKIN FLAPS RATHER THAN GRAFTS

1. When grafts would not pick up an adequate blood supply, for example in irradiated tissue, or over bare cortical bone, bare tendon or bare cartilage. Since a flap brings its own blood supply via the pedicle, it can be used to cover such avascular tissues.

2. When subcutaneous tissue must be transferred as well as skin, to fill in a deep hollow or to provide good wear and tear qualities.

3. When tissue such as bone or muscle is required in the graft, for example to span a gap caused by removal of bone due to carcinoma, or by a fracture.

Local flaps

'Local' flaps consist of tissue adjacent to the defect which is to be covered. They are sutured to the defect on three sides, leaving the fourth side as the pedicle in which the blood supply is carried.

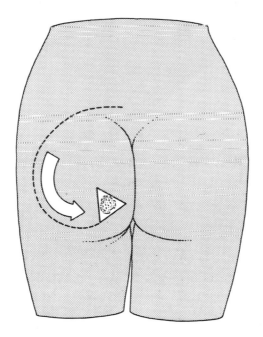

Fig. 12. *Rotation flap to cover an ischial pressure sore.*

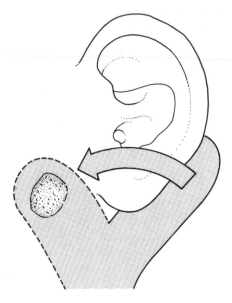

Fig. 13. *Transposition flap from behind the ear into a cheek defect.*

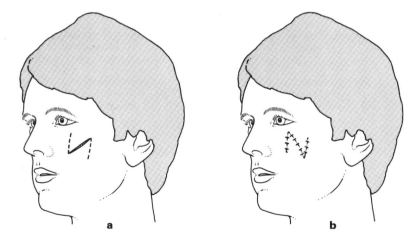

Fig. 14. *(a) Incisions of a Z-plasty to alter the direction of the scar. (b) Scar now running in crease lines.*

Examples of local flaps:

Rotation flap. Skin and fat is rotated round part of a circle (Fig. 12).

Transposition flap. Tissue, usually rectangular in shape, is slid sideways on the pedicle (Fig. 13).

Z-plasty. Two adjacent V-shaped flaps are interdigitated. It is used to lengthen or alter the direction of a scar (Fig. 14).

Advancement flap. Tissue is raised as a trap door and advanced by stretching it into the defect (Fig. 15).

Rhomboid flap. A rhomboid (sloping rectangular) shaped flap moves tissue from a line of low skin tension into the defect. A type of transposition flap.

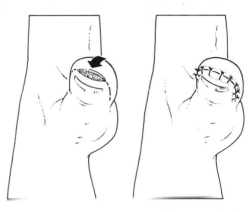

Fig. 15. *Advancement of pulp skin to cover a defecct on the thumb tip.*

Distant flaps

'Distant' flaps require transfer from the donor site, in stages, to a distant recipient site, each stage allowing an adequate blood supply to develop before the next transfer is carried out. Each stage usually takes about 3 weeks.

Examples of distant flaps:

Tube pedicle. Two parallel incisions are made in skin and fat. The bridge in between is undermined, leaving it attached by pedicles at each end. By suturing the long sides of the flap together, the skin is made into a tube, with skin outermost. After 3 weeks, one end of the tube may be detached and sutured to the recipient site. After a further 3 weeks, the other end may similarly be sutured to the recipient site. Tubing the skin reduces the raw surface and therefore the likelihood of infection of the flap.

Delto-pectoral flap. A flap which extends from the sternum to the shoulder, and is supplied by arteries entering it from its sternal end. It may be used to cover defects on the face or neck (Fig. 16).

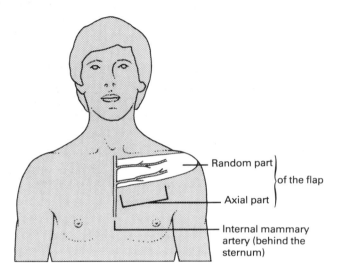

Fig. 16. *Delto-pectoral flap.*

Groin flap. A flap which extends from the groin to the iliac crest, and is supplied by arteries entering from the groin end. It may be used to cover defects on the hand and arm. The resulting defect in the groin can usually be sutured directly.

Cross-leg flap. A flap hinged from the back of the calf of one leg onto the front of the other leg. It is used to cover exposed fractures of the tibia. A skin graft is applied to the back of the calf of the donor leg. (See page 183.)

Axial pattern flaps contain a large artery in the pedicle, and therefore have a more certain blood supply than *random pattern flaps*, in which there is no large supplying artery. Axial pattern flaps may, therefore, be cut longer than random pattern flaps.

Island flap. Skin and fat are completely separated from surrounding and underlying tissue, being left attached by a pedicle which consists only of an artery and vein. If a nerve is also in the pedicle the flap is known as a neuro-vascular island flap.

Subcutaneous pedicle flap. Similar to island flap, but the pedicle consists of subcutaneous fat not covered by skin (Fig. 17).

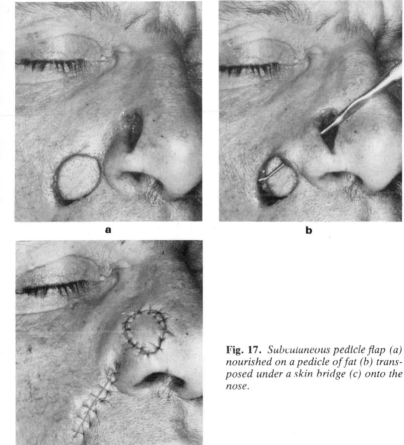

Fig. 17. *Subcutaneous pedicle flap (a) nourished on a pedicle of fat (b) transposed under a skin bridge (c) onto the nose.*

Glabella flap. A transposition of skin and fat at the root of the nose (Fig. 18).

Naso-labial flap. A transposition of skin and fat from the crease between the upper lip and cheek.

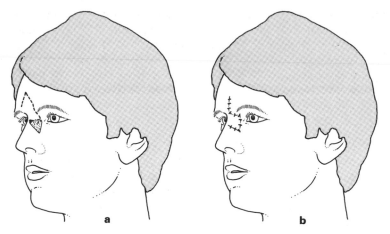

Fig. 18. *(a) Glabella flap raised from the forehead. (b) Glabella flap completed onto the nose.*

Myocutaneous flaps

The skin of some regions of the body obtains its blood supply from perforating vessels from the underlying muscles. Provided, therefore, that the arterial supply and venous drainage of such an underlying muscle is kept intact, the raising of the muscle and the skin over it will result in the skin remaining alive. This observation has been used with advantage in covering, for example, full-thickness defects of the leg (the *gastrocnemius myocutaneous flap*) and of the face (*pectoralis major myocutaneous flap*).

Latissimus dorsi flap. A myocutaneous flap from the upper part of one side of the back may be transposed under the axilla onto the front of the chest in reconstructing a breast.

Pectoralis major flap. A myocutaneous flap from the front of one side of the chest may be used to reconstruct defects of the neck, jaw and mouth.

Tensor fascia lata flap. A myocutaneous flap raised from the outer aspect of the thigh may be turned to cover a pressure sore on the buttocks.

Muscle flaps

A muscle alone, without its overlying skin, can be used as the flap.

The muscle is then covered with a split skin graft. The advantage of a muscle flap over a myocutaneous flap is that a skin defect is not left at the donor site of the muscle. For example, soleus muscle from the back of the calf may be used to cover defects of exposed tibia.

Composite flaps

In the same way that composite grafts consisting of multiple layers of tissue (such as skin, fat and underlying cartilage) can be used for repairing defects, so composite flaps can be raised on a supplying vascular pedicle. Such use of a composite flap is made in the transfer of rib and overlying skin and fat to repair a defect in the mandible.

Microvascular free flap

Tissue supplied by an artery and vein is removed from a donor site. The ends of the artery and vein are carefully dissected out and sutured to an artery and vein at the recipient site, using an operating microscope. Sites from which tissue may be taken include the groin, the dorsum of the foot and the chest. (See Chapter 18.)

'Delay'

Some flaps are *mixed axial and random pattern flaps*, for example the delto-pectoral flap, which consists of an axial portion at the sternal end supplied by a large artery and vein, and a random pattern portion distally on the shoulder (Fig. 16). Before transferring such mixed axial and random pattern flaps, it is usual to incise around three sides and to undermine the random part, and then suture the flap back into the same place in order to improve the blood supply – a 'delay'. After several days, it is then safe to transfer the whole flap to the new site on the axial pattern pedicle.

Since the flap brings its own blood supply via the pedicle, it can be used to cover defects over bare bone, cartilage or tendon, or irradiated tissue, which would not support a graft.

Factors causing flap death

1. *Tension.* Stretching a flap narrows and eventually obliterates the smaller blood vessels. This shows as a white area in the flap. Repositioning the two ends of the flap closer together may restore the circulation provided this is done before thrombosis has occurred.

2. *Kinking* the flap may have the same effect as tension.

3. *Haematomas* beneath the flap may distend it sufficiently to compromise its blood supply, and act as a nucleus for infection.

4. *Pressure.* A flap should be left exposed so it can be inspected for colour and capillary return, and to ensure the blood supply is not occluded by pressure on it.

5. *Gravity.* The venous return in a long dependant proximally based flap may be inadequate so the flap becomes congested and blue.

6. *Arteriosclerosis.* Flaps incorporating arteriosclerotic vessels are more prone to necrosis. Flaps in elderly patients are, therefore, to be avoided if possible.

Methods of attempting to revive a failing flap

1. *Release of tension* and *kinking* of the flap, by repositioning the patient or adjustment of fixation. If these measures are unsuccessful, sutures are removed. If the flap still fails to respond, the patient is taken to theatre to return the flap temporarily to the donor site.

2. *Evacuate the haematoma* from beneath the flap, by removing sutures if necessary, and milking the haematoma out using a roll of gauze.

3. Ensure that fixation apparatus or adjacent tissue does not exert *pressure* on the flap.

4. *Improve venous return* by repositioning the flap to the horizontal, or so that the flap drains downwards instead of upwards. Fixation apparatus is also adjusted.

5. *Cooling by fans* may lower the metabolic requirements of the flap.

6. *Hyperbaric oxygen* temporarily increases the oxygen in the circulation, though the effect of this is lost when the patient is removed from the oxygen chamber (see Glossary).

7. *Intravenous low molecular weight dextran* increases capillary blood flow and reduces blood viscosity.

PRE-OPERATIVE NURSING CARE

● Some flap repair procedures require more than one operation. Ensure that the patient and his relatives are fully informed of all planned surgery and the expected result, especially in relation to the function and appearance of both the recipient and donor sites.

● If fixation apparatus is to be used post-operatively, ensure before surgery that the patient can be nursed satisfactorily in the required position. This will require admission to hospital a few days before operation.

POST-OPERATIVE NURSING CARE

● Frequent nursing observations of the flap are necessary to detect disturbance of the flap circulation. Failure to recognise such signs will result in necrosis of the flap. The flap should be left exposed so that it can be constantly observed.

● The patient is positioned so that the flap can be seen clearly by both night and day staff.

● Treat 'factors causing flap death' (see above).

FURTHER READING

Conley, J. (1976) *Regional flaps of the head and neck*. London: W.B. Saunders.
Gillies, H. & Millard, D.R. (1957) *Principles and art of plastic surgery*. London: Butterworth.
Grabb, W.C. & Myers, M.D. (Eds) (1975) *Skin flaps*. Boston: Little, Brown & Co.
Grabb, W.C. & Smith, J.W. (1979) *Plastic surgery*, 3rd edn. Boston: Little, Brown & Co.
McGregor, I.A. (1980) *Fundamental techniques of plastic surgery and their surgical applications*, 7th ed. Edinburgh: Churchill Livingstone.

4 Congenital deformity: basic concepts

Congenital deformities are deformities present at birth. Since it was shown in 1927 that abnormalities could be produced experimentally by irradiation damage to the genetic material of the cell, interest has increased in the part played by this material in the production of such anomalies.

Genetic information is contained in rod-shaped *chromosomes* present in the nucleus of a cell. In man, each nucleus contains 46 chromosomes. Two of these (the *sex chromosomes*) determine the individual's sex; the remaining 44 *autosomes* determine other characteristics of the fetus.

Ovum and sperm contain 22 autosomes and one sex chromosome. All ova contain one X chromosome; sperm contain either an X or a smaller Y chromosome. Following fertilisation of the ovum by the sperm, the resulting embryo has 44 autosomes plus two X chromosomes (a female embryo) or one X and one Y chromosome (a male embryo).

Each chromosome carries a number of *genes* along its length. These genes consist of molecules of nucleic acid and carry specific pieces of genetic information, depending on how these molecules are arranged. Deformities occur as the result of abnormalities in the sex chromosomes, the autosomes or in individual genes. Such abnormalities may be inherited from the parent chromosome or occur as a spontaneous change (mutation).

Sex chromosome abnormalities

Some congenital abnormalities can be related to alterations in the number of sex chromosomes.

In 1949, the significant discovery was made that a small darkly staining mass is present in the nucleus of cells of females which is absent in the cells of males. Subsequent work has shown that this probably represents a deactivated X chromosome, and it has come to be known as the 'sex chromatin mass'. The presence or absence of this mass can be used to help diagnose sex chromosome abnormalities.

Patients with Turner's[1] syndrome, who are short-statured females with webbed necks and amenorrhoea, have 44 autosomes, only a single X chromosome, and no sex chromatin mass. Patients with Klinefelter's[2] syndrome, who appear to be males with small testes, gynaecomastia and a high-pitched voice, have 44 autosomes, two X and one Y chromosome, with a sex chromatin mass.

The sex chromatin mass can also be used to ascribe a gender to children with indeterminate genitalia at birth.

Autosome abnormalities

In 1952, it was accidentally discovered that individual chromosomes could be separated in hypotonic solutions, allowing their shape and size to be studied. Numbers have been assigned empirically to the chromosomes, beginning with 1 for the longest and 22 for the shortest. Abnormalities in specific numbered chromosomes have been shown to be associated with certain congenital deformities; thus chromosome 21 is abnormal in Down's[3] syndrome and chromosome 13 is abnormal in a syndrome showing mental deficiency, cleft lip and palate, low-set ears and polydactyly (multiple fingers).

Gene abnormalities

The chromosomes in a nucleus are paired, one chromosome of each pair coming from the ovum and one from the sperm. The genes on the chromosomes are, therefore, also paired. When one abnormal gene in the pair causes a congenital deformity in the presence of a normal gene in its partner (i.e. only one of the parents carried the abnormal gene) the gene is termed 'dominant'.

[1] Dr Henry Turner, 1892–1970. University of Oklahoma, USA.
[2] Dr H.F. Klinefelter, Junior, b.1912. Johns Hopkins Medical Institute, Baltimore, USA.
[3] Dr John Langdon Down, 1828–1896. Physician, London Hospital. He wrote a 'classification of idiots' in 1866.

When congenital deformity appears in the baby only if both genes in the pair are abnormal, the gene is termed 'recessive'.

Some examples of congenital deformity caused by dominant and recessive genes are given in Table 3.

Table 3. *Some examples of congenital deformity caused by dominant and recessive genes*

Dominant gene malformations	Recessive gene malformations
Neurofibromatosis	Cutis laxa
Cranio-facial dysostosis	Xeroderma pigmentosum
Ehlers-Danlos syndrome	Polydactyly, obesity and retinal pigmentation
Lobster-claw hand	
Basal cell naevus syndrome	Certain types of intersex
Congenital ptosis (many instances)	
Treacher Collins' syndrome	
Bilateral congenital lymphoedema	
Affected persons married to un-affected persons produce normal and abnormal children in equal proportions	Both parents are required to carry the gene (whether or not they show the abnormality) for a child to be affected
When 2 affected parents marry they produce affected and normal offspring in the ratio 3:1	When 2 affected parents marry all the offspring are affected

CAUSES OF CONGENITAL ABNORMALITY

In addition to inherited disorders, several environmental factors are also known to produce congenital abnormalities in the fetus. Some of these act on the genetic material, for example ionising radiation, causing genetic abnormalities. Others act on the fetus in its growth phase. Since the formative phase of the embryo is during the first 3 months of pregnancy, it is particularly at risk during this time.

Few congenital abnormalities can, with any degree of certainty, be ascribed solely to genetic abnormalities. It seems likely that Turner's syndrome (XO) (Fig. 42, page 111), syndactyly (webbed fingers) and Down's syndrome (mongolism) are examples of mainly genetic mutation. However, it appears that some genetic abnormalities may make a fetus more susceptible to environmental damage. An example of this environmental effect in a genetically abnormal individual is xeroderma pigmentosum. In this disease, inherited as an autosomal recessive character, skin cells are unable to repair themselves when damaged by sunlight and the patients develop skin cancer in their teens or twenties. Another example is malignant hyperthermia, an autosomal dominant inherited condition, in which muscle rigidity, often fatal, is produced by the administration of muscle relaxants and inhalation anaesthesia (see Glossary).

Infection

Syphilis transmitted across the placenta to the fetus produces destruction of the nose, perforation of the palate and peg-shaped incisor teeth. Rubella in the first 3 months of pregnancy may produce cardiac abnormalities (ventricular septal defects and patent ductus arteriosus) and microcephaly (small skull).

Drugs

Some 7000 babies were born deformed after their mothers had taken thalidomide during the first three months of pregnancy; most of these deformities were to the limbs, with absence of the humerus, radius, ulna, femur or tibia. The consequence of this tragedy is that all drugs must be tested for their possible effects on the unborn fetus before they are allowed on the market. Even so, it is generally agreed that, if possible, it is preferable to avoid drug-taking during pregnancy. Smoking, alcohol, steroids, anticonvulsants and warfarin have all been suspected of having adverse effects on the fetus.

Irradiation

The effect of ionising radiation on cells is not fully understood, but it is clear that cells may lose their ability to divide or, if they do divide, they do so in an abnormal fashion. Therefore, in a developing embryo, if spontaneous abortion does not occur, multiple congenital deformities may be caused.

Maternal age

With increasing maternal age, particularly over 35 years, parts of the chromosomes may become fragmented and lost, or become attached to another chromosome during cell division. Such faulty division may give rise to Down's syndrome.

GENETIC COUNSELLING

Parents who have a deformity, or who have given birth to offspring with a deformity, require guidance on the chances of bearing other abnormal children. In most instances, parents who have already given birth to one abnormal infant are more likely to produce another.

To give proper advice, a full family history is required, as well as a knowledge of the incidence and method of inheritance of the congenital anomaly in question. Uninformed advice may be harmful as well as misleading, even though well-intentioned to allay the parents' anxiety. It is essential that parents be referred to the appropriate counsellor with whom the question can be discussed in detail.

The availability of amniocentesis to women at risk of producing a deformed baby has made possible the detection of abnormal fetuses before birth, though failure to detect an abnormality is no assurance that one does not exist. Only some of the many thousands of congenital deformities can, so far, be detected.

FURTHER READING

Emery, A.E.H. (1983) *Elements of medical genetics*, 6th edn. Edinburgh: Churchill Livingstone.

Fraser Roberts, J.A. & Pembrey, M.E. (1978) *An introduction to medical genetics*. London: Oxford University Press.

Gorlin, R.J., Pindborg, J.J. & Cohen, M.M. (1976) *Syndromes of the head and neck*, 2nd edn. New York: McGraw-Hill.

Smith, D.W. (1982) *Recognizable patterns of human malformation: genetic, embryologic and clinical aspects*, 3rd edn. Philadelphia: W.B. Saunders.

5 Cleft lip and palate: early procedures

DEVELOPMENT OF THE FACE

During the second month of intra-uterine development, the head begins to differentiate into recognisable features which will become the brain, face and jaws. The entire embryo is only about 10 to 15 mm long, but already there are thickenings of tissue at the sites of the future ears, eyes and mandible (Fig. 19).

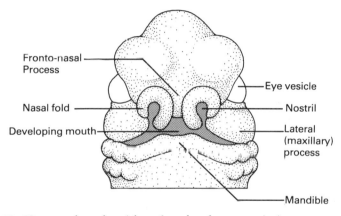

Fronto-nasal Process

Nasal fold

Developing mouth

Eye vesicle

Nostril

Lateral (maxillary) process

Mandible

Fig. 19. *15 mm embryo face (about 6 weeks after conception).*

The tissue around the primitive gills, the *pharyngeal pouches*, differentiates into the external auditory meatus, the pinna, and the ossicles of the middle ear. Failure of the pharyngeal pouches to develop leads to abnormalities such as deformity of the pinna, microtia (small, deformed ear and deafness) and meatal stenosis.

The tissue on the front of the developing face thickens at two points in its centre, the *nasal placodes*, and these sink backwards into the surrounding tissue producing the nostrils (Fig. 19). The tissue between them, the *fronto-nasal process*, will become the philtrum of the lip and the columella of the nose (see Fig. 104, page 386). On each side, at the site of the future cheeks and lateral parts of the upper lip, the *lateral processes* enlarge. The lower parts grow round beneath the mouth to form the lower jaw and chin, while the upper parts grow above the mouth and fuse with the fronto-nasal process to complete the upper lip.

A groove appears between the lateral process of the cheek and the developing nose, deepens and sinks in, forming the lacrimal duct.

Failure of fusion of the lateral processes of the cheeks and upper lip to the fronto-nasal process gives rise to clefts of the lip and alveolus (the primary palate), and persistence of the groove in the cheek results in partial or complete lateral cheek clefts.

Inside the developing mouth, tissue grows downwards on either side from the roof, and during the eighth week of intra-uterine life these *palatal plates* turn horizontally and fuse together in the midline on top of the tongue, thus separating the nose cavity from the mouth cavity with a palate.

If the palatal plates from the roof of the common nose–mouth cavity fail to turn horizontally and fuse together, there is no separation of this common cavity, leaving a cleft palate.

CAUSATION OF CLEFT LIP AND PALATE

Only a small minority of clefts are thought to be due to mutation of genes. When they are, the child often has other congenital abnormalities such as Turner's syndrome (XO), Klinefelter's syndrome (XXY), heart disease or cerebral palsy. The incidence of clefts in both of 'identical' twins is only about 40% suggesting an environmental rather than a genetic cause.

The method of inheritance of cleft lip (with or without cleft palate) may be different from cleft palate alone. Cleft lip is commoner in males, whereas cleft palate is commoner in females (mneumonic: *males* grow moustaches on their *lip*). Cleft lip occurs in the offspring of unaffected parents about once in every 800 births, while cleft palate occurs about once in every 2000.

In laboratory animals, clefts have been produced by vitamin deficient diets, irradiation, corticosteroids, aspirin and cytotoxic drugs, but none of these has been shown to be responsible in man.

Parents or relatives of an affected child may wish to know the likelihood of a cleft occurring in a subsequent pregnancy. This information is obtained by studying large numbers of affected children, enabling the risks of a further deformed pregnancy to be calculated.

For cleft lip (with or without cleft palate) the risks that a baby will be born with a cleft are:

When one parent has a cleft lip:	1 in 30
When normal parents already have a child with a cleft:	1 in 25
When a cleft lip parent already has a child with a cleft:	1 in 10

For cleft palate alone the risks to the baby are:

When one parent has a cleft palate:	1 in 14
When normal parents already have a child with a cleft:	1 in 10
When a cleft palate parent already has a child with a cleft.	1 in 6

CLASSIFICATION OF CLEFTS

Cleft lip and palate abnormalities can be divided as follows:

1. *Pre-alveolar clefts* of the lip, due to failure of fusion of the fronto-nasal process with the lateral maxillary processes (Fig. 19). The gum (alveolus) may also be cleft (Fig. 20).

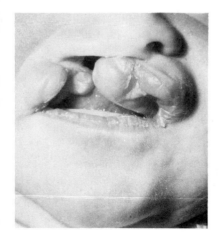

Fig. 20. *Cleft of the lip and alveolus, showing tilting of the premaxilla.*

2. *Post-alveolar clefts* of the palate, posterior to the incisive foramen (which is just behind the incisor teeth in the bony palate), due to failure of the palatal plates to turn medially and fuse (see page 62).

3. *Complete (pre- and post-alveolar) clefts* of lip, gum (alveolus) and palate (Fig. 21).

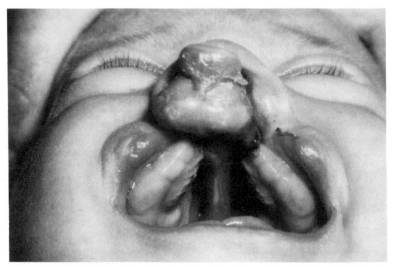

Fig. 21. *Bilateral cleft of the lip, alveolus and palate, with collapse of the alveolar segments inwards.*

These three above are all lateral (not midline) clefts.

4. *Midline (median) clefts* (very rare) are often associated with defects of the nose and brain, and mental retardation.

Dr Fogh-Andersen[1] gives the following incidence for clefts:

Pre-alveolar clefts (lip with or without alveolus)	34%
Post-alveolar clefts (palate)	25%
Complete clefts:	41%
	100%

[1] Påul Fogh-Andersen, Plastic Surgeon, Deaconess Hospital, Copenhagen, Denmark.

Thirty per cent of babies with clefts have some other congenital abnormality, though this may be minor, such as a small mandible, unequal nostrils or flattening of the cheek. The more major associated anomalies include cerebral palsy, cardiac disease, abnormalities of the skeleton, microtia, Down's syndrome and mental deficiency. Babies with clefts tend to have respiratory infections.

NURSING CARE

- The cataclysmic horror of the mother at seeing her deformed baby will be treated by the nursing and medical staff with all the sympathy and support necessary.
- Counselling of the parents, siblings, and often the grand-parents as well is essential to the child's future well-being. Rejection by either parent is not an unnatural reaction to a deformity which the average lay person will view with varying degrees of horror. Censoring such reactions is unhelpful. Sympathetic reassurance and an optimistic attitude will result in a happy child–parent relationship.
- Direct the parents' attention to the baby's normal features, for example remark on what pretty eyes she has, what a lovely sturdy little boy he is.
- As soon as possible after the birth, the surgeon will explain to the parents the expected programme of treatment, the likely outcome and the effect on their baby. The nurse or midwife should be present at this consultation in order that continuity of information is maintained in subsequent nursing interviews.
- Early operation within the first few days of life to satisfy the parents has little to recommend it, for the development of bonds between baby and mother is crucial at this stage, and the operation will still leave stigmata of the deformity.
- Babies with a lip cleft only can suck normally, though if the alveolus (gum) is cleft too there may be spluttering and some nasal regurgitation.
- Encourage breast-feeding. With constant reassurance, the mother quickly gains confidence in her own ability to cope with the deformity. If the mother chooses to bottle-feed her baby, encourage her to do this herself from the first feed. An 'over-helpful' nurse at this stage delays the mother–baby bonding.

- Whilst it is important for the baby to gain weight normally, the mother will lose confidence if the nurse emphasises feeding difficulties. Remind the mother that 'normal' babies sometimes experience feeding problems, and that these are only temporary.
- Explain to the mother that a degree of post-partum depression is normal, especially around the third to fourth day and that this is due to her hormonal changes and not her baby's deformity. Reassure her that the depression will soon pass, and keep telling her how well she is coping.
- Observation of the baby for other, less obvious congenital anomalies must be carried out as unobtrusively as possible, to protect the mother from further anxiety.
- Careful attention to the mother's own observations of her baby assists in highlighting her particular anxieties, and may produce important information regarding the baby's general health.
- Before discharge from hospital, explain the importance of prompt treatment for any signs of respiratory, oral or systemic infection.
- Ensure that after-care is adequate to provide the emotional support and reassurance the parents need to care for the child at home.
- The nurse responsible for community care helps by encouraging the parents to talk about their own feelings and the reaction of their family, friends and the general public.
- There must be close liaison between those caring for the family at home and at hospital.

PRE-ALVEOLAR CLEFTS

The cleft is one of skin, muscle and mucosa. It may vary from a small notch in the lip vermilion to a cleft from the lip to the floor of the nose. A flattened band of tissue may be present below the nostril above the cleft, a 'Simon[2] artz' band, and this is useful tissue in the repair of an incomplete cleft lip (Fig. 22). There is often a shortage of tissue in the lip, maxilla, nose and cheek.

[2] Dr Gustav Simon, 1824–1876. Surgeon, Rostock, Germany.

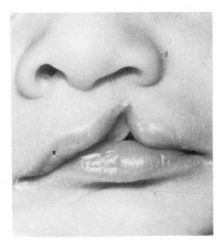

Fig. 22. *Incomplete cleft of the lip, with a 'Simon artz' band.*

Unilateral cleft lip

Left-sided clefts are more common than right-sided; the reasons for this are unknown. There is usually a shortage of tissue in the lip, and the ala of the nose is often flattened in complete lip clefts.

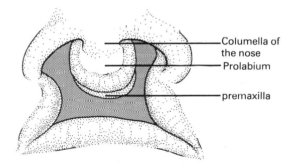

Columella of
the nose

Prolabium

premaxilla

Fig. 23. *Bilateral cleft lip and alveolus.*

Bilateral cleft lip

About 15% of cleft lips are bilateral. The tissue between the two clefts, the *prolabium*, consists of skin covering fibrous tissue where muscle should be. The prolabium hangs like a dew-drop from the columella of the nose. It may be thrust forwards like a duck's bill, or twisted, and is supported on that part of the gum which should give rise to the central incisor teeth, the *premaxilla*. The alveolus is usually cleft as well as the lip (Fig. 23).

Clefts in the alveolus may result in the absence of a tooth, or a misshapen or displaced tooth at the site of the cleft, often the lateral incisor or canine.

The alveolar cleft is closed by operation at the same time as the cleft lip, using flaps of mucosa lying adjacent to the cleft. Skoog[3] advocated placing a small amount of Sterispon under the periosteal flaps between the ends of the cleft, into which bone would grow.

ALVEOLAR CLEFTS

A cleft in the alveolus produces the possibility of:

1. Rotation or tilting of the premaxilla (the gum which will bear the incisor teeth) forwards or laterally, causing a wide cleft on one side and a narrow one on the other. This tilt may need to be corrected by the orthodontist before operation is undertaken. The orthodontic appliance consists of an elastic strap across the lip, attached either onto a head bonnet or adhering to the cheeks. This moulds the premaxilla back into line with the lip. The mother and child are admitted to hospital for this to be fitted, and for the mother to be instructed in its use.

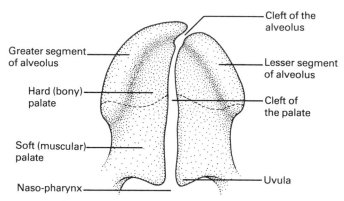

Fig. 24. *Anatomy of cleft alveolus and palate seen from below.*

[3] Tord Skoog, 1915–1977. Plastic Surgeon, Uppsala, Sweden.

2. Collapse of the smaller segment of the gum inwards, so that the larger alveolar segment over-rides the anterior end of the smaller segment (Fig. 24). Collapse of the lateral segments of the alveolus medially results in them falling in behind the premaxilla (Fig. 21). This, therefore, pushes the prolabium forwards so that the premaxilla cannot achieve its correct position between the lateral segments until they are separated. The orthodontist achieves this by inserting into the mouth a dental expansion plate, split in two. The two halves press laterally against the lateral segments of the gum, and pressure is maintained by a screw on the plate, which the mother is instructed to turn once a day.

THE NURSE'S RESPONSIBILITIES FOR ORTHODONTIC APPLIANCES

- If an orthodontic appliance is required, mother and baby are admitted to the Plastic Surgical Unit 24 to 48 hours after birth.
- The baby has dental impressions taken on the first day of admission.
- The dental plate is usually ready for fitting on the second day.
- Explain to the mother that her baby will feed more efficiently with the dental plate in place.
- Teach the mother how to fit and clean the plate.
- Check the baby's mouth before each feed for any signs of mucosal ulceration.
- The baby is discharged when the plate appears to be comfortable, the baby is feeding normally and the mother is confident in her ability to manage his care at home.
- Make arrangements for after-care at home, in the Orthodontic Clinic and Plastic Surgical Clinic.
- Instruct the mother to contact the ward should any problems occur which prove difficult to solve at home.

THE PLASTIC SURGICAL NURSE'S RESPONSIBILITIES FOR THE MOTHER'S POST-PARTUM CARE

- The mother's post-partum care is mainly carried out by a practising midwife. If necessary, the community midwife attends the mother during her admission.
- The mother is nursed on a suitable hospital bed, so she can be safely cared for should a post-partum haemorrhage occur.
- Ensure that the ward has a stock of Syntometrine, should it be needed to control post-partum haemorrhage.

- Should a post-partum haemorrhage occur, the first nurse on the scene summons another nurse immediately and instructs her to call the attending doctor urgently. The first nurse positions the mother on her back and rubs up a contraction. This is done by placing the palm of the hand on the woman's abdomen directly above the uterine fundus, and gently rubbing the abdomen, kneading the fundus with the finger tips firmly but gently.
- Whilst awaiting the doctor's arrival, the second nurse prepares 1 ml of Syntometrine for the doctor to give either intravenously or intramuscularly.
- The attending midwife is notified as soon as possible.

OPERATION FOR CLEFT LIP

To achieve optimum results, the operation needs to be carried out at the optimal time, by an experienced surgeon supported by experienced nurses in the theatre and in the ward, on an optimally fit baby with an anaesthetist fully conversant with this type of problem. In practice this means:

the child is usually 3 to 6 months of age,

weighs more than 4.5 kg (10 lb),

has a haemoglobin more than 10 g/100 ml,

and is free from pathogenic organisms (*Streptococcus haemolyticus* in the respiratory tract, in particular, is likely to produce breakdown of the surgical wound).

The operation room is warm and the child lies on a heated blanket to prevent hypothermia during surgery.

Methods of operation

The technique used for cleft lip closure, which need not be considered in detail, depends on the distribution of the cleft, the deformity of the nose and length of the lip. When an alveolar cleft and cleft of the anterior end of the hard palate are present also, these are closed at the same operation as the lip.

Le Mesurier's[4] *method*. A square flap of tissue is advanced

---

[4] Dr A.B. Le Mesurier, 1889–1982. Surgeon, Toronto, Canada.

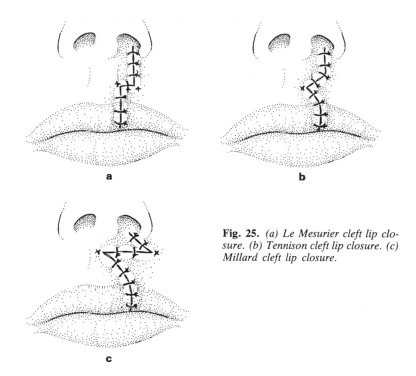

Fig. 25. *(a) Le Mesurier cleft lip closure. (b) Tennison cleft lip closure. (c) Millard cleft lip closure.*

across the lower part of the lip above the vermilion margin to give a right-angled scar (Fig. 25a). The lip tends to be long.

Tennison's[5] method. A triangular flap is moved from the lateral side of the lip into the cleft (Fig. 25b). This method has been used satisfactorily for many clefts, and the scars are usually good.

Millard's[6] method. A flap is rotated downwards from the medial side of the cleft below the columella, and the defect filled by interdigitating a transposition flap from below the ala (Fig. 25c). The design can be altered as the operation proceeds to create the best result.

Bilateral Cleft Lip (Figs. 21 and 23)

Once the premaxilla is properly aligned with the remainder of the

---

[5] Dr C.W. Tennison, Surgeon, San Antonio, Texas, USA.
[6] Dr D.R. Millard, Professor of Clinical Surgery, Miami, Florida, USA.

gum by orthodontic treatment, the narrower cleft can be closed, followed by the wider cleft 3 to 4 weeks later. In a favourable case, both sides may be closed simultaneously.

The prolabium is devoid of muscle. Since an important objective is to bring muscle into the prolabium from the lateral parts of the lip, secondary operation some months later is often required. The preliminary closure of the cleft discards as little tissue as possible, leaving the definitive repair till the muscle approximation may be achieved.

Since the prolabium is sometimes very small, closure of the cleft may leave a central section of lip which is inadequate both in height and in width. This results either in a tight lip or in a nose tip which rests on the lip, lacking a columella strut (see Chapter 6).

PRE-OPERATIVE NURSING CARE

- Baby (and mother if possible) are admitted 48 hours before the operation to a single room with adequate and adjustable heating.
- Check that the baby's weight is consistent with his age.
- Take nose and throat swabs for culture.
- Carry out routine observations including temperature, pulse and respirations to ensure that the baby is fit for surgery.
- The baby will have been stabilised on a successful feeding regime at home before admission for surgery. Ensure that this regime is maintained exactly, according to the mother's instructions.
- Ensure that the baby's normal routine, with regard to sleeping times, bathing, type of nappy and toys, is maintained as closely as possible throughout his admission.
- Fit the baby with the correct size of arm splints before the operation. These will later prevent him from touching the operation site. A useful type of splint for this purpose is made from Plastazote, moulded into a tube but left unsealed along its length. The splint should cover the baby's arm from just above the mound of the biceps muscle to about 2.5 cm above the wrist. The splints are held firmly in position by crepe bandages. These splints are light-weight, comfortable for the baby to wear and easily applied.
- When applying splints, care must be taken not to constrict the blood supply, especially at the wrist.

- Leave the splints on the baby for a few hours to ensure that they are a good fit and do not cause unnecessary discomfort. Encourage the baby to play whilst wearing them and check that he cannot bend his elbows to touch his face.
- Show his mother how to remove and reapply his splints and instruct her in their use post-operatively.
- Explain that the splints can be removed for short periods to allow her baby to exercise his arms, but ensure that she understands the importance of never leaving her baby unattended without his splints on, even when he is asleep.
- Ensure that the parents understand the operative procedure and how the child will look after surgery, with sutures in place and his arms splinted.
- Check the nose and throat swab results to ensure that the baby is free from pathogenic organisms such as *Streptococcus haemolyticus*.
- On the day of operation, the baby will be starved for the shortest time considered safe for anaesthesia, usually 6 hours.

POST-OPERATIVE NURSING CARE
- A nurse remains with the baby until he is fully conscious.
- The baby is nursed on his side, and the airway kept clear by gentle suction.
- As soon as the baby is conscious, arm splints are applied to prevent him touching the operation site.
- It is essential not to allow the baby to cry, thus putting tension on the lip stitches. The baby is cossetted, picked up, fed or cleaned as necessary to comfort him.
- Feeding is resumed 2 hours after recovery from the anaesthetic, or earlier if the baby is crying. The first feed consists of warm water only. If this is tolerated well, then a second feed is given after about one hour. The second feed is of half-strength milk. The strength and quantity of feed is gradually increased according to the baby's needs and tolerance. The normal feeding regime should be re-established within 24 hours.
- The wound is left exposed and cleaned gently with saline as often as is necessary.
- Many surgeons like to have a light film of antibiotic cream applied periodically to the wound. This keeps it moist, pre-

venting crusting, and may reduce the risk of infection.
- Over the next few days, any sutures showing signs of redness in the skin are removed.
- Cleaning of the wound and suture removal requires two nurses, one to hold the baby and restrain his head, while the other undertakes the wound care. The baby should first be wrapped firmly in a sheet to restrain his arms. Cotton buds are useful for cleaning the wound. Suture removal requires good quality, light-weight, fine-pointed scissors (such as iris scissors) and metal dissecting forceps with a fine-pointed end (such as McIndoe[7] forceps).
- On the fourth day, all remaining sutures are removed.
- Heavy-handed removal of sutures can cause small degrees of wound dehiscence, resulting in permanent unsightly scarring.
- After suture removal the wound is supported with Steristrips.

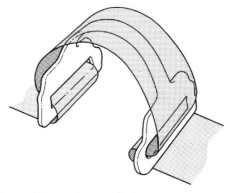

Fig. 26. *Logan bow with strapping attached.*

- A Logan[8] bow (Fig.26) may be placed across the lip at the end of the operation to give support to the suture line. If a Logan bow is used, it should be reapplied for a few days after suture removal.
- If there are any signs of infection, wound swabs are sent for culture and sensitivity. When culture results are known, appropriate antibiotic therapy is commenced.

[7] Sir Archibald McIndoe, 1900–1960. Plastic Surgeon, East Grinstead, Sussex.
[8] William Logan, 1873–1943. Professor of Oral Surgery, Chicago, USA.

- It is helpful before suture removal to sedate the baby (for example with Calpol syrup).
- The arm splints are removed when the wound is soundly healed.
- Throughout the baby's admission, remember to keep directing the mother's attention to her baby's normal features.
- Explain to the mother the importance of early treatment at any sign of infection around the operation site.
- The baby is discharged home approximately 7 days after surgery.

POST-ALVEOLAR CLEFTS OF THE PALATE

The palate is examined by the midwife and paediatrician at birth in order to diagnose these clefts. The diagnosis is difficult only if the mucosa over the cleft is intact, obscuring a muscle gap — a *submucous cleft*. However, the diagnosis can usually be made if the palate is transilluminated with a lighted torch through a nostril, the gap in the muscle becoming apparent when viewed through the mouth. The uvula is often bifid.

Speech

If early diagnosis is missed and operation not undertaken until after the child has started to talk, speech is hypernasal. For normal speech, it is necessary to be able to close off the nasal cavity from the mouth, so that air coming up through the larynx is directed into the mouth and not into the nose. This is achieved in the normal child by the muscles in the palate pulling the palate upwards and backwards so that it touches the posterior wall of the pharynx. In the patient with a cleft in the palate or with a palate that is too short, production of sounds is faulty as air cannot be retained within the mouth. This can be demonstrated by watching the patient's palate when he says 'Ah'. Only the sounds 'N', 'M' and 'NG' require there to be a gap left behind the palate for some air to enter the nose (Fig. 27). The speech therapist sees the child from the age of 2 years onwards, and both aids and monitors the child's speech progress.

More precise investigation of the movement of the palate can be made by:

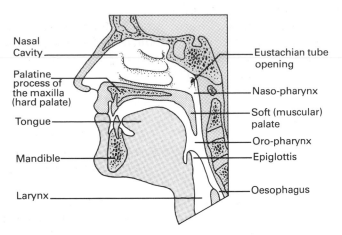

Fig. 27. *Section through the face showing the palate's relationship to the nasopharynx.*

1. Cine X-ray of the palate which has been coated with a film of barium.

2. Looking at the palate indirectly by introducing a nasendoscope through a nostril to the back of the nose.

Nasendoscopy

The endoscope superficially resembles a cystoscope, and consists of lenses and a source of light at the tip. The endoscope may conveniently be attached to a video-recorder so that a permanent record can be kept. It is also useful to have a microphone near the patient which records into the video-recorder, allowing the shape of the pharynx to be related to the sound the patient is making.

The patient is sat comfortably in an upright chair with a head support, and the procedure explained. The nostril and airway is anaesthetised with 4% lignocaine introduced on a cotton wool bud or through a catheter with a syringe attached.

The endoscope is slowly introduced through the nostril into the back of the nose and, when in the correct position, the patient is asked to speak different sounds. The movements of the palate and pharynx can be observed through the endoscope.

FEEDING THE CLEFT PALATE BABY

- Breast-feeding should be encouraged. Although there may be some spluttering and regurgitation, breast-feeding is almost always possible and helps the mother gain confidence in her ability to manage her baby's care.

- Instruct the mother to hold her baby in an upright position with his mouth slightly above the nipple. She then lifts the nipple to the baby's mouth and, as he commences sucking, she directs the nipple to the side of his mouth. This prevents the flow of milk being delivered directly into the cleft. Remain with the mother for the first few feeds, to advise and reassure her.

- Breast-feeding a baby with a cleft palate may take longer than for a normal baby at first, but as both mother and baby gain experience in the technique, they reduce the feeding time to near normal.

- As cleft palate babies tend to swallow a lot of air, teach the mother to wind the baby frequently.

- If the mother chooses to bottle-feed her baby, try various teats. If the baby is still having difficulty in sucking, then cut a larger hole, directed to one side, in a standard teat. Lamb's teats are effective but often worry the mother, making her feel that her baby will not be able to feed unless she uses a special teat. Not all chemists stock lamb's teats, and the mother may become anxious if she finds difficulty in obtaining one. As a general rule, it is considered bad practice to cut a larger hole in a teat. But while this may be true for a normal baby, this simple procedure eliminates the need for other cleft feeding aids, such as lamb's teats and special spoons. These aids are useful, but tend to emphasise the baby's deformity.

OPERATION FOR CLEFT PALATE

Closure of the cleft palate is usually undertaken between the ages of 9 and 24 months, preferably before speech is established. The same careful pre-operative preparations are taken as for cleft lip (see above).

Methods of operation

Veau–Langenbeck[9] method (Fig. 28). The edges of the cleft are pared with the scalpel on either side. A long relieving incision is made just inside the alveolar margin on either side of the palate. The mucosa and periosteum are separated from the bony palate. Tendons and muscles which tend to pull the palate laterally are cut, and the palate allowed to fall medially towards the cleft. The cleft is then sutured in two layers with stitches in the nasal mucosa, the muscle and the oral mucosa.

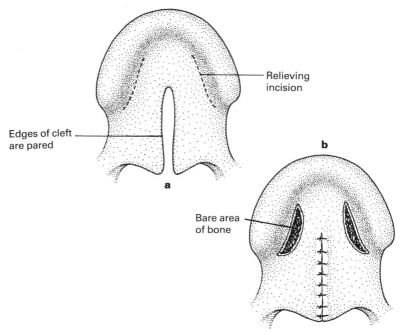

Fig. 28. *Veau–Langenbeck cleft palate closure. (a) Incisions. (b) Completed.*

The bare area of bone inside the alveolar margin spontaneously covers with epithelium within 10 days. Some surgeons pack these grooves with Whitehead's Varnish on ribbon gauze.

[9] Victor Veau, 1871–1949. Foundling Hospital, Paris; Bernhard von Langenbeck, 1810–1887. Berlin.

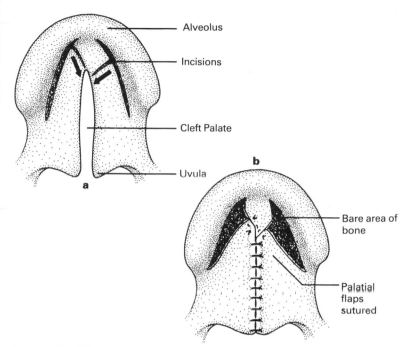

Fig. 29. *Wardill's cleft palate closure. (a) 3 flap cleft palate repair incisions. (b) 3 flap cleft palate repair completed.*

Wardill's[10] method (Fig. 29). In order to lengthen the palate in a posterior direction, Wardill used the muco-periosteum as flaps cut asymmetrically from either side. Though it often does lengthen the palate, the blood supply to the flaps is less certain than with the Veau-Langenbeck method, so fistula formation is more common.

The overall operative mortality for cleft lip and palate is less than 1 per 1000. Further surgery, for example to close partial breakdowns in the closure or to lengthen the palate further, is needed in about 5% of patients.

PRE-OPERATIVE NURSING CARE
- Pre-operative nursing care is as for the baby with a cleft lip (see above).

[10] William Wardill, 1893–1960. Surgeon, Newcastle.

- The importance of not allowing the baby to cry after the operation (thus straining the suture line) is emphasised to the mother before surgery. The action of crying uses the palatal muscles, which exert considerable pull on the suture lines. Explain this to the mother, and encourage her to stay with her baby as much as possible after surgery. Instruct her to inform a nurse every time she leaves her baby unattended, so that the nurses are alert and respond to the baby's crying immediately in her absence.

POST-OPERATIVE NURSING CARE
- The nurse remains with the baby until he is fully awake.
- The baby is nursed on his side, with his body on a pillow and his head slightly lower on the mattress.
- Should there be respiratory difficulty, the tongue is held forwards. If a tongue stitch has been inserted, this is pulled on gently.
- The airway may be cleared by very gentle suction. The suction catheter must be of soft rubber with a rounded tip, and should be introduced cautiously along the side of the tongue, keeping well clear of the palatal repair. If necessary the nostrils may be sucked out gently, but care must be taken not to insert the catheter into the pharyngeal area.
- As soon as the baby is conscious, arm splints are applied as for cleft lip repairs, to prevent the baby from touching his mouth.
- Every effort is made to prevent the baby from crying. If cuddling, feeding or distraction fail to calm the baby, analgesia and/or sedation must be given promptly.
- The feeding regime is the same as for cleft lip repair (see above), commencing with warm water, and gradually increasing to full-strength feeds.
- Very careful observation is maintained, especially for any signs of respiratory distress or bleeding from the palate.
- Temporary respiratory distress may be alleviated by use of a humidifier.
- Should haemorrhage occur, examine the palate carefully using a torch, and identify the bleeding point. Apply gentle direct pressure with the tip of the finger to control the bleeding until medical help arrives.
- Position the baby on his side, with his body on a pillow and his

head on the mattress so that blood is not inhaled or swallowed.

- It may be necessary to return the baby to theatre to obtain haemostasis.
- Reassure the mother that the bleeding will be controlled. Be sympathetic, and firmly optimistic.
- Because of the possibility of secondary haemorrhage around the tenth post-operative day, the child remains in hospital under close observation for 10 to 12 days after surgery.
- Sutures are not removed. If non-absorbable stitches have been used, they will eventually come away of their own accord.
- Arrange for after-care in the Out-Patients Department, and also instruct the mother to telephone the ward if she needs advice on any problems connected with her baby's surgery.

PIERRE ROBIN[11] SYNDROME

The baby has (Fig. 30):

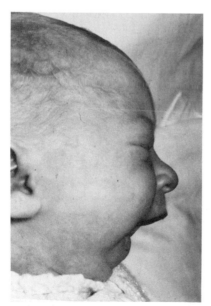

Fig. 30. *Micrognathia of Pierre Robin syndrome.*

[11] Pierre Robin, 1867–1950. Stomatologist, Paris.

1. A relatively small mandible.
2. A relatively large tongue.
3. A cleft of the palate.
4. Difficulty with respiration.

The neonate does not breathe through its nose for several days, or even weeks, after birth. When the mouth is obstructed by a relatively large tongue accommodated in a relatively small jaw, the child is in danger of suffocating. While awake respiration may be laboured, and when asleep cyanosis may be apparent.

NURSING CARE

- The parents and family are counselled as described for cleft lip (see page 65).
- Immediately after birth, the baby must be nursed prone to allow the over-large tongue to fall forward, clearing the airway as far as possible. A full body and head splint assists in maintaining the prone position, whilst leaving the baby's face and mouth free for any treatment required to maintain a clear airway.
- The most effective splintage for this purpose is produced by casting a full anterior plaster of Paris shell of the baby's entire body, including the limbs, but leaving the head and neck free. A head-band to support the forehead firmly is then incorporated into this anterior shell. The whole splint is lined with orthopaedic felt, and then mounted onto wooden blocks with a slight head-up tilt. The baby should be fully clothed, including a nappy, whilst this plaster bed is being cast, so that the cast will fit comfortably when he is normally dressed.
- An apnoea mattress (a device which will emit an alarm signal if the baby stops breathing) may be placed between the baby and the splint to assist in his nursing observations.
- A silk suture through the tongue, by which the tongue can be drawn forward, may be life-saving.
- An airway, sucker and oxygen are kept at the cot side.
- Tracheostomy is rarely needed, but is considered if pneumonia occurs.
- The baby may have difficulty with feeding because of the large tongue. The fitting of an acrylic dental plate may assist sucking, but its size further reduces space in the mouth, and this may outweigh its advantages.

- If the deformity is severe, breast-feeding may be too hazardous. The mother is encouraged to express milk for her baby's bottle-feeds.
- A wide-bore teat is used, and the hole in the teat can be adapted as described for cleft palate.
- To assist feeding, the baby is held as upright as possible, and the jaw held forwards by gently pushing with one finger behind the angle of the mandible.
- These babies tend to swallow air and must be winded frequently during and after each feed.
- Teach the mother how to hold and feed her baby. Explain that as he grows his feeding difficulties will be overcome. Encourage, reassure and help the mother, but do not appear to 'take over' her baby's care, as this will only reinforce her natural fear that she will not be able to cope with him.

FURTHER READING

Grabb, W.C., Rosenheim, S.W. & Bzoch, K.R. (Eds) (1971) *Cleft lip and palate: surgical, dental and speech aspects.* Boston: Little, Brown & Co.

Jackson, I.T. (Ed.) (1981) *Recent advances in plastic surgery*, Vol. 2. Edinburgh: Churchill Livingstone.

Mustardé, J.C. (Ed.) (1979) *Plastic surgery in infancy and childhood*, 2nd edn. London: E. & S. Livingstone.

Skoog, T. (1974) *Plastic surgery*. Stockholm: Almquist & Wiksell.

6   Cleft lip and palate: later procedures

CORRECTION OF NASAL SPEECH

The inability to close off the nasal cavity from the mouth during speech permits air coming up from the lungs through the larynx to issue partly through the mouth, but also partly through the nose. The speech is, therefore, hypernasal. The muscles of the palate and pharynx cannot contract sufficiently to close the gap behind the palate (Fig. 27). Nasendoscopy (page 76) has permitted the investigation of the shape of the gap between the back of the palate and the posterior and lateral pharyngeal walls which allows this air to escape into the nose.

The decision to perform a further operation is taken jointly with the speech therapist.

The short palate

A palate which is too short to reach the posterior pharyngeal wall during speech may be 'lengthened' by 'push-back' procedures. This may be feasible at the time of the primary closure of the cleft, as examination of Figure 29 will show. However, this primary lengthening is sufficient only for small degrees of 'shortness'. Despite several attempts at different techniques, this Wardill procedure remains one of the more satisfactory, and can be used as a subsequent procedure if primary closure by the Veau–Langenbeck technique (see page 78) results in a short palate.

The 'wide' pharynx

Hynes[1] (1950) described a procedure to narrow the pharynx from side to side (Fig. 31). A vertical flap of muscle and mucosa from

[1] Wilfred Hynes, Plastic Surgeon, Sheffield.

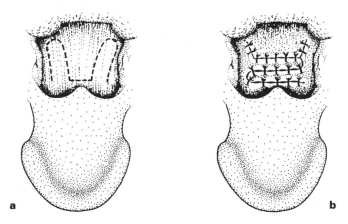

Fig. 31. *Hynes pharyngoplasty. (a) Flaps incised on the posterior pharyngeal wall and (b) transposed transversely to narrow the pharynx.*

each side of the pharynx is turned through 90°, and sutured across the back of the pharynx. This can reduce the size of the pharynx by 40%, and so improve speech.

The inadequate posterior pharyngeal wall

Like the mouth, the pharynx can be thought of as a sphincter with muscle around its circumference. If the posterior wall (Passavant's[2] ridge) does not bulge forwards during speech, it will not reach the palate.

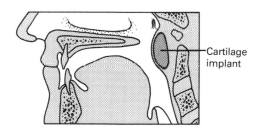

Cartilage implant

Fig. 32. *Cartilage implanted behind the posterior pharyngeal muscles.*

[2] Philippus Gustavus Passavant, 1815–1893. Berlin and Frankfurt.

Various materials have been placed behind the muscles of the posterior pharyngeal wall to move them closer to the palate (Fig. 32). Cartilage, fat, fascia, silicone, Teflon and bone have been inserted, but are subject to extrusion, infection or reabsorption.

Pharyngeal flap procedures ('Rosenthal[3] operation)

To reduce the cross-section of the gap of the pharynx, a muscle–mucosa flap from the posterior pharyngeal wall (based superiorly or inferiorly) is sutured to the posterior end of the palate (Fig. 33). A space is left on either side of this flap through which air can pass, to permit nasal breathing. During speech, these two small spaces can be closed by the muscles of the lateral pharynx.

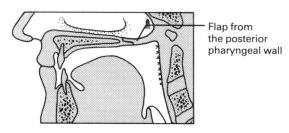

— Flap from the posterior pharyngeal wall

Fig. 33. *Pharyngeal flap sutured to the palate.*

Free muscle transplants

Thompson[4] (1974) narrowed the pharyngeal space with an actively contracting muscle graft transplanted to the pharynx.

NURSING CARE
- Explain to the patient and his parents that he should not try to talk for the first 2 to 7 days post-operatively (the length of time depends on the type of surgery).
- Explain that a toothbrush must not be used for 10 to 14 days after surgery. Mouth-washes should not be used as an alterna-

---

[3] Dr Wolfgang Rosenthal, 1884–1971. Professor of Jaw Surgery, Hamburg.
[4] Noel Thompson, Plastic Surgeon, The Middlesex and Mount Vernon Hospital, Northwood, London.

tive, as the action of swilling fluid around the mouth involves the use of the muscles of the palate and pharynx. Ensure that the patient understands the importance of this and instruct him to take a drink of plain water after every meal or drink to keep his mouth as clean as possible.

- Feeding commences with clear fluids only for 24 to 48 hours, followed by a full liquid diet. Soft food is gradually introduced, and a soft diet is continued for three weeks.
- Because of the possibility of secondary haemorrhage the patient remains in hospital for 10 to 14 days after surgery.

ALVEOLAR CLEFT BONE GRAFTING

The gap between the premaxilla and the lateral segment of the alveolus which occurs in alveolar clefts (Figs. 20 and 24) represents a failure of development of bone. Surgeons, therefore, considered that this tissue should be reconstructed with bone grafts. Attempts to do this with tibial or iliac bone grafts at the time of closure of the cleft have been disappointing. Disappointment has centred mainly around the failure of bone grafts to grow as the baby grows, their failure to prevent collapse of the lateral segments, and the failure of teeth to erupt spontaneously through the grafts.

Grafting is now usually postponed until the secondary teeth have erupted. Until then, the orthodontist bands the deciduous teeth and maintains the lateral segment alignment with appropriate dental splints and plates.

Most cases of cleft do not require bone grafting, but it may be indicated:

1. In bilateral clefts when the premaxilla is mobile, with little or no union other than to the nasal septum (Fig. 21).

2. For malocclusion of teeth, or in order to move teeth into the area of the cleft.

3. To build up a flat nasal ala base to improve the appearance of a flat lip or nostril.

CLOSURE OF PALATAL FISTULA

The breakdown of part of the repair of the palate results in a fistula between the nasal and oral cavities. Food and air are then free to pass into the nose.

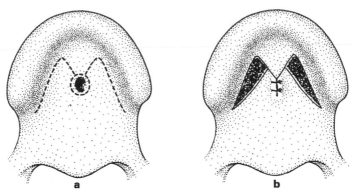

Fig. 34. *Palatal fistula. (a) Incisions for local muco-periosteal flaps. (b) Fistula closed.*

Most fistulae require re-operation on the palate in order to close them (Fig. 34).

NURSING CARE
- Nursing care for the repair of a palatal fistula is as for correction of nasal speech.

INADEQUACY OF TISSUE IN THE UPPER LIP

Although the maxilla may be in correct relationship with the mandible, tissue in the upper lip may be insufficient. A full-thickness flap of skin, muscle and mucosa (Abbe[5] flap) may be transposed through 180° from the lower lip into the upper lip, nourished on the lower lip (labial) artery (Fig. 35). After 10 to 14 days the artery can be cut and the flap inset into the upper lip.

PRE-OPERATIVE NURSING CARE
- The routine paediatric admission procedure is followed.
- Ensure that the child and his parents understand that the operative procedure requires two operations.
- Explain carefully to the child and his parents the post-operative appearance. Be confident and optimistic.

[5] Robert Abbe, 1851–1958. Surgeon, New York, USA.

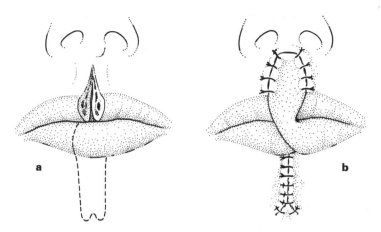

Fig. 35. *Abbe flap. (a) Incisions in the lower lip. (b) Flap transposed into the upper lip.*

- Explain that the child will be able to drink and eat by passing the food through the gaps at either side of the flap. Demonstrate how this is done, by gently holding the child's lips together and giving him some food he likes. In the same way, show him how to use a feeding cup with a spout.
- Explain that drinking straws must not be used. Sucking through a straw involves the use of the muscles encircling the lips. This action will cause unnecessary pull on the suture lines.
- Show the child how to use a mouth-wash solution for oral hygiene post-operatively, using a feeding cup with a spout.
- Tell him not to touch the wounds after his operation.
- If pre-operative explanation and reassurance are inadequate, the child will panic on recovery from the anaesthetic, and may tear his lips apart.

POST-OPERATIVE NURSING CARE
- As the child is coming round from the anaesthetic, constantly remind him not to open his lips, but keep telling him that all will be well.
- The wound is left exposed, and kept clean and dry.
- Commence oral hygiene on the first post-operative day by using mouth-washes via a 'feeder'. Should this prove difficult

initially, due to swelling of the lips, then a syringe may be used, such as a Higginson's syringe.

- Start feeding with fluids only, rapidly progressing to soft food, and then to normal food cut very small. Teach the child to use his little finger to push the food in from a teaspoon.

- Do not allow the child to put the spoon into his mouth, as this will pull on the suture line. It is possible for the child to eat any kind of food, provided that it is cut small enough or crushed, for example crisps can easily be crushed up and are still palatable to a child who really likes them.

- The child is allowed up and about as desired from the first post-operative day.

- Sutures are removed on the fifth day.

- Continue to encourage the child throughout the 10 to 14 days until his lips are separated. Keep reminding him how much the operation will improve his appearance.

THE SHORT COLUMELLA

Because of a lack of tissue in the upper lip, the tip of the nose may appear depressed and flat. The nose tip rests on the lip without an intervening columella and the nostrils are splayed. Releasing the tip upwards, providing tissue by vertical advancement of skin from the lips, gives a more normal appearance.

This procedure is usually performed at the age of 10 to 16 years.

NURSING CARE

- Pre-operative care consists of clipping the nasal hairs using fine scissors, such as iris scissors. This procedure should be carried out with the patient sitting up so that the hairs do not fall back into the nasal cavity, causing sneezing. Smearing the scissors with liquid paraffin makes the clipped hairs stick to the scissors, preventing the hairs from being inhaled into the nasal cavity.

- Explain to the patient that post-operatively he may not be able to breathe through his nose for a few days, because of nasal swelling, and that nasal packs may be used. The swelling may cause him to feel as if he has a head cold for up to 2 weeks.

- Advise him not to use a nasal decongestant or similar 'cold cures'. The symptoms will resolve spontaneously as the swelling reduces.

- Advise the patient to sleep with his head on a high pillow for about a week after his operation.
- Explain that he will be allowed to be up and about as desired from the first post-operative day but, to prevent increase of the nasal swelling, he should not stoop or bend his head for 7 to 10 days.
- Post-operatively sit the patient up in bed as soon as possible after recovery from the anaesthetic. This will both reduce oedema and assist in preventing post-operative haemorrhage.
- Keep the suture lines and upper-lip clean and dry.
- Instruct the patient not to attempt to blow his nose, but to clean his top lip very gently if there is any discharge.
- Nasal packs are removed after 2 to 4 days.
- Tell the patient that after removal of the nasal packs he may still find that he cannot breathe through his nose for a few days. Explain that this is due to swelling inside the nose, and is a normal reaction of the tissues following surgery.
- Sutures are removed after 3 to 5 days.
- Explain to the patient that the final results of this surgery cannot be judged for about a year.
- The patient is usually discharged after 3 to 5 days.

NASAL SEPTUM AND NASAL CARTILAGE CORRECTION

Rhinoplasty is usually reserved until the nose is fully grown, at about the age of 16 years (see Chapter 20).

The growth of the nose, septum and nasal cartilages is deficient on the cleft side. Consequently, the nostril is flattened and the nose may be deviated to one side. As a result of lack of growth of the alveolus, the floor of the nostril is often depressed on the side of the cleft.

While attempts will have been made at the first cleft operation to correct any deformity then present, the full extent of the nose deformity is not complete until nasal growth has finished, at about the age of 16.

MIDDLE EAR DISEASE

The incidence of middle ear infections, mastoiditis and deafness is higher among cleft palate children than normal children. This may be due to abnormalities of the Eustachian[6] tubes, which lead from the middle ear to the pharynx. These children, therefore, have their hearing tested by an audiologist and, if necessary, appropriate treatment instigated.

● Explain to the parents the need for prompt treatment of any upper respiratory infection.

Tonsillectomy and adenoidectomy

In cleft palate children, recurrent ear infections often do not respond to tonsillectomy and adenoidectomy. It is not uncommon for hypernasal speech to deteriorate after adenoidectomy because the palatal gap is increased by removing the adenoids.

● Ensure the parents understand that if the child suffers from recurrent head colds and tonsillitis, they should attend the Plastic Surgery 'Cleft' Clinic for advice.

FURTHER READING

Converse, J.M. (Ed.) (1977) *Reconstructive plastic surgery: principles and procedures in correction, reconstruction and transplantation*, 2nd edn. Philadelphia: W.B. Saunders.

Goldwyn, R.M. (Ed.) (1980) *Long-term results in plastic and reconstructive surgery*. Boston: Little, Brown & Co.

Holdsworth, W.G. (1970) *Cleft lip and palate*. London: Heinemann Medical.

---

[6] Bartolommeo Eustachio, 1524–1574. Professor of Anatomy, Rome.

7 The face, head and neck

CRANIO-FACIAL MICROSOMIA
(First and Second Branchial Arch Syndrome)

Usually unilateral, this deformity consists of under-development of the mandible, zygoma and maxilla, the muscles and other soft tissues of the ear, cheek and nose. The cheek is sometimes cleft. The abnormality occurs about once in every 5000 births, but there was a rise in incidence around 1960, during the taking of thalidomide in the first three months of pregnancy.

Since the mandible is short, the chin is deviated to the side of the deformity. The asymmetry worsens as the child grows, and the dental bite is affected.

The ear may be absent or hypoplastic (*microtia*), and there may be one-sided deafness.

Management

The contour of the soft tissues may be improved by expanding them with rib grafts or implants applied under the cheek skin, by dermo-fat grafting, or by silicone injection (see Romberg's disease, page 94). The mandibular deformity may be partially corrected by osteotomies and the insertion of bone grafts (iliac or rib) between the bone ends.

The age at which the correction is attempted depends on the state of the deformities. It is probably wise to attempt to expand the soft tissues by the insertion of grafts or implants into the cheek during growth. When facial growth is complete, or earlier, the osteotomies and bone grafts to the mandible are carried out. Prior to mandibular osteotomy, dental casts are taken and dental cap splints made to fit the teeth in the position of correction. In this way, the mandible can be held in the correct alignment while the bone graft and osteotomies are consolidating.

TREACHER COLLINS' SYNDROME[1]
(Mandibulo-facial Dysostosis)

A rare disease inherited as an autosomal dominant comprising:
1. Outward slanting of the eyes.
2. Notching of the lower eyelids (coloboma).
3. Underdevelopment of the zygoma and regression of the mandible.
4. Abnormalities of the ear, especially shell and cup deformities.
5. High arched or cleft plate.

Bone, cartilage or silastic may be implanted into the cheek to build up the contour. The mandible is advanced forwards by making osteotomies in the rami and symphysis, drawing the freed bone forwards and wiring it into its new position (*sliding genioplasty*). Alternatively, the regressed chin may be camouflaged by placing a silastic chin implant in front of the symphysis of the mandible, through an incision either below the chin, or in front of the teeth in the mouth.

NURSING CARE
- See Chapters 5 and 19.

PROGRESSIVE HEMI-FACIAL ATROPHY
(Romberg's[2] Disease)

An adolescent or child develops a progressive atrophy of the subcutaneous tissue of a cheek. This is followed by atrophy of the overlying skin and underlying muscles, loss of hair and eyebrows and sometimes epileptic fits. The cause is unknown.

The disease usually abates after between 2 and 10 years. Reconstruction of the forehead and cheek is carried out using de-epithelialised skin flaps embedded beneath the skin, or by inserting grafts of dermis, fat or fascia. However, these tend to be absorbed. More promising is the injection of liquid silicone into

---

[1] E. Treacher Collins, 1862–1932. Ophthalmic Surgeon, Moorfields Eye Hospital, London. On his honeymoon in Persia he was summoned to treat the eyes of the Shah's eldest son.
[2] Moritz Heinrich von Romberg, 1795–1873. Professor of Medicine, Berlin.

the cheek in small amounts, to build up facial contour. A maximum of 2 ml may be injected at one treatment, and ten or more injections may be necessary.

NURSING CARE
- See Chapters 3 and 22.

CONGENITAL PTOSIS OF THE EYELID

The upper eyelid is normally elevated by the levator palpebrae superioris muscle. Weakness, or absence of action, of the levator muscle results in the eyelid drooping. When the eyelid droops over the cornea of the eye, the retina fails to receive the appropriate light stimuli. If the ptosis remains uncorrected, the retina fails to develop, and some degree of blindness occurs in the affected eye.

Operation aims to shorten the muscle in the eyelid, so pulling up the lid.

Complications

1. Corneal abrasion from an eyepad on an open eye.
2. Failure of closure of the eye (lagophthalmos) due to over-tightening the muscle (uncommon).

Post-operative management

The eye is kept covered with chloramphenicol eye ointment.

Sutures tied over rubber capillary tubing hold the ends of the muscle steady during healing. They are, therefore, left in situ for rather longer than is usual for eyelid skin sutures, perhaps for 7 to 10 days.

If lagophthalmos persists, it may be necessary to prescribe 'artificial tears' of methylcellulose, or for the patient to wear protective glasses.

NURSING CARE
- Nursing care is as described for blepharoplasty (eyelid reduction) in Chapter 20.

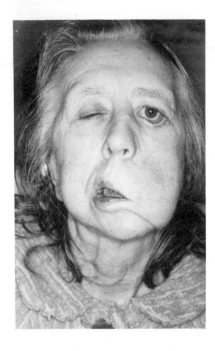

Fig. 36. *Left facial palsy.*

FACIAL PALSY

Seventh cranial nerve (facial nerve) paralysis affects the muscles of facial expression (Fig. 36). Causes of facial palsy include:

1. *Congenital*: for example Moebius syndrome[3]. Bilateral paralysis of the face and lateral rectus muscles of the eyes produces a mask-like, doleful, expressionless face.

2. *Traumatic*: lacerations of the facial nerve, fractures of the skull.

3. *Infective*: meningitis, poliomyelitis, Bell's[4] palsy, otitis media.

4. *Neoplastic*: intracranial acoustic neuroma, carcinoma of the parotid (see Chapter 17).

5. *Vascular*: intracerebral vascular accident (angioma or atheroma).

---

[3] P.J. Moebius, 1853–1907. Munich.
[4] Sir Charles Bell, 1774–1842. Surgeon, Middlesex Hospital, and later Professor Edinburgh University.

There is usually inability to close the eye, drooping of the angle of the mouth, asymmetry of the lips and loss of wrinkling of the forehead. The eye waters and develops conjunctivitis and keratitis. On the non-paralysed side the muscles appear hyperactive accentuating the grimace.

Management

When possible, primary repair of the lacerated facial nerve should be undertaken. Facial muscles lose their tone rapidly, and various external slings and supports and faradic stimulation have been used to try to delay this.

If treated early with steroids, the majority of cases of Bell's palsy (probably a neuritis of the cranial nerve within the bony canal of the skull) have a considerable degree of recovery.

When recovery is not expected because, for instance, it is known that a segment of nerve has been destroyed, or when recovery has not occurred within 9 months or so of the onset of the paralysis, reconstruction is considered. This falls into 6 categories:

1. *Nerve transfers.* Suture of the hypoglossal (twelfth cranial) nerve to the facial nerve produces movement of the facial muscles when the tongue is moved. Facial movement therefore occurs when eating and is somewhat unnatural.

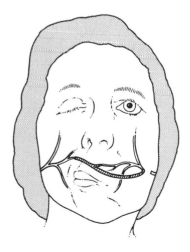

Fig. 37. *Cross-facial nerve graft (shown cross-hatched) for left facial palsy sutured to a cut branch of the right facial nerve.*

2. *Nerve grafts*. A donor graft, such as the sural nerve from the calf, is sutured to the proximal stump of the facial nerve on the paralysed side if it is identifiable, or, if not, to a small branch of the facial nerve on the non-paralysed side, so re-innervating the muscles (Fig. 37).

3. *Static suspension*. (a) Fascia lata or tendon (from the forearm or calf) is secured to the angle of the mouth and fixed to the zygomatic bone to lift the corner of the mouth (Fig. 38). (b) Excisions of an ellipse of skin above the eyebrow or a face-lift limit the droop of paralysed tissue.

Fig. 38. *Fascia lata sling attached to the malar beneath the skin.*

4. *Dynamic suspension*. The pull of the masseter or temporalis muscles is transferred to move the cheek, lips or eyelids.

5. *Correction of hyperactivity* on the non-paralysed side. The grimace caused by hyperaction of the muscles of the non-paralysed side of the face is reduced by dividing those muscles (myectomy), or by division of their nerve supply (neurectomy).

6. *Tarsorrhaphy*. The lateral third of the upper eyelid is stitched to the lower eyelid. This narrows the amount of eye exposed, and so reduces conjunctivitis and keratitis.

NURSING CARE
● Depending on the operative procedure, see nursing care of

nerve grafts, tendon grafts (Chapter 3) or face-lifts (Chapter 20).

● Nursing care may involve care of the grafts or flaps used to close the defect (see Chapter 3).

CRANIO-FACIAL DYSOSTOSIS

A rare inherited abnormality causing premature fusion of the sutures of the skull produces a prominent forehead, shallow orbits, exophthalmos, an excessive width between the eyes (hypertelorism), mental deficiency and relative prominence of the mandible (Crouzon's[5] syndrome).

Some of these children also have congenital abnormalities of the hands including syndactyly, short or rudimentary digits and clinodactyly (acrocephalosyndactyly or Apert's[6] syndrome). This abnormality occurs about once in every 160 000 births.

Pre- and post-operative assessment involves the expertise of several specialities:

Paediatric	Ophthalmic
Neurological	E.N.T.
Neurosurgical	Anaesthetic
Surgical	Radiological
Dental	Social
Orthodontic	Speech therapy
Psychiatric	Genetic counsel

Meticulous pre-operative planning is necessary, and includes:

1. Radiological studies and computerised axial tomography (CT scan).
2. Ophthalmic tests.
3. Mental and neurological assessment.
4. Dental impressions and splintage construction.
5. Medical photography.

Surgery encompasses three principles:

1. To decompress the brain if intracranial pressure increases, to prevent loss of vision, paralysis and mental retardation.

---

[5] Dr Octave Crouzon, 1874–1938. Physician, France.
[6] Dr Eugene Apert, 1868–1940. Paediatrician, Paris.

2. To remove bone from between the orbits to correct the hypertelorism.

3. To release the backwardly displaced maxilla, and insert bone grafts behind it to maintain its forward position.

Principles of operation

The skull bones are exposed through an incision across the top of the scalp from ear to ear. The forehead skin is turned downwards to the level of the top of the rim of the orbits. A segment of skull is removed to expose the brain, and the frontal lobes of the brain are retracted backwards to expose the bone in the roof of the orbits.

Osteotomies are made in the maxilla, through cheek and/or intra-oral incisions, to complete the mobilisation all around the orbits. Bone is resected from between the roofs of the orbits to allow them to come closer together. Once these have been moved, iliac bone grafts are placed behind them to maintain their forward position. Where necessary, dental splints, applied pre-operatively, are wired or cleated together.

The skull is replaced and the soft tissues closed with drainage.

NURSING CARE

- Pre- and post-operative care requires intensive nursing by nurses with experience in all the specialities involved, i.e. neurosurgery, ophthalmology and facio-maxillary surgery, in a specialised unit.
- The patient is nursed in an Intensive Care Unit.
- Endotracheal intubation (or tracheostomy) may have been performed, and is maintained until the patient is conscious and breathing easily.
- The eyelids are sutured or taped, and an encompassing bandage supports the face. Continuous reassurance that his blindness is only temporary is needed for the child whose eyes are covered.
- Oral feeding by a catheter or straw is instituted within 24 to 48 hours while the dental splints are in place (for care of dental splints see Chapter 19).
- Alternatively, or in association, feeding may be by a nasogastric tube.
- A drain is placed where the bone grafts have been removed,

probably from the iliac crest.

- A spinal drainage catheter, inserted into the subarachnoid space of the spinal cord in the lumbar region, is connected to a closed measuring system. The removal of about 60 ml of cerebrospinal fluid (CSF) prevents it leaking from the skull.

Complications

1. Bleeding, often rapid and profuse, from a torn vein or artery in the face or scalp.
2. Epileptic fits, in patients who have had intracranial surgery.
3. Confusion, disorientation and clouding of the consciousness (indicates cerebral oedema).
4. Wound infections.
5. Resorption of the bone graft, or bone of the face.
6. Corneal ulceration.
7. Anaesthesia of the cheek due to division of a nerve.
8. Cerebrospinal fluid leak from a defect in the meninges of the brain.
9. Respiratory difficulty.
10. Intestinal bleeding due to a stress ulcer in the stomach or duodenum.

SCALP INJURIES AND DEFECTS

Neonatal scalp defects

A baby, more commonly female, born with an ulcer in the midline of the scalp, often with exposure of the dura, may succumb to meningitis or haemorrhage. Small ulcers will epithelialise from the edges if protected with moist dressings. Larger ones require skin grafting. If bone or cartilage grafts are needed for the skull defect, local scalp flaps are needed to cover these grafts.

Avulsion of the scalp

When long hair is caught in rotating machinery, the scalp may be avulsed. The injury bleeds profusely, and early blood transfusion is required to prevent shock.

Management depends on the extent of the loss:

1. Skin grafts will 'take' on bared periosteum. They do not, of course, grow hair.

2. Avulsed skin may be defatted and replaced as a full-thickness graft. Hair growth is sparse.

3. Local scalp flaps, or flaps from the arm or abdomen, provide full-thickness cover for extensive scalp loss.

4. Provided the avulsed skin has not been crushed in the machinery, it may be possible to anastomose its arteries and veins to vessels of the occiput or forehead, replacing it as a 'free flap'.

Skull defects

Initial cover of holes in the skull produced by trauma can be achieved by skin grafts, which 'take' well on dura mater. For later, definitive replacement of missing bone, autogenous bone grafts from the ribs or cancellous iliac bone are laid in the skull defect. It has been shown that bone from the skull defect edges will grow over and join up with the bone grafts.

Vitallium, silicone and stainless steel plates have been used to cover such defects, though they tend to become infected and to be extruded.

Radiation and burn injuries of scalp

Radiation was formerly used in the treatment of ringworm and of haemangiomata. This may result many years later in the development of scalp ulceration and neoplastic change to basal and squamous cell carcinoma. Skin grafts on heavily irradiated areas 'take' poorly, so scalp flap cover may be required.

Full-thickness burns of the scalp can usually be covered with split skin grafts, provided the galea aponeurotica or the periosteum is intact. When cortical bone is exposed, trephining the outer table of the skull permits granulation tissue to grow from the marrow, onto which skin grafts can be applied.

EAR DEFORMITIES

The anatomy of the normal pinna is shown in Figure 39. Congenital deformities of the pinna range from total absence, through

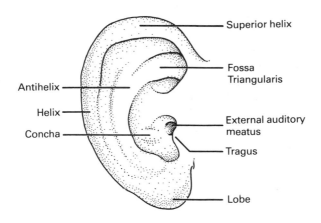

Fig. 39. *Anatomy of the normal pinna.*

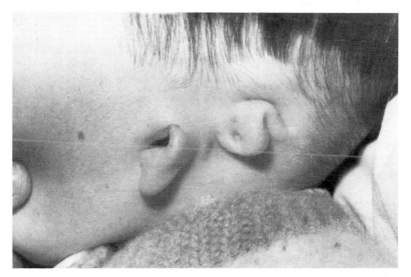

Fig. 40. *Microtia.*

microtia (a small malformed ear, see Fig. 40), to the presence of an accessory auricle, a tag of skin containing cartilage, usually close to the tragus of an otherwise normal ear. Microtia occurs once in every 20 000 births and is usually unilateral.

NURSING CARE
- General nursing care at birth is similar to that of any baby born with congenital deformity (see Chapter 5).
- Specific care involves careful explanation to the parents of the exact nature of the deformity and the prognosis.
- When there is total absence of the pinna (very rare) or microtia, the external auditory meatus may also be absent. This results in impaired hearing on the affected side, but, if the internal hearing mechanism is unaffected, hearing may be restored by an operation to construct the external auditory meatus.
- If the middle ear is also deformed, it may be possible to improve the hearing by surgery to reconstruct the sound-receiving mechanism. For these children the prognosis for hearing is uncertain.
- The middle ear may be deformed even if the external auditory meatus is present. Therefore the external appearance of this deformity gives no guide to the prognosis for the child's hearing.
- It is not feasible to conduct accurate hearing tests until the child is 2 to 3 years old. Therefore the parents will have to wait for a few years before the extent of their child's disability can be accurately assessed.
- All aspects of the child's condition will be explained to the parents as soon as possible after the birth.
- Fortunately this congenital deformity is usually unilateral, so the child is seldom totally deaf.

Microtia (Fig. 40)

When the cartilaginous skeleton of the pinna needs to be reconstructed, it is usual to employ a scaffold of rib cartilage or silicone rubber, which is covered with local skin flaps. When surgery to the middle ear or auditory meatus is proposed, this is carried out before reconstruction of the pinna is commenced. Reconstruction involves a multi-staged operation, and some patients may accept a prosthetic ear instead of operation. The stages of the operation are:

1. Removal of the rib cartilage from the eighth, ninth and tenth right ribs. The cartilage is sculptured and implanted under the skin

of the scalp at the site of the future ear. It is held in position in contact with the skin with mattress sutures.

2. After 2 or 3 months, the cartilage and overlying skin is raised from the scalp, and a skin graft placed in the groove behind it. A local tube pedicle flap is raised.

3. After a further 2 months, the tragus of the ear is constructed from the external skin, and a further skin graft placed onto the future concha.

4. Finally, usually with a composite graft from the opposite normal ear, the concha is constructed and the helix completed from the tube pedicle.

Operation to reconstruct the pinna is delayed until the child is at least 8 years of age, by which time the pinna is fully grown. Since the pinna is one of the most difficult shapes to reconstruct, reconstructive surgery will provide a pinna which is less acceptable cosmetically than a prosthetic pinna.

When the child reaches the age where he becomes self-conscious about his deformity, a prosthesis may be provided. This relieves the child's anxiety about his appearance, until he is old enough for surgery. It also allows both the child and his parents the opportunity to make an informed decision as to the relative advantages and disadvantages of opting for surgical reconstruction.

The disadvantages of wearing a prosthetic pinna are:

1. It has to be stuck onto the side of the head each day with special glue. This is a rather time-consuming procedure which has to be accomplished each morning before the child goes to school.

2. The prosthesis may be knocked off, causing social embarrassment and drawing attention to his deformity.

3. If the child has to wear a hearing aid, it cannot be attached satisfactorily to the prosthetic pinna.

4. If the child requires spectacles there is nowhere to hang them. Attaching spectacles to a prosthetic pinna is unsatisfactory, as the weight of the spectacles dislodges the prosthesis. Therefore specially adapted spectacles are required and this draws attention to the deformity.

The disadvantages of surgical reconstruction are:

1. The cosmetic result in many instances is not good. This type

of surgery is best explained to the child and the parents as an attempt to produce an apology for an ear. All parties concerned will then be pleased rather than disappointed at the result.

2. The surgical procedure requires a minimum of 4 operations over a period of about 12 to 24 months. The child is discharged home between each stage of the surgery. Once surgery has been commenced he is not able to wear his prosthesis. Therefore, for about 12 months, he has to face his friends and the general public with an incomplete pinna. The child needs to be very well motivated to tolerate both the surgery involved and social embarrassment between operations.

3. The surgery may leave scars on the chest and neck. If a composite graft is taken from the opposite pinna (stage 4), the scar is small and usually hidden at the back of the pinna. The donor sites used for the skin grafts usually heal with minimal scarring.

Before a decision is made to construct a pinna surgically, the child's wishes, as well as those of the parents, will be considered.

POST-OPERATIVE NURSING CARE

● Post-operative nursing care involves general care of the child undergoing surgery, and specific care of the grafts and flaps used to provide the tissues from which the pinna is constructed (see Chapter 3).

Protruding or lop ear

Prominence of the pinna due to the ear bending forwards at an angle to the side of the head, or due to the superior pole lopping forwards, causes emotional problems amongst children teased at school. The deformity is usually not corrected before the age of 7 years, when the pinna is approaching adult size and the cartilage is firm enough to hold its reconstructed position. In the majority, the deformity is due to the absence of the antihelix fold (Fig. 39) in the cartilage, and the reconstruction of this corrects the deformity. In a minority, the concha is too deep, so the entire pinna is displaced laterally from the side of the head, and the concha requires reduction. The operation scar lies behind the ear, so it is rarely noticed.

Many people express the opinion that this type of surgery is a purely cosmetic procedure. However, the child with protruding ears may become so emotionally disturbed by the teasing of his peers that at school he either becomes the 'class clown' or a persistent truant. Therefore the operation to set the ears closer to the head may change the whole academic course of the child's life.

This operation may be performed under local anaesthesia as an out-patient, or under general anaesthesia which requires admission to hospital for a few days. The optimum time for surgery is when the child himself requests it to correct his protruding ears. The child will then be well motivated to tolerate the post-operative discomfort. This is usually after the child has reached 7 years, but may be delayed until he reaches his teens. However, if the child is suffering from severe emotional problems, it may be desirable to persuade a reluctant child to undergo surgery.

PRE-OPERATIVE NURSING CARE
- Explain to the child that his ears will be heavily bandaged after his operation.
- Tell him that post-operative pain will not be severe, but the dressing will be uncomfortable.
- Explain that he must not interfere with his dressings, as it is the packing around his ears and the firm bandage which hold his ears in the corrected position. Therefore, dislodging the dressing may spoil the outcome of the operation.
- Explain that he will not be able to hear very well as the dressings will muffle sound.
- If the dressing is discarded or displaced too soon, then the unhealed and weakened cartilage of the pinna may 'spring' back into its old position, so destroying the objective of the operation. Ensure that the child and his parents understand that the dressing must remain undisturbed for at least 7 days, until the remoulded cartilage has started to heal in the correct position.
- The child's hair is washed on the morning of the operation.
- It is not necessary to trim or shave the hair around the ears. To do so may cause the child unnecessary embarrassment when the bandages are removed.

POST-OPERATIVE NURSING CARE
- The child may suffer severe nausea for a few hours after this

operation. To overcome this problem the child is given an anti-emetic drug with his pre-anaesthetic medication. Anti-emetic therapy is repeated as necessary post-operatively.

- Until the child is fully awake and aware of his surroundings, careful observation is required to ensure that his dressings are not disturbed.
- A haematoma forming behind the ear will produce a 'cauliflower ear' unless treated promptly.
- Leakage of blood through the dressings or persistent pain may indicate haematoma formation. The dressings are removed very carefully so the position of the pinna is not disturbed. Care must be taken not to disturb the moulded packing which is placed over the pinna. The function of this packing is to mould the cartilage of the pinna to the correct position. Removal of the dressing therefore requires at least two nurses, one to undo the bandage and one to hold the packing in place. The wound behind the ear is inspected. If a haematoma is present, it may be possible to evacuate it gently from between the sutures. If not, the child is returned to theatre for evacuation and haemostasis.
- The bandage must be applied firmly to hold the dressings in the correct position. However, if the bandage is too tight it may cause sufficient pressure to produce skin necrosis over the new antihelix. If there is persistent pain and no haematoma, then the front of the pinna is inspected for signs of ischaemia.
- Displacement of the dressing, such as may occur whilst the child is asleep but restless, may cause the pinna to become folded back onto itself. If the cartilage heals in this position the ear will be deformed. Therefore, if there is any sign of displacement, the dressing is carefully removed so the position of the pinna can be checked and corrected if necessary.
- Before his discharge home, ensure that the child and his parents understand the importance of prompt treatment in the event of persistent pain or displacement of the dressing.
- Sutures are removed 7 to 10 days after the operation.
- The bandage may be discarded during the daytime 1 or 2 weeks after surgery, depending on the extent of the surgery and the age of the child.
- Bandages are applied at night, to prevent damage to the delicate cartilage, for 4 weeks after surgery.

Shell or cup ear

In this condition the helix is too short to surround the concha and is cupped around the pinna. The helix is lengthened either using a composite graft from the opposite ear, or by releasing the superior helix from the side of the scalp.

NURSING CARE
● Nursing care is the same as for protruding ears (see above).

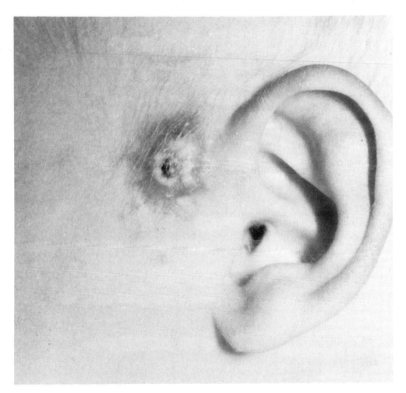

Fig. 41. *Preauricular sinus.*

Preauricular sinus

This is a congenital pin-hole opening in front of the pinna which leads down to a labyrinth of bifurcating tracks (Fig. 41). It is liable to repeated infection. The asymptomatic sinus may be left alone, but excision is necessary after infection has occurred. To mark the tracks, methylene blue may be injected into the pin-hole before dissection is begun. The skin is closed by direct suture after the tracks have been excised.

NURSING CARE
- The wound is closed by direct closure. It must be kept clean and dry.
- Sutures are removed after 3 to 5 days.

Traumatic amputation ('Garden of Gethsemane' ear)

Because of the unique configuration of ear cartilage, it is never discarded after amputation if there is any possibility of conserving it. If primary ear reconstruction is not feasible, the cartilage may be banked by implanting it under the abdominal skin.

NURSING CARE
- Nursing care is the same as for reconstruction for congenital absence, plus care of the wound caused by the amputation.

Otohaematoma ('cauliflower' ear)

Haemorrhage between the ear cartilage and its perichondrium is converted into fibrous tissue if untreated, producing an irreversible 'cauliflower' ear. Blood is, therefore, evacuated early and any dead space obliterated by pressure dressings or mattress sutures.

NURSING CARE
- Nursing care is the same as for protruding ears.

THE NECK

Webbed neck

This is a congenital deformity in which webs of skin and subcutaneous tissue extend from the mastoid to the shoulder regions (Fig. 42). Sometimes the deformity is associated with:

1. *Turner's syndrome*. An apparent female with only a single X sex chromosome (XO), and infantile uterus, vagina and breasts.

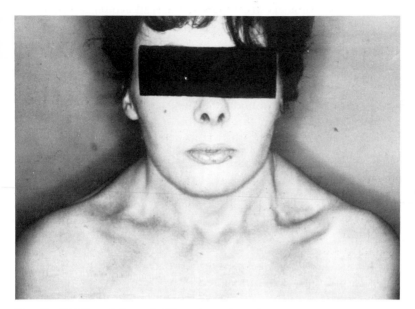

Fig. 42. *Webbing of the neck (Turner's syndrome).*

2. *Sprengel's[7] shoulder.* The shoulder, and particularly the scapula, is higher on the affected side.

3. *Klippel–Feil[8] syndrome.* A congenital fusion of the cervical vertebrae, resulting in limitation of movement of the short neck, sometimes accompanied by squint, deafness and cleft of the palate.

Treatment is by multiple Z-plasties (see page 49) of the webs.

NURSING CARE

● See nursing care of flaps in Chapter 3.

Wry neck (Torticollis)

This may result from:

1. Squint

---

[7] Otto Sprengel, 1852–1915. Surgeon, Brunswick, Germany.
[8] Maurice Klippel, 1858–1942; André Feil, b. 1884. Neurologists, Paris.

2. Pain in the neck, for example cervical lymphadenitis.

3. Congenital deformities of the cervical vertebrae.

4. Hysteria.

5. A haemangiomatous malformation of the sternocleidomastoid muscle, usually present at or soon after birth.

Management of torticollis due to haemangioma begins with physiotherapy, to manipulate the head and massage the sternocleidomastoid muscle. If this fails, the angioma becomes replaced by fibrous tissue, necessitating a sternocleidomastoid tenotomy. A padded collar support is worn post-operatively.

Cystic hygroma (lymphangioma)

This is a collection of lymph sacs which fail to drain. They therefore progressively enlarge from birth onwards, usually as swellings in the side of the neck, or occasionally in the axilla. Large ones may cause respiratory embarrassment, and they are liable to infection. Careful dissection is necessary for their total removal, since they tend to grow as isolated separate sacs. Leaving one sac behind may give rise to a recurrence.

NURSING CARE

- The wound is usually closed by direct closure, with suction drainage. Therefore, nursing care involves care of the wound and drains.
- If vacuum suction is used, the vacuum should be reinstated every 6 hours, or more frequently if drainage is copious.
- If the drains appear blocked, for example if there is no drainage and the area beneath or around the wound is swelling, milk the tubes to free the blockage. If this fails to produce adequate drainage, the doctor is notified urgently. It may be necessary to remove a few sutures to release the collection of fluid, or the patient may be returned to theatre for reinsertion of the drainage tubes.
- The drains are removed 24 hours after the last drainage.
- Sutures are removed 5 to 7 days after the operation.

Thyroglossal cyst and fistula

A thyroglossal cyst occurs in the midline of the front of the neck, moves on swallowing, and arises from an embryological track between the tongue and the pharynx. It is liable to recurrent infection. Incision into or incomplete removal of the cyst and track produces a fistula or sinus which opens into the front of the neck.

Branchial cyst and sinus

Branchial cysts lie on the side of the neck, usually over the carotid artery. They are lined with squamous epithelium, and arise from a fetal remnant of the embryonic gill (branchial) arch (see Chapter 5). Less commonly, a track may extend from the remnant to the skin surface as a sinus.

Branchial cysts and sinuses may become infected. They are treated by excision, though if an abscess is present this requires drainage, with definitive excision later. Following definitive excision the wound is closed by direct closure.

Surgery is usually performed before the child starts school.

NURSING CARE

- Nursing care involves general pre- and post-operative care of the child and specific care of the wound.
- If a fistula has been excised, oral feeds and fluids are withheld until the wound is healed, usually 5 to 7 days.
- Nasogastric feeds are commenced a few hours after recovery from the anaesthetic. For the feeding requirements of the child see page 340.
- For care of wound drainage see nursing care for cystic hygroma.
- Sutures are removed after 5 to 7 days.

FURTHER READING

Jackson, I.T. (Ed.) (1981) *Recent advances in plastic surgery*, Vol. 2. Edinburgh: Churchill Livingstone.

Longacre, J.J. (1968) *Cranio-facial anomalies*. Philadelphia: J.B. Lippincott.

Mustardé, J.C. (1980) *Repair and reconstruction in the orbital region: a practical guide*, 2nd edn. Edinburgh: Churchill Livingstone.

Peet, E.W. (1971) *Congenital absence of the ear*. London: E. & S. Livingstone.

Rubin, L.R. (1977) *Reanimation of the paralysed face*. St Louis: C.V. Mosby.

Wynne-Davies, R. (1973) *Heritable disorders in orthopaedic practice*. Oxford: Blackwell Scientific.

8 The thorax and breast

PECTUS EXCAVATUM
(Funnel Chest)

The sternum and anterior chest are depressed as a developmental abnormality (Fig. 43). Two theories are postulated as to its formation:

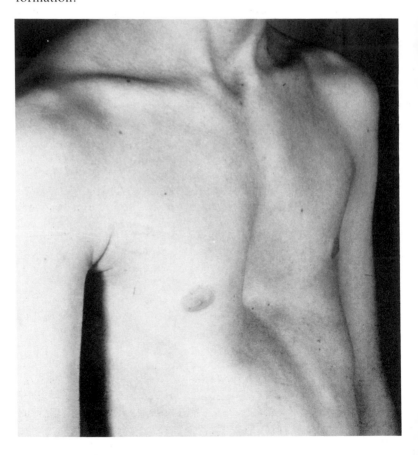

Fig. 43. *Pectus excavatum.*

1. The muscular pull of the diaphragm deforms the costal cartilages in infancy, drawing them inwards.

2. Overgrowth of the costal cartilages forces the sternum posteriorly.

Symptoms are usually confined to the embarrassment of a school-child about the appearance of his chest. Occasionally, breathing difficulties and palpitations may be the predominant symptoms.

Treatment

Explanation of the developmental nature of the condition and emotional support may assuage the child's anxiety.

If this is insufficient, the deformity may be camouflaged by subcutaneous introduction of rubberised silicone (Dow Corning Medical Grade Elastomer 382) through a presternal incision, to build out the funnel depression. The fluid silicone hardens when mixed with a catalyst, stannous octoate, to a firm rubbery consistency. Surgery is usually performed after the thorax has reached adult size.

The patient is anaesthetised and laid supine on the operating table. The hollow of the funnel chest is filled with water. Since the specific gravity of Elastomer 382 is approximately one, the number of millilitres of water required to fill the hollow is equal to the number of millilitres of Elastomer needed.

The requisite amount of Elastomer is autoclaved. At the same time the quantity of catalyst recommended by the manufacturers to give a setting time of 15 to 20 minutes is separately autoclaved in a bowl.

The chest skin is carefully sterilised and towelled during this autoclaving process. An incision is made over the sternum, the necessary dissection carried out, and a suction drain laid in the bottom of the wound.

The Elastomer is now poured into the bowl containing the catalyst. The two are thoroughly mixed with a sterile tablespoon and then poured into the sternal incision. The wound is closed in two layers, and while the Elastomer is hardening it is moulded to conform with the contours of the chest.

If the deformity is severe, causing respiratory problems or palpitations, surgery to elevate the sternum may be indicated.

Through a midline incision, the sternum is separated from the xiphisternum and the manubrium sterni. The perichondrium of the depressed rib cartilages is stripped off, and the cartilages are cut across at both ends and removed. The sternum is manipulated forwards and held with non-absorbable sutures. If the pleura is punctured during the procedure, the pneumothorax is eliminated by inflating the lungs by positive pressure ventilation, and the tear is repaired. A chest drain may then be inserted and attached to an underwater seal. Positive pressure ventilation is discontinued when the underwater seal is seen to be working satisfactorily. The underwater seal is maintained until the pleura is healed, usually after 5 to 7 days.

PRE-OPERATIVE NURSING CARE

- The patient is admitted the day before the planned surgery, and the routine pre-operative and pre-anaesthetic preparation is carried out.
- Ensure that the patient understands the nature of the surgery involved.
- Tell the patient that this type of surgery is usually successful, but do not enhance his expectations of the cosmetic result of the operation. This will already have been explained to the patient by his surgeon. This type of surgery usually produces a marked improvement in the patient's appearance, but encouraging the patient to expect absolute perfection may result only in dissatisfaction with the final result.
- There is a small risk that a silicone implant may have to be removed if it becomes infected. This slight risk is explained to the patient by the surgeon before the patient makes his decision to have the operation performed. Further discussions about this may cause the patient unnecessary anxiety.
- Similarly, for patients undergoing elevation of the sternum, all the risk factors, including the possibility of the need for an underwater seal post-operatively, will have been explained to him by the surgeon. Reassurance that the outcome of this type of surgery is invariably successful is more helpful to the patient than discussions of possible complications.
- Post-operatively the patient may be reluctant to breathe deeply because of pain or fear of disturbing his surgical repair. The importance of breathing exercises to prevent chest infec-

tion is explained to the patient, and the physiotherapist teaches the patient his exercises pre-operatively.

- On the day of operation the patient's entire chest is shaved, taking care not to cause any abrasions or nicks in the skin.
- The patient is starved for 6 hours before the operation, and instructed to remain in the position he finds himself on waking from the anaesthetic (i.e. lying on his back or sitting up in bed).

POST-OPERATIVE NURSING CARE

- The patient is nursed lying on his back, gradually moving to a semi-recumbent, and then a sitting position as soon as his blood pressure is stable.
- If the wound has been left exposed, it is kept clean by swabbing with sterile saline.
- If dressings are in situ, these are inspected frequently for any signs of bleeding.
- Excessive pain in the operation site may indicate haematoma formation. The dressings are removed and the wound inspected.
- If a haematoma is present, evacuation is carried out either by 'milking' it out gently between the sutures, or by removal of one or two sutures if necessary. If sutures are removed, Steristrips may be applied once drainage of the haematoma has ceased.
- Careful observations of the wound for any signs of infection are continued until the wound is healed.
- If wound infection is suspected, wound swabs are sent for culture and sensitivity, and the appropriate antibiotic therapy commenced when the organism has been identified.
- The patient is usually allowed up on the first post-operative day. He is instructed to move carefully and not to stretch his arms above his head, so putting tension on the operation site.
- The patient is instructed not to touch the operation site until at least 7 days after surgery.
- Sutures are removed after 7 to 10 days.
- Throughout the post-operative period the patient is encouraged to carry out his deep-breathing exercises conscientiously.
- If any signs of chest infection present, sputum is sent for culture and sensitivity, and appropriate antibiotic therapy

commenced when the organism has been isolated.

● If an underwater seal has been used, routine observations are continued to ensure that the seal remains effective until the chest drain is removed, usually after 5 to 7 days.

● The patient is discharged after 3 to 14 days, depending on the exact nature and extent of his surgery.

POLAND'S[1] SYNDROME

Absence of the pectoralis major muscle causes little physical disability, but may be associated with underdevelopment of the breast and syndactyly of the hand on the same side.

Reconstructive procedures involve breast augmentation (see below) and correction of the syndactyly (see Chapter 10).

PECTUS CARINATUM
(Keel or Pigeon Chest)

This is the opposite deformity to pectus excavatum. The sternum protrudes prominently in front of the rib cage like a keel of a ship. The deformity is much rarer than funnel chest.

Treatment

Through a midline incision, the costal cartilages on either side of the sternum are removed, leaving their periosteum. The expanding lung lifts the periosteum into alignment with the sternum. The operation is normally done in two stages, one side at a time.

NURSING CARE
● Nursing care is as for pectus excavatum (see above).

THE BREAST

The organ which distinguishes mammals from the lower animal classes is a specialised sweat gland, the site of disease and an inspiration of artists.

Patients who request surgery to improve the appearance of their

---

[1] Alfred Poland, 1820–1872. Surgeon to Guy's Hospital, London.

breasts do so because they feel a great need to seek some improvement in their 'body image'. Whatever their reasons for this, they tend to feel a sense of guilt at requesting what may be regarded as non-essential surgery. When the patient is admitted to the ward this sense of guilt may be greatly increased when she sees other patients in the ward whose need for surgery is obviously essential and acute. The patient may, therefore, be in a state of emotional conflict, feeling a great need for surgery but at the same time feeling intense guilt at having acknowledged that need. This may result in the patient either becoming very anxious and appearing very demanding, or becoming aggressive towards the staff and over-defensive.

The Plastic Surgical nurse understands the cause of this reaction from the patient, and learns how to reassure her that the nurses appreciate her need for surgery, are sympathetic to her problems and do not regard her request for surgery as frivolous. It may help to explain to the patient that nurses working in Plastic Surgery regard quality of life as important as life itself.

BREAST AUGMENTATION

Breast augmentation may be indicated for:
1. Asymmetrical development of the breasts (Fig. 44).
2. Involution following pregnancy or weight loss.
3. Failure of development of both breasts (micromastia).
4. Burn injury to the chest. Destruction of the breast disc before puberty may lead to failure of breast growth.
5. Post-mastectomy reconstruction.

Historically, a large range of substances have been used to augment the breast. Implants have included free dermo-fat grafts from the buttocks, sponge and polythenes, but the most satisfactory are the silicone implants. A patch of Dacron, a polyester fibre, may be attached to one surface if it is desired that the implant should adhere to the chest wall fascia; the free-floating implant is, however, now more in fashion (see Chapter 22).

Implants are inserted through an axillary or submammary incision to lie in front of the pectoralis major muscle or, less commonly, behind the muscle. The implant, therefore, lies behind the breast and does not interfere with the anatomy or functions of

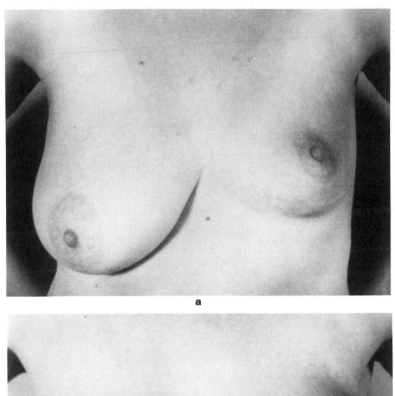

a

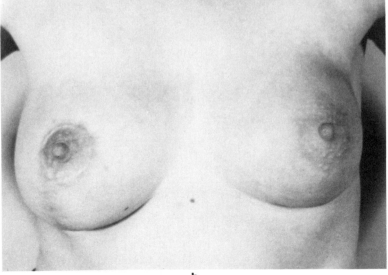

b

Fig. 44. *Breast asymmetry (a) before and (b) after left augmentation and right reduction.*

the breast. It may be possible for the patient who has had an implant to breast-feed.

Types of silicone implant

1. *Gel-filled.* A silicone envelope surrounds a gel of semi-fluid silicone. The implants are available in various sizes from 120 ml to 450 ml and differ in shape from round to tear-shaped.

2. *Inflatable.* An envelope of silicone is attached to a filling tube and valve; the lumen of the envelope is filled to the desired volume with dextran or saline when the implant has been inserted. These have the advantage that they can be inserted through a smaller incision than the gel-filled implants; for example a periareolar incision may be used. They also permit a greater variety of sizes than the pre-filled gel implants, but sometimes deflate due to leakage of the valve. (See Chapter 22.)

Pre operative preparation

Scrupulous preparation of the implant and the patient's skin is essential. If the prosthesis is not supplied sterile, the manufacturer's directions for sterilisation are followed meticulously. Just before insertion into the patient, the implant is washed in saline to remove all adherent matter.

Complications

1. Haematoma around the implant is often followed by its extrusion.

2. Infection may necessitate removal of the implant.

3. The prosthesis may rupture or leak (particularly with an inflatable prosthesis).

4. A capsule may form. About 10 to 15% of patients develop a capsule of scar tissue around the implant producing an unacceptable degree of hardness of the breast. Attempts have been made to prevent formation of this capsule by:

(a) Incorporation of steroids into the prosthesis or wound cavity.

(b) Minimising the collection of blood around the implant, by meticulous haemostasis and wound drainage.

(c) Instituting massage of the breast by the patient after the first post-operative week.

(d) Capsulotomy for the refractory case, involving surgical division of the scar and enlarging the space in which the implant lies.

(e) Surrounding the silicone envelope with a second outer envelope (double lumen implant). There is some suggestion that leakage of silicone gel through the envelope may contribute to thicker capsule formation.

PRE-OPERATIVE NURSING CARE

- Pre-operative nursing care involves preparation of the patient and explanation that the nurses understand and support the patient's need for surgery.
- Ensure that the patient understands the operative procedure and that there will be small scars at the site of insertion of the prosthesis.
- Be optimistic that the outcome of this type of surgery is usually successful. Exactly what the patient may expect as a result of her operation will already have been explained to her by her surgeon. It is very important that the nurse does not encourage her to fantasise about the degree of improvement she may anticipate.
- When augmentation is carried out on one breast only, for example for asymmetry or post-mastectomy, it is never possible to achieve an exact match with the other breast. Ensure that the patient understands this, but reassure her that this will not be a serious problem. Explain to her that many women have one breast slightly larger than the other, just as many people have one foot slightly larger than the other. Point out that this fact is not normally observed.
- Instruct the patient not to raise her arms above shoulder-height for 7 to 14 days after her operation. Explain that this avoids putting unnecessary strain on the prosthesis, so preventing displacement.
- Explain to the patient that post-operatively she may have drains in situ. Ask her to remain in the position she finds herself when she wakes up, until the nurse has instructed her on what position she needs to maintain, and how to move herself about in bed.

POST-OPERATIVE NURSING CARE

- The patient is nursed on her back, moving to a semi-recumbent position as soon as her blood pressure is stable.

- If drains are in situ, frequent observations are necessary to ensure that they are working correctly, so preventing haematoma formation.
- The amount of drainage is accurately recorded and any excessive blood loss reported to the doctor promptly.
- The type of dressing and supporting bandage used depends upon the exact nature of the operative technique, and on the individual preference of the surgeon. Ensure detailed instructions are received before the patient is transferred from the theatre to the ward.
- Remind the patient not to raise her arms above shoulder height for 7 to 14 days.
- Warn the patient to be very careful not to knock the breasts as the prostheses may easily be displaced during the first few weeks after implantation.
- The patient is usually allowed up on the first post-operative day.
- The drains are removed 24 hours after the last drainage.
- If any signs of infection present, the wound is inspected and wound swabs sent for culture and sensitivity, so that appropriate antibiotic therapy can be commenced when the organism has been identified.
- Urgent evacuation of any haematoma may avert the need to remove the implant.
- Skin sutures are removed after 5 to 7 days.
- Ensure that the patient understands the importance of wearing a suitable bra to give adequate support to the augmented breast.
- Explain and demonstrate the technique of massaging the breast to prevent capsule formation.
- Ensure that the patient understands that 'heavy-handed' manipulation of the breast during the first few weeks after surgery may displace the prosthesis and encourage scar tissue and adhesions to form around the implant.
- Many patients ask about the effect that their monthly cycle may have on the augmented breasts. Many women experience a feeling of 'fullness' and sometimes slight discomfort in the breasts in the few days prior to menstruation. Explain that this is a normal occurrence and that, since the implant is behind

the breasts and not within it, this will not affect the implant.
- The patient is usually discharged from hospital after 3 to 7 days, depending on the operative technique used.
- Ensure that the patient's follow-up arrangements include instructions to contact the hospital immediately if she is concerned about her wound or the state of the breasts.

BREAST REDUCTION

The overlarge breast in the female may be:
1. A developmental abnormality at puberty or pregnancy.
2. A familial characteristic.
3. The result of weight gain due to obesity.
4. The result of an endocrine abnormality, such as oestrogen-secreting tumours.
5. Produced by pathology within the breast, for example a cystic fibro-adenoma.

The symptoms produced by breast hypertrophy are:
1. A feeling of heaviness on the chest and shoulders, often interfering with work and sports.
2. Backache.
3. Itching and intertrigo under the breast.
4. Social embarrassment.
5. Respiratory difficulties.

Treatment

While considerable overall weight loss has to be achieved to produce a detectable reduction in breast size, pre-operative weight reduction may be in the interests of the patient in reducing the risks of anaesthesia.

Surgery to reduce the size of the breasts leaves extensive scars which tend to be of indifferent quality. The scars are usually sited on the lower half of the breast and within the mammary fold. Scars encircling the nipple are less noticeable as the line of the scar tends to blend into the natural demarcation around the areola. The extent of the operative scars and the expected results are carefully explained to the patient before operation is decided upon.

On the night before operation, the patient's skin will be marked

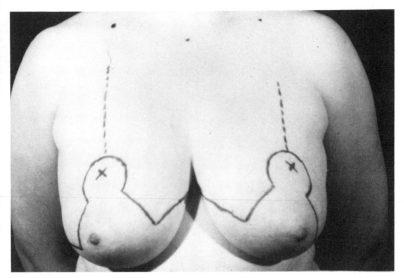

Fig. 45. *Pre-operative breast reduction skin marking.*

out with a skin pencil to define the incisions to be made and the amount of the reduction to be undertaken. For this the patient is in a sitting position, comfortably relaxed, with the arms to the sides (Fig. 45).

Methods of operation

1. Reduction with free nipple graft (Thorek[2] technique). For gross hypertrophies, the areola and nipple are removed, thinned and replaced in the corrected position as a full-thickness graft after breast reduction. The excess breast tissue is removed by excising a segment of skin and breast from the inferior quadrants (Fig. 46). Breast function is lost post-operatively, and there is an incidence of about 20% of partial or complete failure of the nipple grafts.

2. Reduction leaving the nipple nourished on a pedicle, or pedicles, of breast tissue (McKissock[3], Pers[4], Skoog, Strombeck[5]).

[2] Max Thorek, Surgeon, Chicago, USA.
[3] P.K. McKissock, Plastic Surgeon, California, USA.
[4] Michael Pers, Plastic Surgeon, Copenhagen.
[5] J.O. Strombeck, Plastic Surgeon, Stockholm.

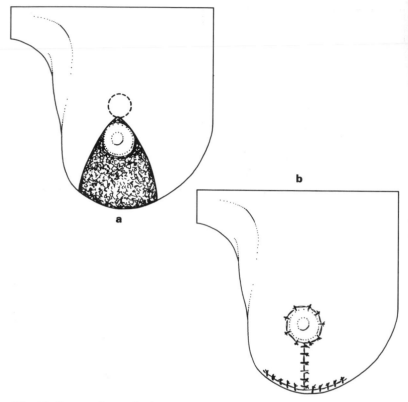

Fig. 46. *Breast reduction by free nipple graft method. (a) Incisions. (b) Completed.*

The resection of breast tissue is carried out to either side of a pedicle of breast tissue to which the nipple is attached (Fig. 47). The pedicle may lie vertically or horizontally. Breast function may continue as the ducts to the nipple remain intact.

3. Separation of the skin envelope from the breast with subsequent resection of breast tissue laterally and inferiorly. The nipple is rotated on the breast (Biesenberger[6]). The incidence of nipple

[6] H. Biesenberger, Vienna, 1931.

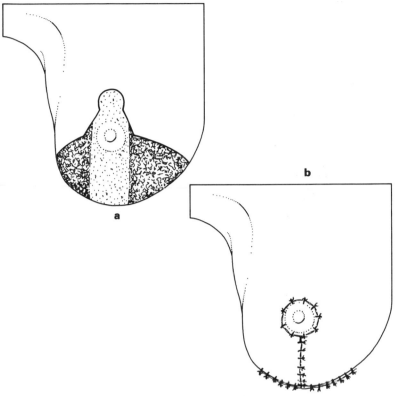

Fig. 47. *Breast reduction by McKissock's method. (a) Incisions. (b) Completed.*

and skin necrosis is higher than with some other techniques, and symmetry is somewhat more difficult to achieve.

4. Lateral quadrant excision of skin and breast tissue, leaving the nipple attached to the main breast remnant (Dufourmentel–Mouly[7]) (Fig. 48). The advantage of this method is that a linear scar is obtained which runs obliquely from the nipple towards the lateral chest wall. Only relatively small reductions can be achieved

[7] Claude Dufourmentel and Roger Mouly. Surgeons, Paris.

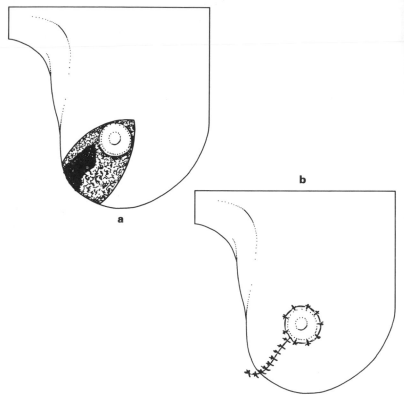

Fig. 48. *Breast reduction by Dufourmentel–Mouly method. (a) Incisions. (b) Completed.*

and symmetry is more difficult to obtain. However, breast function is maintained.

Post-operative complications

1. The operation may involve blood transfusion and lengthy anaesthesia. Precautions are taken to prevent deep vein thrombosis by the use of intermittent pressure (Flowtron) stockings on the legs during and after operation and by early physiotherapy.

2. Haematoma formation. If gross, evacuation in theatre is necessary.

3. Skin loss and partial wound dehiscence are treated with regular wound toilet and dressings.

4. Breast gangrene, fortunately rare, requires excision of dead tissue and secondary repair.

PRE-OPERATIVE NURSING CARE

- Pre-operative nursing care is the same as for breast augmentation.

POST-OPERATIVE NURSING CARE

- Before collecting the patient from the theatre ensure clear instructions have been given as to the exact operative procedure, for example whether free nipple grafts have been used.
- Blood transfusion is usually required. This may have been completed in the theatre. Ascertain how much blood has already been given, how many more units are to be given, and how much blood remains in the bank for this patient, should post-operative haemorrhage occur.
- On return to the ward the patient is nursed lying on her back until the blood pressure is stable. She is then raised to a semi-recumbent position, which is maintained for the next 24 hours.
- Until the patient is fully awake and orientated after the anaesthetic, careful observations are required to ensure that she does not turn onto her side, causing pressure on any of her wounds.
- Remind the patient not to move her arms above shoulder-height for 10 to 14 days after surgery. Explain that to do so will put additional strain on the wounds and may lead to post-operative bleeding or wound breakdown.
- Intravenous infusion is usually continued for 24 hours in order to keep the vein open should further blood transfusion be required.
- A fluid balance chart is maintained, and routine observations for any sign of reaction to the blood transfusion are carried out.
- If drains are in situ these are observed frequently to ensure that they are draining adequately. Blockage of a drain may result in haematoma formation and subsequent breakdown of the wound.

- All drainage from the wounds is recorded.
- If excessive amounts of blood are draining, the doctor is informed immediately. Additional blood transfusion may be needed, and if haemorrhage persists it may be necessary for the patient to be returned to theatre for haemostasis.
- The drains remain in situ until 24 hours after the last drainage.
- If Flowtron stockings are in use, ensure that these are working correctly and remain comfortable for the patient.
- The Flowtron stockings are usually removed after 24 hours. Physiotherapy is then commenced to prevent deep vein thrombosis.
- The type of dressing and supporting bandage used will depend on the operative procedure and the particular preference of the surgeon. Inspect the dressings frequently for signs of bleeding.
- Severe pain beneath the dressings may indicate haematoma formation. The dressings are removed and the wound inspected.
- If attempts to express the haematoma are unsuccessful, it may be necessary to return the patient to the theatre for evacuation.
- Failure to recognise and treat a haematoma may result in skin necrosis. It may then be necessary to close the wound by skin grafting, resulting in additional scarring.
- Pressure from a haematoma situated deeply within the wound may result in fat necrosis. This is seen at a late stage as liquefied globules of fat leaking from the wound. If fat necrosis is extensive the actual size of the breast is reduced by the amount of fat lost in this way.
- If there are any signs of infection, wound swabs are sent for culture and sensitivity and appropriate antibiotic therapy commenced when the organism has been isolated. Wound infection may result in both breakdown of skin and necrosis of actual breast tissue.
- The patient is usually allowed up and about on the first to third post-operative day.
- If free nipple grafts have been used these are treated as full-thickness (Wolfe) grafts (see Chapter 3).
- Failure of a nipple graft will necessitate later reconstruction of the nipple. Fortunately this complication is rare, but the fact

that it exists at all highlights the need for very careful observations for signs of haematoma formation or infection which may result in the loss of the free nipple graft.

- Nipple sutures are removed after 5 to 7 days.
- The other skin sutures are removed in stages after 10 to 14 days.
- Once the dressings and supporting bandages are removed, ensure that the patient understands the importance of wearing a correctly fitting bra, which does not exert pressure on the wounds.
- The patient is usually discharged from hospital after 7 to 14 days, depending on the operative procedure carried out.
- Ensure that after-care arrangements include instructions for the patient to contact the ward for advice if any untoward symptoms occur.

BREAST PTOSIS

Normal volume breasts may droop so that the nipple lies below the level of the submammary crease. Ptosis occurs when the pectoral ligaments attaching the breast skin to the fascia of the pectoralis major muscle stretch and rupture.

The correct anatomical relationship of the breast to the chest wall (overlying the second to the sixth ribs) is restored by excising the excess of breast skin, and repositioning the breast tissue within the smaller skin envelope (*mastopexy*). The amount of skin to be removed is estimated and marked out before the operation with the patient in a sitting position with her arms to the sides.

If ptosis accompanies involution of the breast, mastopexy may be combined with implant augmentation.

NURSING CARE
- Nursing care for correction of breast ptosis is a combination of nursing care for breast augmentation and breast reduction (see above), and depends on the exact operative procedure employed.

POST-MASTECTOMY BREAST RECONSTRUCTION

Mastectomy for breast carcinoma or other breast disease not only

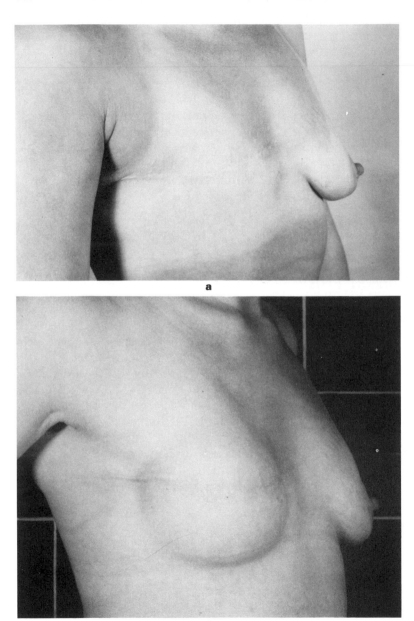

Fig. 49. *Post-mastectomy (a) before and (b) after reconstruction.*

disfigures, but is also a cause of severe emotional loss to many women. In general, the younger the woman, the greater is this emotional stress, but post-menopausal patients are not exempt. For the woman who is facing the possibility of removal of her breast because of disease, the knowledge that some later reconstruction is possible will help to allay some of her anxieties (Fig. 49).

Indications for mastectomy include:

1. Severe fibroadenosis (chronic mastitis).
2. Gross breast pain (mastodynia) unrelieved by other means.
3. Pre-malignant disease, such as multiple intraduct papillomata.
4. Breast carcinoma. The breast is responsible for 10% of all cancers, and occurs in 4 per 10 000 women.

To permit scars and tissue to soften, reconstruction is usually carried out not earlier than 6 to 12 months after the mastectomy.

Types of procedure

1. Insertion of a silicone-gel prosthesis behind the chest skin is suitable when little or no skin has been excised at the mastectomy, and when the skin is of a good texture. A prosthesis large enough to permit symmetry with the other normal breast is used. If, however, the opposite breast is very large, it may be necessary to carry out a reduction on that side so as to produce symmetry.

2. Replacement of chest skin by a flap, and the insertion of a silicone-gel prosthesis behind the flap, is required when there is skin shortage or there is severe radiotherapy damage to the chest skin. Local skin flaps are available from the side of the chest, the abdomen or the back over the scapula. The last usually also incorporates the latissimus dorsi muscle, on which the skin ellipse is carried (a myocutaneous flap – see Chapter 3).

Nipple reconstruction

Mastectomy frequently involves removal of the nipple along with the breast tissue. Some 3 to 6 months after breast reconstruction has been performed, the nipple–areola complex is simulated using:

1. The nipple excised at mastectomy, preserved by banking it temporarily as a graft on the abdomen until it is needed for reconstruction. The possibility exists of preserving cancer cells on the nipple, so this method is not applicable for reconstruction following carcinoma.

2. Part of the nipple from the other normal breast. This method is useful when the other nipple is large (nipple-sharing technique).

3. A full-thickness graft of pigmented skin from the groin or medial thigh, to simulate the areola.

4. A full-thickness graft of pigmented skin from the labia minora, to simulate the areola.

5. A partial-thickness skin graft from the buttock (whose pink colour may simulate the nulliparous areola).

6. Tattooing with inorganic pigments a circle corresponding in size and tone with the areola of the opposite breast.

When methods 1 or 2 are used, reconstruction of the areola and nipple is achieved.

Methods 3, 4, 5 and 6 only provide areola reconstruction. The nipple may then be simulated by a composite graft from the earlobe.

NURSING CARE

- Nursing care varies with the exact procedure required for the reconstruction.
- Skin flaps may be required, the nursing care for which is described in Chapter 3.
- Nursing care for breast augmentation, mastopexy and reduction is described under the appropriate headings in this chapter.
- Patients who are undergoing reconstruction following mastectomy for cancer often express some anxiety that the reconstruction may mask any recurrence of the disease. Should the patient express such anxiety, explain to her that reconstruction is not undertaken unless the surgeon is satisfied that it will not mask future symptoms.

SUPERNUMERARY NIPPLES

Nipples may occur anywhere on a line from the axilla to the groin, and represent the condition of multiple teats found in some other mammals. The amount of underlying breast tissue is usually very small. Treatment consists of simple excision of the supernumerary nipple and any underlying breast tissue.

ABSENCE OF NIPPLES

Absence of the nipples may occur as a congenital deformity or as a result of trauma, such as a severe burn injury to the chest.

The nipples have a psychological role in the development of normal puberty. Reconstruction of the nipples should, therefore, be carried out before the child reaches puberty.

To reconstruct areolae for this purpose full-thickness grafts may be used:

1. From the labia, since the skin of the labia has similar colour and appearance to that of the areola.

2. From the skin, particularly to match a nulliparous contralateral areola which is lighter in colour than the multiparous areola.

NURSING CARE
● Nursing care is as for full-thickness skin grafts (see Chapter 3).

GYNAECOMASTIA

Enlargement of the breast in the male may be an isolated abnormality or part of a generalised disease. Causes include:
1. *Physiological.*
    Neonatal. The newborn baby's breast is enlarged under the influence of the mother's hormones in utero.
    Pubertal. Some tenderness and enlargement is usual during puberty between 14 and 16 years of age.
2. *Genetic.*
    Klinefelter's syndrome, in which the sex chromosomes are XXY, producing testicular atrophy in an apparent male.
3. *Endocrine.*
    Testicular tumours.
    Hyperplasia of the adrenal glands.
    Pituitary tumours.
    Hyperthyroidism.

Bronchial carcinoma.
Castration.
4. *Drug induced*.
Oestrogens.
Steroids.
ACTH.
Androgens.
Monoamine oxidase inhibitors.
Spironolactone.
5. *Metabolic*.
Haemodialysis for renal failure.
Cirrhosis of the liver.
Starvation.

Treatment is directed to the cause if known. Breast tissue may be removed through an incision around the lower half of the areola of the nipple. The skin is undermined and the breast tissue freed from its attachments to the pectoral fascia. Suction drainage post-operatively is usually necessary. Haematoma requires expressing or evacuating in theatre.

PRE-OPERATIVE NURSING CARE
- The patient is usually admitted the day before the planned operation, so that pre-operative and pre-anaesthetic preparation may be carried out.
- Reassure the patient that the operation is a simple procedure and is invariably successful.
- Explain that drains may be in situ post-operatively. Instruct the patient to remain in the position he finds himself on waking from the anaesthetic, until the nurse has shown him how to move about the bed without disturbing his drains.
- On the morning of the operation the patient's chest is shaved, taking care not to cause abrasions or nicks in the skin.

POST-OPERATIVE NURSING CARE
- The patient is nursed lying flat on his back for the first 24 hours. This ensures the skin of the chest remains taut over the operation site, so discouraging any collection of fluid beneath the nipples. It also makes early detection of such fluid collection easier to recognise.

- The drains are inspected frequently to ensure that they are draining the wounds satisfactorily.
- All drainage is recorded. If there is excessive blood loss this is reported to the doctor immediately. Blood transfusion may be required, and if bleeding continues it may be necessary to return the patient to theatre for haemostasis.
- The wound may usually be left exposed so that haematoma can be detected and evacuated as quickly as possible. If dressed, it is inspected at 48 hours.
- The patient is allowed up and about from the first post-operative day.
- The drains are removed 24 hours after the last drainage, usually 2 to 3 days after the operation.
- Nipple sutures are removed after 5 to 7 days.
- The patient is usually discharged from hospital on the fifth post-operative day.

FURTHER READING

Converse, J.M. (Ed.) (1977) *Reconstructive plastic surgery: principles and procedures in correction, reconstruction and transplantation*, 2nd edn. Philadelphia: W.B. Saunders.

Gant, T.D. & Vasconez, L.O. (Eds) (1980) *Post-mastectomy reconstruction*. Baltimore: Williams & Wilkins.

Jackson, I.T. (Ed.) (1981) *Recent advances in plastic surgery*, Vol. 2. Edinburgh: Churchill Livingstone.

9 The trunk and abdominal wall

OMPHALOCOELE

This is a failure of formation of the abdominal wall, so that the intestines are covered at birth only by a lining of amnion. The abdominal contents have never lain in the abdominal cavity, and attempts to make them do so force up the diaphragm, causing death from respiratory failure.

Complications include rupture of the lining, peritonitis and strangulation of the bowel, and are often fatal.

Treatment as an emergency is imperative if the baby's life is to be saved. The sac is covered with swabs soaked in Ringer's[1] solution to prevent it drying out. A nasogastric tube is passed and the stomach kept decompressed. As soon as practicable, the baby is taken to theatre. The sac is opened and the intestines examined for other congenital anomalies. The skin and fat on the sides of the trunk and the back are mobilised, if necessary with relieving incisions, and used to cover the abdominal contents.

ABDOMINAL WALL DEFECTS

Causes include:
1. Congenital malformation (omphalocoele).
2. Massive infections and gas gangrene, most usually following intestinal surgery.
3. Tumour excision.
4. Post-operative incisional hernia (Fig. 50).
5. Gunshot wounds.

Methods of reconstruction include:
1. Fascia lata graft from the thigh.

[1] Sydney Ringer, 1835–1910. Physician, University College Hospital, London.

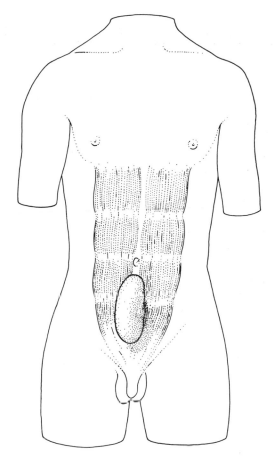

Fig. 50. *Lower abdominal herniation between the rectus muscles.*

2. Local muscle flaps.
3. Local fascia flaps.
4. Synthetic materials such as nylon, Teflon, Dacron, Marlex (polyethylene).

NURSING CARE
- Babies are nursed in a specialised paediatric Intensive Care Unit.

- Adults are nursed in a Plastic Surgery Intensive Care Unit.
- Nursing care specific to Plastic Surgery involves care of the skin flaps used to close the abdomen. This is described in Chapter 3.

ABDOMINOPLASTY

'He who does not mind his belly will hardly mind anything else.'
Dr Samuel Johnson, 1709–1784. Georgian writer and perceptive commentator.

Reduction of the skin and fat from the abdominal wall may be combined with strengthening of the abdominal muscles with non-absorbable sutures inserted into the sheath of the rectus abdominis muscle.

Indications

1. Abdominal skin flaccidity (for example following several pregnancies or a twin pregnancy, or resulting from loss of abdominal fat).

2. Marked striae of pregnancy. Striae gravidarum are caused by disruption of skin proteins. The skin loses its elasticity when overstretched.

3. Separation of the rectus abdominis muscles, permitting a bulge of the midline fascia between these two vertical muscles (Fig. 50).

4. Abdominal obesity. Patients with true lipodystrophy may not lose fat even on a strict diet. Other obese patients should be induced to lose fat prior to abdominoplasty to facilitate the operation.

5. Repair of umbilical herniae, or herniae through abdominal laparotomy scars.

Technique

Where possible, scars are kept very low in the abdomen so as to be hidden below the bikini. With briefer bikinis this is becoming increasingly difficult! The scar is transverse from below the iliac crest to below the opposite iliac crest. It may be necessary to extend the scar vertically towards the umbilicus from the pubis if there is much lateral skin excess, and to reposition the umbilicus.

Complications

1. *Wound haematoma*. These extensive wounds are often drained with vacuum suction. Significant pain, swelling or blood loss post-operatively alert the nurse to continued bleeding.

2. *Wound infection*. Unless treated swiftly and effectively, wound breakdown may occur.

3. *Deep vein thrombosis and pulmonary embolus*. Stagnation of venous blood in the leg and pelvic veins during and after operation requires prevention by leg elevation, bandaging, physiotherapy and protection of the calf veins from pressure.

PRE-OPERATIVE NURSING CARE

- The patient is admitted the day before the planned operation so that pre-operative and pre-anaesthetic preparation may be carried out.
- Ensure that the patient understands the operative procedure and the approximate position of the scar.
- Explain that post-operative drains will be in situ. Instruct the patient to remain in the position she finds herself on waking from the anaesthetic, until shown how to adjust her position in bed without disturbing the drains.
- Blood transfusion may be required. Explain to the patient that an intravenous infusion will be in progress when she wakes from the anaesthetic, and reassure her that this is nothing to become anxious about.
- Explain that post-operatively she will be nursed in a semi-recumbent position with hips and knees slightly flexed, as this position will prevent tension on the wound.
- On the morning of the operation the abdominal and pubic hair is shaved carefully, ensuring that no abrasions are made in the skin.

POST-OPERATIVE NURSING CARE

- Before collecting the patient from the theatre, ascertain how much blood has been given during the operation and the intravenous regime required for the post-operative period.

- In case post-operative haemorrhage occurs, the quantity of blood retained in the blood bank for this patient is checked.
- Internal haemorrhage may proceed unobserved if the drains fail to drain the operative site adequately. Therefore, frequent observation of the pulse and blood pressure is maintained for the first 24 hours after the operation.
- As soon as the blood pressure is stable, the patient is nursed in a semi-recumbent position with knees and hips slightly flexed.
- If open drains are used, inspect the dressings frequently for signs of haemorrhage.
- If vacuum drains are used these are re-charged every 6 hours, or more frequently if drainage is copious. If large volumes of blood are draining, summon the doctor urgently, as the patient may require further blood transfusion and may need to return to theatre for haemostasis.
- The drains are removed 24 hours after the last drainage.
- Bed rest is maintained for 2 to 3 days, after which the patient is gradually mobilised.
- Before helping the patient out of bed, explain to her how to manage her drains, and that she should walk with a slightly stooped posture, with knees and hips slightly flexed, to prevent exerting any strain on the wound. Explain that she may gradually regain a normal posture 5 to 7 days after the operation.
- Inspect the dressings daily for any sign of infection. If infection is suspected, wound swabs are sent for culture and sensitivity so that antibiotic therapy can be commenced as soon as the organism has been isolated.
- Sutures are removed after 7 to 10 days.
- The patient is discharged from the hospital 5 to 7 days after surgery. Ensure that after-care instructions include directions to telephone the ward for advice if any symptoms occur relating to the operation.
- Instruct the patient not to lift anything heavy for a further 3 weeks after discharge.

UPPER ARM AND THIGH REDUCTION

Conditions which may warrant reduction include:

1. Collection of fat on the medial aspect of the upper arms.

2. Collection of fat on the medial thighs.

3. Collection of fat over the femoral trochanters of the thighs ('riding breeches' deformity).

4. Drooping buttocks.

Operation may be undertaken for lipodystrophy, but is frequently unsatisfactory for dietary obesity if the dietary habit is not altered prior to surgery.

In these conditions, scars tend to be of poor quality. Operation is, therefore, undertaken only after very full explanation by the surgeon of the expected result, and a full realisation and acceptance by the patient. Wound healing is slow.

NURSING CARE

- Nursing care is the same as for abdominal reduction (see above), except that the post-operative position will be dependent upon the site of the operation. The patient will be positioned so as to reduce tension on the wound.

SPINA BIFIDA

Spina bifida is a developmental defect in the vertebral column through which the contents of the spinal canal may protrude. It occurs once in every 800 births. Parents who have one child with spina bifida have a 1 in 25 chance of producing a subsequent child with the same abnormality.

Spina bifida occulta. A hairy naevus or an area of atrophic skin over the lumbar or sacral area suggests that a vertebra is affected, but there is no protrusion of spinal canal contents. This condition is symptomless and requires no treatment. Later in life, tingling or weakness of the lower limbs may occur, should the spinal cord drag on the vertebral column. The patient will then be assessed by the neurologist.

Meningocoele. A midline swelling on the back consisting of a herniation of meninges through the vertebral gap. The overlying skin soon ulcerates.

Meningomyelocoele. A midline swelling on the back containing nerve elements from the spinal cord. There is usually paralysis of the legs, bladder and rectum, and often talipes equinovarus and hydrocephalus.

Management

The prognosis, particularly regarding paraplegia, the risk of meningitis and hydrocephaly, is carefully discussed with the parents. About 85% of patients with spina bifida (other than occulta) are paraplegic and require repeated hospital admission. The early mortality is about 40%. The Plastic Surgeon may be involved with the baby with a meningomyelocoele, the aim being to obtain skin cover over the spinal defect within the first 24 hours of life by using skin flaps. Decisions as to the advisability of this operation are made jointly with the paediatrician, neurologist and the parents.

NURSING CARE

- The baby is nursed in a specialized paediatric unit.
- Post-operative care of the flaps used to achieve closure is described in Chapter 3.

SACROCOCCYGEAL TUMOURS

These occur as swellings between the coccyx and anus, and may be confused initially with a meningomyelocoele. The tumours contain nerve, bowel and respiratory elements, and are often cystic. Excision within the first few days of life is usually curative; the longer they remain, the higher the risk of malignancy.

POSTANAL PITS

These occur over the coccyx. Some contain hair (pilonidal sinus). In children, a pit over the midline of the back related to an angioma will raise suspicion of an underlying connection to the spinal canal, in which case infection in the sinus may produce meningitis.

FURTHER READING

Grabb, W.C. & Smith, J.W. (1979) *Plastic surgery*, 3rd edn. Boston: Little, Brown & Co.

10   The hand

Such is the importance of the hand as an organ of manipulation and sensation that one of the largest single areas of the cortex of the brain is responsible for its function. Man's ability to fully oppose his thumb across the palm, in order to achieve an accurate pinch grip, is shared by no other animal, and gives him a unique advantage in using his hand for power and precision. It will, therefore, be appreciated why deformity, injury or disease of the hand, especially the thumb, is of such serious significance.

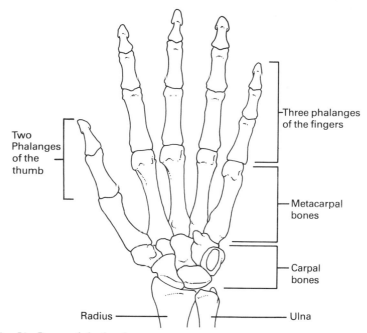

Two Phalanges of the thumb

Three phalanges of the fingers

Metacarpal bones

Carpal bones

Radius

Ulna

Fig. 51. *Bones of the hand.*

Anatomy of the hand (Fig. 51)

The wrist joint attaches the eight small carpal bones of the palm to
  (a) the broad lower end of the radius (which lies on the outside,

thumb side or lateral side of the forearm) and

(b) the head and styloid process of the ulna (on the medial side or little finger side of the forearm); a mnemonic for this is 'before you answer which side the ulna is on, say 'UM'.

Beyond the carpal bones, the five metacarpal bones, one for each digit, extend up as far as the knuckles (the *metacarpophalangeal joints*). Beyond the metacarpophalangeal joints, the index, middle, ring and little fingers each have three phalangeal bones; the thumb has two.

On the volar (palmar or flexor) surface of the hand, a superficial and a deep tendon run from the forearm (where they arise from muscles) into each of the fingers. The *deep tendon* flexes both interphalangeal joints of the finger and the *superficial tendon* flexes the proximal interphalangeal joint. Both flex the knuckle (metacarpophalangeal) joint. The thumb has only one long flexor tendon, not two.

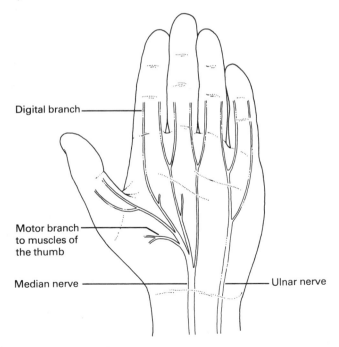

Fig. 52. *Nerves on the volar (palmar) surface of the hand.*

The sensation of the skin of each finger is carried along two nerves, one running on each side of the digit (Fig. 52). The nerves from the thumb, index, middle and ring fingers join in the palm to form the *median nerve*. The nerves from the little finger, and the side of the ring finger nearest to the little finger, join up in the palm to form the *ulnar nerve*. The median nerve also sends branches to muscles of the ball of the thumb. The ulnar nerve sends branches to the lumbrical and interosseus muscles, producing separation of the fingers and fine manipulative movements. Each nerve on either side of the finger is accompanied by an artery and a vein.

On the back of the hand, extensor tendons run to each digit from muscles in the forearm. Sensation from the back of the hand is carried in nerves that join to form the *radial nerve*, which runs up across the back of the wrist joint into the forearm.

NURSING CARE

- When caring for a patient with a hand deformity or injury, two factors which will cause the patient and his family anxiety must be considered:

  1. *Function of the hand.* The hand is such a valuable organ in everything he does that any malfunction will affect the way in which the patient can care for himself and the type of work and hobbies he is able to pursue. Therefore, *restoration of function* is the primary aim in hand care.

  2. *Appearance of the hand.* It is almost as difficult to hide a disfigured hand as it is to hide a disfigured face. Constantly wearing a glove over a deformed hand both draws attention to the hand and makes good function more difficult to achieve. When it is impossible to achieve full function of the reconstructed hand, the patient must be taught how to adapt what function he does have to make his damaged hand as useful as possible.

- As the child with a congenital deformity learns manual dexterity in the normal manner, he finds ways of using whatever function he can obtain from his deformed hand (see nursing care for congenital deformities of the hand, page 158).

- The adult who is suddenly faced with the problem of a hand which no longer functions normally may have to adapt to radical changes in his way of life. He may have to change both his work and his hobbies.

- Rehabilitation of these patients should start from the moment the extent of the damage and the prognosis are known. The first steps in this direction are to encourage the patient to use his other hand for all his needs, and to provide him with aids to enable him to become as independent as possible. If it is the dominant hand which is disabled, the patient may become depressed and despondent about his ability to cope. Encouragement, optimism and sympathy must be offered in the correct proportions.

- The patient who is unable to use his hand, even temporarily following surgery, needs help with most of his normal activities. Simple aids should be provided immediately so that he can maintain his independence.

- Some simple aids for one-handed patients:

    1. A one-handed knife/fork has a cutting blade, which tapers to a blunt curved end where there are prongs like a fork.

    2. A non-slip pad can be placed beneath the plate to steady it.

    3. A half-rim may be clipped to the plate, providing a surface for the patient to push the food against.

    4. A book-stand enables the patient to turn the pages easily.

    5. If the patient smokes, ensure that he has a lighter, not matches.

    6. Replacing standard shoe laces with elastic ones allows the shoe to be pulled on with the lace permanently tied.

- Some simple aids for patients unable to use either hand:

    1. A drinking cup mounted on a stand, so balanced that it can be tipped by mouth control, allows the patient to take a drink unassisted and at his own pace.

    2. A book-stand, with a page turner that can be held in the mouth, may help the patient to keep himself occupied.

    3. A rubber-tipped stick, positioned so that the patient can easily pick it up in his mouth, may enable him to manipulate the controls of a radio or television.

    4. If the patient smokes, a cigarette holder mounted onto a

swivel stand, with an ashtray attached to catch the ash, enables the patient to enjoy a cigarette without assistance, once it has been lit.

- There are many more aids available from the Occupational Therapy Department which assist the patient who is to be discharged from hospital with one or both hands out of action.
- It is pointless to spend time and resources reconstructing a damaged hand if, on leaving hospital, the patient is so self-conscious of the appearance of his hand that he puts it in his pocket and no longer uses it.
- Watch for any sign of the patient hiding his disfigured hand and offer counselling if necessary.
- The patient should be encouraged to socialise on the ward, and then to go into the hospital grounds, so that he may experience other people's reaction to his disfigured hand.
- If the patient is very distressed about the appearance of his hand, before discharge he should be encouraged to go out of the sheltered atmosphere of the hospital for a few hours, preferably accompanied by his relatives. A shopping trip or a visit to the local pub allows the patient to become accustomed to public reaction to his deformity.
- The need for counselling in this respect should not be over-stressed as this may render the patient more self conscious.

POST-OPERATIVE AND POST-INJURY NURSING CARE
- Following any hand surgery or injury, the hand requires elevation to reduce oedema and assist venous drainage. There are many ways of elevating a hand. The method chosen will depend on the site of surgery or injury and the amount of elevation required.

METHODS OF ELEVATING THE HAND
- If the arterial blood supply to the hand has been jeopardised, for example when the radial or ulnar artery has been cut or is in spasm, high elevation of the hand will increase ischaemia. The hand is, therefore, supported at heart level on pillows.
- High elevation can be maintained comfortably with Tubigauze and a drip stand. Tubigauze of a size that fits comfortably over

the arm and dressings is applied to the whole arm, extending to the mid-part of the biceps muscle. The stockinette is firmly attached to the arm with adhesive tape which should not completely encircle the arm (circumferential taping may produce distal ischaemia). The stockinette is then extended over the hand and tied onto the drip stand, raising the hand to the required height. The elbow is supported on pillows. A hole may then be cut at the hand level to allow freedom of movement of the fingers and inspection of the dressings. Elasticated tubular bandages are not as efficient in maintaining elevation, as they stretch, allowing the hand to slip down. They are also considerably more expensive than straightforward stockinette.

- If very high elevation, including extension of the elbow, is required, this is more comfortably achieved by bandaging the whole arm onto an extension splint. Cramer[1] wire (15 cm × 1 m) makes a suitable frame for this sort of splint, and can readily be bent and adjusted to suit each patient. The wire frame is padded to prevent direct pressure points, and a hook is attached to the top of the splint by which it can be tied to a drip stand.

- When the patient is up and about, elevation of the hand can be continued either by use of a mobile drip stand, if high elevation is required, or by slings. With a collar and cuff sling, the patient can easily remove his hand from the sling to exercise his elbow and shoulder joints. For children, the cuff part of the sling can be bandaged onto the wrist to prevent the child removing his hand irresponsibly. A collar and cuff sling is generally more comfortable than a full arm sling.

- When the patient is sitting in an arm-chair, he can elevate his hand by simply resting his elbow on the arm of the chair.

- Intermittently changing the method of elevation may help to prevent stiffness of the shoulder and elbow joints. This is especially important if the patient is elderly or arthritic.

- Following surgery or injury, the hand frequently requires immobilisation or support by some form of splintage. There are many types of hand splint available with various functions.

---

[1] Freidrich Cramer, 1847–1903. Surgeon, Würzburg, Germany.

Fig. 53. *Position of the joints for bandaging.*

HAND SPLINTAGE

- When total immobilisation of the hand and fingers is required, it is usual to immobilise all the joints in the optimum position of use. This means that the wrist will be in slight extension, the metacarpophalangeal joints in flexion, the thumb in abduction and the interphalangeal joints in extension (Fig. 53).

- A *'boxing glove'* dressing will provide adequate immobilisation if correctly applied. The wound is covered with gauze swabs, which are also placed firmly between each finger, ensuring that they fit right down into the web space.

  The wrist, hand and space between each finger is then padded with good quality cotton wool, adding wool layer by layer until the wrist, hand and fingers are entirely encased in cotton wool, A firm crepe bandage is then applied to compress the cotton wool. Start bandaging around the hand and wrist with a 7.5 cm bandage. Then using 5 cm bandages, compress the wool between the fingers, applying the bandage as one does a stump bandage.

  Apply more layers of cotton wool and rebandage as before, until only the finger tips remain exposed. Provided adequate cotton wool packing has been applied and the bandaging is firm enough, the hand will be immobilised and comfortable. The finger tips are inspected frequently to ensure that the dressing is not restricting circulation.

- Plaster of Paris may be used either as a full plaster cast or an anterior or posterior plaster slab. If a full cast is used it is bivalved (split along its length) so it can be opened a little to accommodate any oedema.

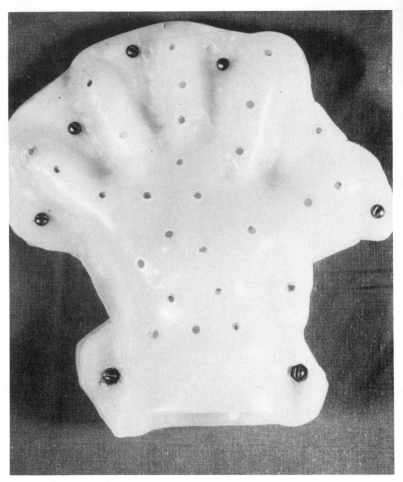

Fig. 54. *The 'oyster' splint.*

- If the fingers need to be kept straight and spaced apart, a bivalved *'oyster'* splint may be used (Fig. 54). This type of splinting is particularly suitable for small children. The splint is made of Aquaplast. The Aquaplast is softened in hot water and moulded onto the palmar aspect of the whole hand. With the fingers held in full extension, it is pushed up between each finger and thumb, separating them, and held in place until it

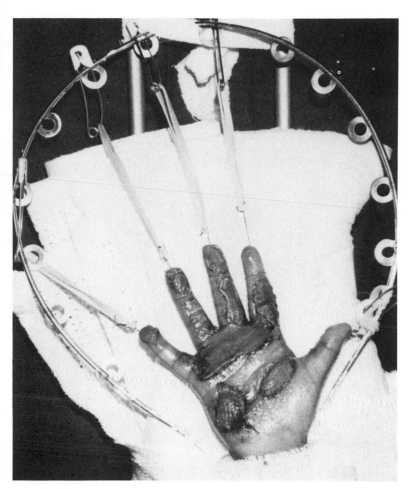

Fig. 55. *The 'banjo' splint.*

hardens. With the palmar splint held firmly in position, the same process is repeated on the dorsum of the hand. The two halves of the splint may be fastened together with strong press-studs or Velcro. This type of splint is light-weight and easily removed and reapplied for wound inspection. However, it tends to make the hand sweat, leaving the skin constantly moist, unless it is perforated with holes.

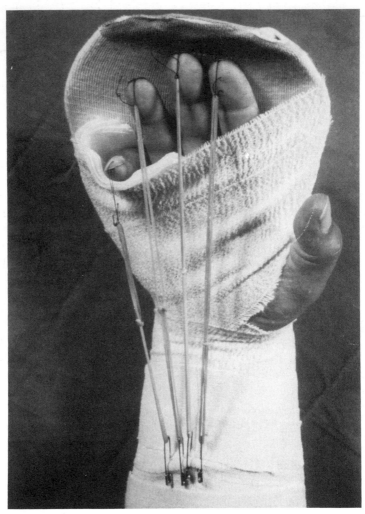

Fig. 56. *Dynamic splintage.*

- Another method of keeping the fingers in extension and separated is a *'banjo splint'* (Fig. 55). This type of splint is very useful when it is desirable to leave the wounds exposed. It is light-weight and comfortable.
- Following flexor tendon repairs of the fingers, *dynamic*

Kleinert[2] *splintage* is frequently employed (Fig. 56). The finger nails are attached by means of adhesive hooks to elastic bands which run to the flexor aspect of the forearm. The bands flex the fingers, so protecting the repaired flexor tendons from strain, but permit the patient to straighten the fingers himself. The gliding mechanisms of the finger tendons are thus preserved while the tendon is healing.

Complications following hand surgery or trauma

1. *Haematoma.* Haematomas forming anywhere in the hand may exert pressure causing irreparable damage, so urgent evacuation is essential. Careful observations of the wound will detect haematomas early. Undue pain beneath a bandage requires careful removal of the dressings to inspect the wound.

2. *Ischaemia.* Prolonged pressure over the front (palmar aspect) of the wrist damages both nerve and blood supply. This fact must always be taken into account when applying bandages, splints, and apparatus to elevate the hand. Frequent observations may be required to ensure that appliances have not moved to a position where pressure is being exerted on the wrist.

Circumferential dressings applied to the fingers or wrist may act like a tourniquet if applied too tightly. Whenever possible the finger tips should be left exposed so that the colour and temperature of the skin can be observed for signs of ischaemia or venous congestion.

If severe oedema develops beneath a splint which will not expand, the blood supply will be constricted. Circumferential splints are therefore bivalved.

3. *Volkmann's*[3] *ischaemic contracture.* This is a very serious complication which may be caused by badly placed splintage or tight bandaging. The brachial artery passes superficially over the front of the elbow, before it divides into the radial and ulnar arteries. This artery can be felt as the pulse point at which blood pressure recordings are usually taken. Pressure from a bandage or splint may occlude this artery, cutting off the major blood supply to the

---

[2] Harold Kleinert, Hand Surgeon, Louisville, Kentucky, USA.
[3] Rickard von Volkmann, 1830–1889. Professor of Surgery, Halle, Germany.

forearm and hand. The ischaemic muscles and nerves then die. As atrophy progresses the muscles contract, pulling the joints into the typical position known as Volkmann's ischaemic contracture. The wrist is fully flexed, the metacarpophalangeal joints are hyper-extended, and the interphalangeal joints are all fully flexed. Once established this condition is irreversible.

Before applying a bandage or splint to the forearm, place two fingers below the crease over the front of the elbow. Mark the skin lightly with ink immediately below the two fingers. The bandage or splint should not extend above this ink mark. It will be seen that, when the elbow is fully flexed, this space below the joint crease is just sufficient to ensure that no pressure is exerted on the front of the elbow.

4. *Traumatic syndactyly*. If a hand wound involves two adjacent fingers, they may become joined together by scar tissue. There-fore, dressings must be applied so that the fingers are separated right down to the web space.

5. *Stiff joints*. The patient with a hand injury usually tends to hold the wrist in flexion. When the wrist is fully flexed it is impossible to make a fist, i.e. to fully flex the metacarpophalangeal joints and all the interphalangeal joints at the same time. In order to assist the patient's physiotherapy, the wrist should always be in extension, except when contra-indicated (for example by flexor tendon repair).

6. *Sudeck's[4] atrophy of the hand*. If the patient's hand has been immobilised for some time, it is essential for him to get the joints moving again as quickly as possible. A hand which is not used for many weeks following trauma may develop Sudeck's atrophy. This condition commences with swelling of the whole hand after the initial trauma has healed. If the early signs are not recognised, or corrective treatment fails, the condition progresses to loss of bone substance (osteoporosis). When the condition reaches this stage it is irreversible.

The patient may fail to get his stiff hand joints moving for various reasons. Getting the joints moving again may be painful and will certainly require hard work. The patient may be unco-operative because of associated psychiatric illness, or simply lack

[4] Hermann Sudeck, 1866–1938. Professor of Surgery, Hamburg.

sufficient intelligence to accept the need for intensive physiotherapy. He may lack motivation because he hopes to receive more money in a compensation claim, if he cannot use his hand.

The underlying cause of the patient's apparent inability to move his hand joints must first be identified if intensive physiotherapy is to be effective.

7. *Accidents caused by dressings on the hand.* Patients who smoke should be advised that the dressing on their hand may be highly inflammable. When the patient is discharged from hospital wearing a hand dressing, he should be reminded to be careful when cooking. If a patient is to return to work wearing a dressing, it is very important to find out exactly what his work involves. For patients who work with power machinery, the dressing may present a hazard by becoming caught in the machinery.

CONGENITAL ABNORMALITIES

Hand development

The hand is fully formed by the eighth week after conception. Malformations in the third and fourth weeks result in absence or deformity of the arm, in the fifth and sixth weeks in deformity of the hand, and in the seventh week in deformity of the digits. Thereafter development is confined to one of growth.

About 1960, the taking of the drug thalidomide by mothers in the first three months of pregnancy produced limb deformities, mostly *phocomelia* (where the hand articulates with the shoulder since the arm fails to develop). These children have now entered adulthood.

A congenital hand deformity in the parents slightly increases the likelihood of a deformity in the offspring. Other non-inherited abnormalities have no known cause, but occur about once in every 600 to 800 live births.

If operative treatment is decided upon, it is usually desirable that this be carried out before the age of 5 years. After this age, the child finds it increasingly difficult to adapt to the new conditions, and tends to try to revert to his old manipulative habits. Very small hands, however, are technically difficult to operate on, so in practice a compromise at about the age of 3 or 4 years is usually set.

The wearing of a prosthesis, by covering up the hand, means the child loses sensation, and the prosthesis tends not to be worn. Later on, at school or in adolescence, a prosthesis may be requested for cosmetic reasons or to improve function for particular occasions.

NURSING CARE

- The parents' distress at seeing their baby's deformed hand (or hands) is treated with all the sympathy and understanding necessary by the doctors and nurses.

- It is obviously very important to the parents that they are given accurate information about the amount of function their baby is likely to achieve from his deformed hand. The baby is examined by a hand surgeon as soon as possible after birth, so that an accurate assessment can be made.

- The surgeon explains the deformity to the parents, what treatment is needed, and the prognosis. The midwife/nurse should be present at this interview, to maintain continuity of information in subsequent counselling of the parents.

- The amount of counselling the parents need naturally depends on the severity of the deformity. However, irrespective of the degree of deformity, all parents of children with hand deformities should be warned that the constant use of mittens to hide the deformity will prevent their child from developing hand dexterity.

- On discharge from hospital, the after-care arrangements should include a detailed report to the health visitor on the baby's deformity, so she may check that the parents are allowing the child freedom to move his hand as much as possible.

- As the child grows and begins to use his hands, he should be encouraged to obtain the fullest range of movement possible. Physiotherapists and occupational therapists assess the child's manual dexterity and teach the parents how to help their child achieve optimum function.

- There are toy libraries in most districts, run by various voluntary organisations. These can be very helpful in providing the handicapped child with a constant supply of different toys designed to help him overcome his handicap.

- If the child's hand deformity is unilateral and severe, he may become reluctant to use his deformed hand at all. He may become so adept with his normal hand that his parents become less anxious about his deformed hand, and consequently less inclined to encourage him to use it. The parents should be warned of this possibility and advised to keep the child supplied with toys which require both hands to operate.

● The child is examined in the Out-Patients Department at 6- or 12-monthly intervals, in order to monitor his hand development and to determine the optimum time for surgery. During these visits prepare the child and his parents for his future admission to hospital. Lend the child interesting toys during his visits, talk to the child and the parents about the ward and encourage the child to talk to other children attending the clinic who have been in hospital.

Webbing of the fingers (syndactyly)

Syndactyly implies a web, usually only of skin, between adjacent fingers, most commonly the middle and ring fingers. The web may involve only the proximal part of the fingers, or may extend along the entire length. Two fingers only may be affected, or two and two or all four. The condition may be unilateral or bilateral. Correction involves division of the web and skin grafting of the resulting defects on the sides of the fingers. To prevent graft contracture, full-thickness or thick partial-thickness grafts are used.

The grafts are held in place with a 'tie-over' dressing (see Chapter 3). The hand is elevated in a 'banjo splint' (see above). The tie-over dressing is removed in the ward on the fifth postoperative day. The splint is retained until the grafts are sound. If more bulky dressings are used at operation, it is often necessary to give the child a second anaesthetic at about the tenth day to re-dress the fingers.

Camptodactyly

Congenital flexion of the fingers, most commonly the little finger, involves the flexor tendons, the joints and the phalangeal bones. Gentle stretching of the fingers over a number of years by the mother may improve the contracture. The condition should be distinguished from *congenital triggering*, usually of the thumb. This triggering is corrected by incision of the fibrous sheath, which is restricting the free movement of the flexor tendon of the thumb.

Clinodactyly

Sideways deviation of the fingers, often the little, causes no functional interference and is best left alone.

Polydactyly (supernumerary digits)

Extra digits on the ulnar (medial) side of the hand are often attached to the little finger by a flimsy skin pedicle which can be tied off with a piece of silk. Larger digits require formal amputation.

On the radial (lateral) side of the hand, a double thumb requires amputation of the smaller, less-used of the two. If the two thumbs are fused together, a V-shaped wedge will be removed from the middle of the two, and the skin and nail sutured. The two half-phalanges may be held with a Kirschner[5] wire, which will be removed when the bones are stable.

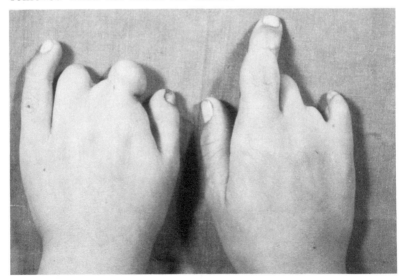

Fig. 57. *Congenital amputation and constriction rings.*

[5] Martin Kirschner, Professor of Anatomy, Heidelberg, Germany.

Constriction rings (Fig. 57)

A congenital constricting band around a finger, toe or, less frequently, the arm, leg or trunk occurs about once in every 2500 births. The cause is thought to be a band of amnion wrapping around the finger or toe in the uterus, like a piece of elastic.

Distal to the band there is a tendency for lymphatic swelling to occur, especially when the groove is deep.

Surgical treatment of the constriction band commences within the first year of life. Half the circumference of the band is excised and lengthened with a Z-plasty.

About 6 months later, the remaining half is similarly excised and lengthened. Excision of the entire circumference at one occasion may jeopardise the blood supply of the digit.

Ectrodactyly (absence of digits)

Digits may be strangulated in utero by a band of amniotic membrane wrapping round them and causing ischaemic amputation. Absence of the thumb seriously impairs the function of the hand. When both thumbs are absent, the index finger may be used to construct a thumb. The metacarpal bone of the index finger is cut across and rewired onto the metacarpal base of the absent thumb, attaching it so that the new thumb flexes across the palm (*pollicisation*). The nerves and vessels of the finger are left intact, and the intrinsic and flexor tendons are repaired. The new thumb will be immobilised in plaster of Paris until the bone has united (about 6 weeks).

Lobster-claw hand

Absence of the middle finger and its metacarpal (Fig. 58) still permits good function, and does not usually require treatment. However, if the index, middle and ring fingers are no more than useless tissue, it may be better to remove them and their metacarpal bones so that the thumb and little finger can grasp.

Radial club hand

The radius and the thumb are usually absent, so that the hand is

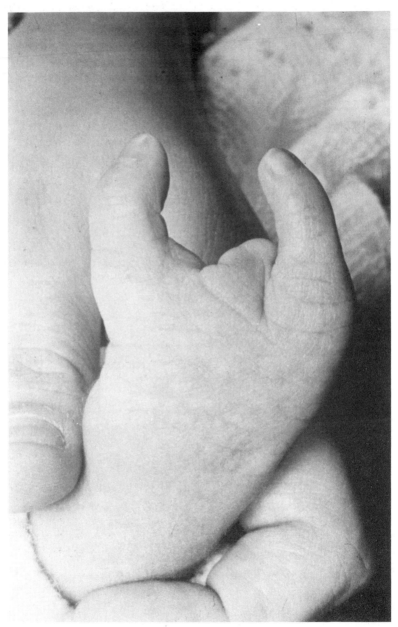

Fig. 58. *Lobster claw deformity.*

severely bent laterally at the wrist. The child learns to use the fingers, especially the little and ring fingers, with remarkable dexterity.

The wrist is splinted from an early age. Any operation which is done to improve the function will probably take the form of a pollicisation of the index finger (see above), or arthrodesis of the wrist to centralise the carpal bones.

Gigantism

An excess growth of all the tissues may involve one digit or more. The index and middle fingers are the most commonly affected. A congenital arterio-venous fistula (a direct communication between artery and vein without any intervening capillaries) may give rise to gigantism which becomes apparent in adult life. Arteriography is used to identify the fistula, which is then excised or the digit amputated. Neurofibromatosis (von Recklinghausen's[6] disease) produces gigantism by excessive growth of nerve tissue.

HAND TRAUMA

A comparatively minor injury to the hand is sufficient to put out of work a technician who depends on manual dexterity, or a labourer who requires hand strength. Hand injuries, therefore, contribute significantly to loss of employment. Causes vary widely from domestic accidents with scissors, needles and window panes, to industrial accidents involving rotating cogwheels, power crushers and steam presses.

The overall aim of treatment at the time of injury is to obtain primary wound healing, while not prejudicing the possibilities for later reconstruction. The management of hand injuries should, therefore, be firmly placed in the care of those with specialist knowledge. The only emergency situation requiring immediate treatment is of vascular injury causing ischaemia. Other treatment may safely be deferred for an hour or two until specialist management is

---

[6] Friedrich von Recklinghausen, 1833–1910. Professor of Pathology, Strasbourg, France.

available. The main factors contributing to a worsening outcome of the injury are:

1. Infection.
2. Swelling, progressing to fibrosis and deep scar formation.
3. Haematoma, becoming replaced by scar.
4. Joint stiffness

FIRST-AID TREATMENT

- Bleeding may be significantly reduced by elevating the hand above shoulder level. Digital pressure on the artery on either side of the base of the finger, or over the radial and ulnar arteries at the wrist pulses, may also arrest bleeding.
- Primary toilet of the dirty or oil-stained hand may be carried out by the patient himself seated in front of a bowl of Cetavlon or povidine-iodine 1%. The hand is rinsed in normal saline solution at the end of this toilet so that the antiseptic solution does not remain in contact with the tissues.
- If the patient has had no previous tetanus prophylaxis, this is given in the form of tetanus toxoid 0.5 ml i.m. repeated at six weeks and again at six months. In addition, either an antibiotic (Triplopen 1 ampoule i.m.) or anti-tetanus serum 1 ml (Humotet 250 units/ml i.m.) is given.
- The cleaned hand is now again elevated in a sterile towel, and arrangements made for examination and debridement under regional or general anaesthesia.

Regional anaesthesia

Local infiltration. Minor lacerations may be treated by infiltrating plain lignocaine 1% into the skin and soft tissues.

Ring block. A finger or thumb may be rendered anaesthetic by infiltrating the two digital nerves at the base of the finger with plain lignocaine 1% (Fig. 52).

Wrist block. Infiltration with plain lignocaine 1% around the median, ulnar and radial nerves at the wrist produces anaesthesia of the hand.

Intravenous (Bier's[7]) block. Two inflatable tourniquets are

[7] August Bier, 1861–1949. Professor of Surgery, Berlin. He introduced the 'tin helmet' in World War I, and gave the first deliberate spinal anaesthetic.

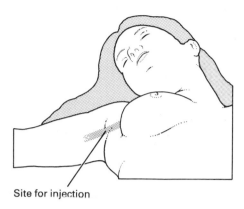

Site for injection

Fig. 59. *Axillary nerve block.*

placed around the upper arm. The arm is exsanguinated using an Esmarch[8] bandage and the proximal tourniquet inflated. Forty millilitres of plain lignocaine 0.5% is injected into a vein in the hand. The distal tourniquet is inflated and the proximal one removed. Since the distal tourniquet is on the part of the arm containing lignocaine, pain from the tourniquet pressure is absent. At the end of the operation, the tourniquet is deflated slowly and then reinflated, so that the lignocaine in the veins is released slowly into the body. Failure to do this may result in an epileptiform fit or circulatory collapse. (See 'Tourniquet' in Glossary.)

Brachial block anaesthetises the hand, forearm and most of the upper arm. There are two methods:

(a) *Axillary brachial block.* The arm is abducted and a tourniquet is applied below the axilla. Twenty millilitres of plain bupivacaine 0.5% with 20 ml of lignocaine 1% and adrenaline 1:200,000 is infiltrated around the nerves surrounding the brachial artery in the axilla (Fig. 59).

(b) *Supraclavicular brachial block.* The brachial plexus above the clavicle is infiltrated with bupivacaine, lignocaine and adrenaline. It is, however, possible to puncture the top of the pleura of the lung, producing a pneumothorax.

---

[8] Friedrich von Esmarch, 1823–1908. Military surgeon and later Professor of Surgery, Keil, Germany. He developed the bandage during the Franco-Prussian war to control haemorrhage.

Operative principles

1. Thorough wound cleaning and excision of non-viable tissue.
2. Assurance of adequate circulation.
3. Adequate fixation of bone fractures.
4. Restoration of nerve and tendon.
5. Provision of skin cover with skin grafts or flaps.
6. Meticulous haemostasis to prevent haematoma formation.

Hand elevation will be instituted while the patient is on the operating table.

POST-OPERATIVE NURSING CARE

- The hand is elevated to prevent oedema from the moment the patient leaves the operating theatre (see 'Methods of elevating the hand' on page 149).
- After the first 6 hours, intramuscular analgesia is rarely necessary. Persisting pain arouses the suspicion that a haematoma is developing under the dressings. The wound is inspected and the haematoma, if present, evacuated.
- The dressing is applied so it is progressively less tight up the forearm than on the hand. A tight proximal dressing will prevent venous and lymphatic drainage from the hand. It needs to be comfortably supportive and sufficiently snug to immobilise the part. Shearing of grafts by movement will hinder their 'take'.
- Tight dressings may render marginally viable tissues non-viable, may produce cyanosis of the fingers, and be responsible for causing pain.
- Plaster of Paris casts should be split longitudinally (bivalved) so that any swelling of the hand or arm can be accommodated (see 'Volkmann's ischaemic contracture' on page 155).
- Dressings are normally first changed after 2 to 5 days, though pain, haematoma or infection may make earlier inspection necessary.
- If there are any signs of infection, wound swabs are sent for culture and sensitivity. Antibiotic therapy is commenced as soon as the organism has been identified.

JOINT INJURY

Exposure of a finger joint by injury is likely to result in stiffness. If damage is severe, it may be decided that the best outcome will be achieved by fixation or arthrodesis in a position which provides the most useful function. Two main methods achieve this:

1. A Harrison–Nicolle[9] polypropylene peg is inserted into the bone ends in place of the joint. An aluminium splint is used to immobilise the finger externally until the bone ends have fused by fibrous or bony union around the peg.
2. Kirschner wire is driven through the bones of the joint after the joint cartilage has been removed. Bone chips are packed into the space, and the finger is dressed. External splintage is unnecessary. The wire may be removed when the bones are solidly united.

TENDON INJURIES

Since tendon heals slowly, hands with tendon repairs will normally be immobilised in plaster of Paris, for about 4 weeks in the case of flexor tendons, 3 weeks for extensor tendons. A course of graduated physiotherapy will then be instituted to regain movement.

Late tendon repairs

Tendons which have not been repaired soon after injury may be repaired later, but with less satisfactory results. In order to try to improve the gliding qualities of flexor tendon repairs, the operation may be done in two stages separated by 3 to 4 months.

Stage 1. The old lacerated tendon is removed and replaced by a rod of silicone. The purpose of this is to induce the growth of a sheath around the rod in which the new tendon graft can glide.

Stage 2. The silicone rod is replaced with a tendon graft (see Chapter 3). The commonly used donor tendons are palmaris longus from the forearm or plantaris from the back of the calf. (Removal of these tendons produces little disability.) Post-

---

[9] S.H. Harrison, Plastic Surgeon, Wexham Park Hospital, Slough, Bucks; F.V. Nicolle, Plastic Surgeon, Hammersmith Hospital, London.

operatively, the hand is immobilised in plaster of Paris and elevated for 4 weeks. After this, physiotherapy is instituted.

Boutonnière injury (Fig. 60)

Either due to a blow or a cut over the dorsum of the bent proximal interphalangeal joint of the finger, the central part of the extensor finger tendon is divided. Reattachment of the tendon to the bone is possible within the first few days after injury. Later repair is often impossible, and less satisfactory procedures such as arthrodesis of the joint may be the best that can be achieved.

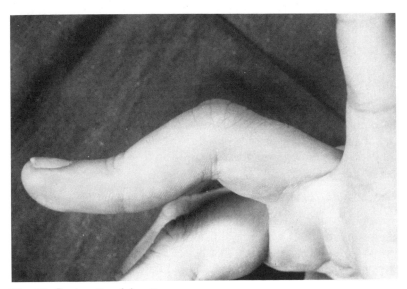

Fig. 60. *Boutonnière deformity.*

Mallet deformity

Forcible flexion of the tip of the finger pulls the extensor tendon off its attachment to the distal phalanx of the finger. Early splintage in a plastic 'mallet Stack[10] splint' (Fig. 61) for 6 to 8 weeks may be successful in allowing the tendon to reattach to bone.

[10] Graham Stack, Hand Surgeon, Billericay and Harold Wood, Essex.

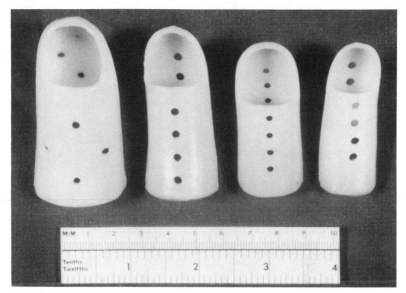

Fig. 61. *Mallet finger splint.*

NERVE INJURIES

The nerve filament along which the electrical impulse passes is the axon. This is encased in a tube (the endoneurium). Several thousands of tubes, collected into bundles, are surrounded by a fibrous sheath, the perineurium. Several sheaths (about 12 to 15 in the case of the median nerve at the wrist) are surrounded by the outer covering of the nerve, the epineurium (Fig. 62).

When a nerve is cut, the axon beyond the cut degenerates, but its tube remains. The axons proximal to the cut grow across into the tubes in the distal part of the nerve.

The tubes, of course, lead either to organs of sensation (such as those responding to touch or temperature) or to muscles. If an axon which is carrying an impulse intended to activate a muscle grows instead into a tube which ends in a touch sense organ, then its impulse is ineffective (see Fig. 11, page 43).

Surgical repair of a nerve, therefore, aims to realign the two cut ends of the nerve so that as many as possible of the axons grow down their 'own' tubes. This is done by carefully matching up the

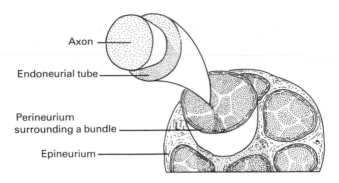

Fig. 62. *Section of a nerve showing its constituent parts.*

bundles in the cut ends of the nerve. It is, of course, not possible to suture individual axons or tubes. The best results of nerve repair are achieved when the repair is carried out within the first 2 or 3 weeks after injury. Provided the wound is clean, nerve repair may be done at the time of the initial surgery to the hand injury. If dirty, the wound will be cleaned, the skin closed and a subsequent operation carried out to repair the nerve when the infection is controlled. If the two ends of the nerve cannot easily be brought together without tension, a nerve graft (see Chapter 3) will be used to bridge the gap.

A nerve repair will be protected from movement by splinting for about 3 to 4 weeks post-operatively.

BURN INJURY TO THE HAND

In adults, burns of the hand often occur during attempts to beat out flames engulfing the individual or another victim. Palmar skin is thick compared to dorsal skin, so that flame burns are more frequently full-thickness on the dorsum and expose joints and extensor tendons. Injury in children is frequently due to the grasping of a hot electric fire filament. Burns of this nature are frequently full-thickness. Once the burn has been assessed, it will be cleaned with Cetavlon or Hibitane. Dead tissue will be removed with forceps and scissors. Blisters will be snipped to evacuate the serum.

Full-thickness burns

The hand which has sustained a full-thickness burn is covered with skin grafts within the first 3 or 4 days, so that early mobilisation by the physiotherapist can be achieved. During the necessary immobilisation to permit the grafts to 'take', the hand is elevated to limit oedema, and splinted with the metacarpophalangeal joints flexed to 90° and the interphalangeal joints straight (Fig. 53). The grafts are inspected and redressed on the fourth or fifth postoperative day.

Partial-thickness burns

The hand with a partial-thickness burn can be expected to heal within 10 to 14 days provided infection does not occur. The hand is placed in a polythene bag bandaged lightly around the forearm and containing silver sulphadiazine cream. Physiotherapy is instituted immediately and the hand kept elevated.

Circumferential burns

Circumferential burns around the forearm and wrist may act as a tourniquet causing ischaemia to the hand and fingers. Emergency division of the constricting tissue must be carried out with a scalpel to prevent gangrene of the hand (escharotomy).

Graft contracture

Some contracture of grafts which are partial-thickness is inevitable and may necessitate later insertion of further grafts. Children's fingers tolerate splintage for several months without becoming stiff. In babies, a bivalved 'oyster' splint of Aquaplast (Fig. 54) is a convenient way of retaining splintage.

CARPAL TUNNEL SYNDROME

Applied anatomy

The median nerve at the flexor surface of the wrist runs beneath an unyielding fascial band, the flexor retinaculum. Compression on the nerve beneath this band causes damage to the nerve axons resulting in 'pins and needles' in the fingers, pain in the hand and forearm, and weakness and wasting of muscles in the ball of the thumb.

Causes of compression include:
1. Rheumatoid synovitis.
2. Fluid retention at the menopause or in pregnancy.
3. Incompletely reduced wrist fractures.
4. Cysts, lipomas or other swellings under the flexor retinaculum.

Management

Steroid injection. One dose of carefully administered triamcinolone 10 mg injected under the retinaculum may reduce the swelling temporarily. Recurrence of symptoms occurs in 50% of cases within 6 months. There is a danger of injecting into the median nerve, producing permanent damage, or into a tendon causing rupture.

Splintage. Temporary relief may be given by splinting the wrist while awaiting surgery.

Surgery. Under regional or general anaesthesia with a tourniquet on the arm, the retinaculum is exposed and fully divided to decompress the nerve. Complications of the operation include haematoma formation and division of branches of the nerve producing painful neuroma.

STENOSING TENDOVAGINITIS
(De Quervain's[11] Disease)

A thickening of the sheath surrounding the tendons on the wrist at the base of the thumb, of unknown cause, causes friction and pain. Splintage, injection of steroids or, if these measures are unsuccessful, division of the tendon sheath relieves the symptoms.

[11] Fritz de Quervain, 1868–1940. Professor of Surgery, Berne, Switzerland.

RHEUMATOID DISEASE IN THE HAND

The progressive loss of function in the hand is one of the principal causes of incapacity of the rheumatoid patient. Due to pain, weakness or stiffness, the patient is increasingly unable to carry out even basic day-to-day household tasks. The disease may conveniently be considered in three phases, which overlap one another.

1. The swelling of the synovial membrane of joints, chiefly wrist and metacarpophalangeal, progressively leads to deformity by destruction of joint ligaments, cartilage and bone. *Synovectomy* during the phase in which the synovitis is proliferative reduces pain (thereby improving hand function), and limits future ligamentous destruction.

2. Once ligaments have been destroyed, the typical rheumatoid deformities of *ulnar deviation* of the fingers and *dislocation* of the wrist and metacarpophalangeal joints become apparent. Surgery is directed to reconstruction of ligaments or to stabilisation of joints by arthrodesis.

3. The gross instability of joints with advanced bone erosion and loss of function precludes soft tissue reconstruction, and makes *prosthetic* (artificial) *joint replacement* or *arthrodesis* the only procedures possible.

POST-OPERATIVE CARE

Since rheumatoid disease usually affects many joints, which tend to stiffen when inactive, parts of the body not requiring immobilisation for post-surgical reasons are exercised fully. Immobilisation of joints may be needed to permit healing and for joint arthrodesis to become firm. A plaster of Paris, metallic or plastic split will have been applied at operation and is retained for as short a time as is commensurate with adequate healing.

'Lively' (dynamic) splints are used where support without immobilisation is needed, for example in tendon repair and replacement arthroplasty. Within the restraints of the splint, the patient's movement is supervised by the physiotherapist.

Where joint mobility is of paramount importance, for example after synovectomy or tenolysis (freeing of scarred tendon), graduated supervised physiotherapy will be commenced as soon as pain permits, within 48 hours of operation.

As with all other types of hand surgery, elevation of the hand to the level of the shoulder or above is maintained from the moment of leaving the operating table until healing is complete, in order to reduce post-operative swelling and pain.

DUPUYTREN'S DISEASE

A disease of unknown cause produces thickening in the fascia of the palm which spreads to the fingers, chiefly the little and ring fingers. Sir Astley Cooper[12] in 1822, and Baron Guillaume Dupuytren[13] in 1832, drew attention to the fact that the flexion contracture of the finger was due not to shortening of the flexor tendon, but to disease in the palmar fascia. Fifteen per cent of patients with Dupuytren's disease have a close relative who also has the disease. The disease becomes increasingly common over the age of 60 years.

Associated conditions include:
1. Alcoholism.
2. Pulmonary tuberculosis.
3. Chronic trauma (vibrating tools).
4. Epilepsy.
5. Cirrhosis of the liver.
6. Local palmar injury.

If the finger contracture interferes with function, the palmar band is carefully excised (*fasciectomy*). The complications of this operation are:
1. Damage to the digital nerves, which may run within the diseased tissue.
2. Haematoma in the palm which, if not evacuated, leads to skin necrosis.
3. Recurrent contracture (especially in young patients with a strong family history of the disease).

Other procedures occasionally used in debilitated patients are:

---

[12] Sir Astley Cooper, 1786–1841. Surgeon, Guy's Hospital, London.
[13] Baron Guillaume Dupuytren, 1777–1835. Surgeon, Hospital Hotel-Dieu, Paris.

Fasciotomy. Through a short longitudinal incision in the palm, a scalpel is introduced under the fascial band and the band divided. The likelihood of damage to the digital nerves is high.

Chemical fasciotomy. The injection of chymotrypsin 2.5 mg, hyaluronidase 1500 units and lignocaine 2% to 20 ml into the palmar band will digest it and allow the finger to be snapped straight.

Amputation of a digit. This may be necessary in the final resort if contracture has recurred after repeated fasciectomy.

TUMOURS OF THE HAND

Ganglion

This arises from a joint or a tendon as a gel-filled cyst. It expands slowly, occasionally ruptures and may subside spontaneously. Recurrence after excision is not uncommon.

Exostosis

A benign tumour which grows out from the phalanx or metacarpal bones, forming a knobbly swelling. Excision, if necessary, is curative.

Enchondroma

A benign tumour containing cartilage grows into the phalanx or, less often, the metacarpal. The bone is expanded and may fracture. At operation, curettage of the tumour leaves a cavity which is filled with bone chips.

Osteoid osteoma

A painful benign nidus of growth, found in any of the bones in the hand, which consists of many small blood vessels surrounding bone-forming tissue. It is cured by excising it with a block of surrounding bone.

Osteogenic sarcoma

A rare malignant tumour of the phalanges or metacarpals which spreads by the blood stream. Survival for 5 years occurs in only 10 to 20% of patients. Excision of the entire half hand or amputation may confine the tumour.

The hand is also subject to the tumours of skin and soft tissue discussed in Chapter 16.

FURTHER READING

Boyes, J.H. (1970) *Bunnell's surgery of the hand*, 5th edn. Philadelphia: J.B. Lippincott.

Eriksson, E. (1979) *Illustrated handbook of local anaesthesia*, 2nd edn. Copenhagen: Munksgaard.

Flatt, A.E. (1977) *The care of congenital hand anomalies*, St Louis: C.V. Mosby.

Flatt, A.E. (1982) *Care of the rheumatoid hand*, 4th edn. St Louis: C.V. Mosby.

Nicolle, F.V. & Dickson, R.A. (1979) *Surgery of the rheumatoid hand*. London: Heinemann Medical.

Malick, M.H. (1976) *Manual on hand splinting*. Pittsburgh: Hamarville Rehabilitation Centre.

Rank, B.K., Wakefield, A.R. & Hueston, J.T. (1973) *Surgery of repair as applied to hand injuries*, 4th edn. Edinburgh: Churchill Livingstone.

Seddon, H. (1975) *Surgical disorders of the peripheral nerve*, 2nd edn. Edinburgh: Churchill Livingstone.

11　Lower limb injury

The relatively poor arterial blood supply and venous drainage of the leg compared with, for example, the face results in slower and less predictable healing. The position of the tibia just beneath the skin at the front of the calf implies that fractures are commonly compound, and that delayed union and infection are frequent occurrences.

General management

Large quantities of blood can be lost from lacerations in the veins of the leg if the limb is allowed to remain dependent. Even when no skin break has occurred but vessels have been ruptured by a blunt blow, large haematomas can develop; these frequently lead subsequently to skin necrosis. Provided the leg is elevated before a haematoma has developed, these complications are avoided; but once present, haematoma requires evacuation to avoid widespread skin loss.

External bleeding can be controlled by localised pressure, leg elevation and, if arterial, by subsequent vessel ligation.

Adequate resuscitation with blood or blood substitutes such as dextran precede operation, which is best performed under general anaesthesia.

EMERGENCY NURSING CARE

* Urgent elevation of the injured limb is mandatory. However, if a fracture is evident or suspected, the first priority is to apply splintage to prevent the fractured bone ends causing further soft tissue damage. Simple traction, applied by pulling on the foot of the injured limb, temporarily overcomes the muscle spasm which causes further displacement of the fractured bone ends and consequently increases soft tissue damage and pain. Traction and elevation of the limb can be applied at the same time, by one or two people, according to the severity and extent of the injury. This considerably reduces the patient's

pain. Another person then applies a suitable temporary splint. High elevation of the leg is maintained throughout the remainder of the patient's emergency care.

- Adequate analgesia, such as intravenous or intramuscular morphia or pethidine, is given as soon as possible.
- If administration of a systemic analgesic is contra-indicated, for example when the injuries include a head injury, Entonox may be used to relieve pain. Entonox does not mask the signs of neurological complications. Within two to three minutes of discontinuing the administration of Entonox, neurological signs return to normal, and therefore accurate head injury observations can be carried out.

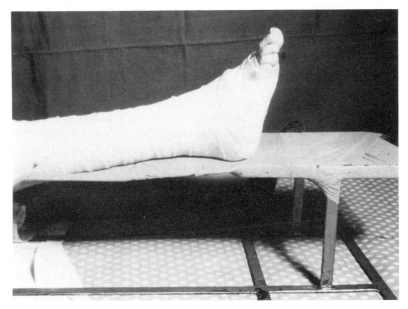

Fig. 63. *Elevation of the leg on a Braun's frame.*

Incised wounds

The swelling which accompanies trauma of the leg makes primary suture of any but the smallest wounds liable to produce wound breakdown, infection, and loss of otherwise viable skin. Many of these patients, therefore, need to be admitted to hospital if for no other reason than that this permits continuous elevation of the leg (Fig. 63). Dressings and bandages are applied loosely so the skin circulation is not restricted.

Muscle damage

Wounds involving muscle require immobilisation of the leg in a plaster of Paris backslab to prevent ankle and/or knee movement.

Contaminated wounds

Wounds older than 12 hours have already permitted ingress of infection. These, and grossly contaminated wounds, are treated by urgent debridement of foreign material and non-viable tissue. Skin grafting or secondary suturing can be carried out when the oedema and infection are controlled.

Skin loss

Slicing injuries to the leg raise trap-doors or triangles of skin and frequently result in necrosis of that skin after it has been sutured back into place. This is particularly so if the patient is on corticosteroid therapy, is a diabetic, has arteriosclerosis or varicose eczema, or is elderly. Such injuries require the removal of skin of doubtful viability, and its replacement with a skin graft, as a primary procedure.

Any tension in closing skin wounds is liable to produce skin necrosis.

Degloving injuries

A leg that has been run over by a tyre may have its skin shorn off; the skin remains only partially attached to the leg. As a primary procedure, doubtfully viable and non-viable skin may be totally removed, cut on the Gibson–Ross dermatome (Fig. 4 in Chapter 2), and reapplied as partial-thickness grafts. To determine whether the skin is viable the patient may be given an intravenous injection of 20 ml of fluorescein (5%) and observed in an ultra-violet light; viable skin fluoresces yellow, while non-viable skin looks black.

Bullet wounds

High velocity bullets travelling faster than 340 m (1100 feet) per second produce a small entry and exit wound but, by producing a pressure wave, cause massive destruction of muscle and bone in between. Such wounds require wide debridement and packing with Eusol dressings. They are covered with skin grafts when all necrosis has ceased, usually some 4 or 5 days later.

Low velocity wounds produce larger skin lacerations but less internal destruction. Debridement of the superficial wound may be followed by spontaneous healing.

In either degloving injury or bullet wounds, swelling deep to the fascia may produce compression on the femoral or tibial arteries and veins. To relieve this pressure, fasciotomy may be necessary as an emergency procedure. Major arteries and veins need immediate repair, but nerve ends can be temporarily tacked together. Joints are irrigated. External fixation with Steinmann[1] or Denham[2] pins is preferable to internal fixation, because of the high possibility of bone infection.

Crush injury

Extensive crushing of the limb, for example by being trapped beneath fallen masonry, produces muscle death which releases myoglobin into the circulation. When the limb is released, the capillaries extravasate large quantities of blood. The result is hypovolaemic shock often accompanied by oliguria from renal damage by the myoglobin.

The hypovolaemia is treated by rapid replacement with plasma and blood. The products of muscle necrosis may be kept in solution in the urine (so that they do not precipitate out into the kidney tubules) by rendering the urine alkaline with intravenous sodium lactate or sodium bicarbonate.

The swelling of devitalised muscle may need to be released by a fasciotomy to prevent further gangrene from compression of major vessels.

It may be helpful to cool the leg with a fan. The bed linen is

---

[1] Fritz Steinmann, 1872–1932. Professor of Surgery, Berlin.
[2] Robert Denham, Orthopaedic Surgeon, Portsmouth.

arranged as a divided bed, so that the injured limb can be left exposed. Cooling ischaemic tissue to about 32°C reduces the oxygen and nutrient requirements of the cells. The cooler the ischaemic cells the longer they remain viable. However, cooling to actual freezing point causes thrombosis of the blood vessels and cell destruction resulting in frost bite (see page 189).

COMPLICATIONS

Complications include:
    Gas gangrene.
    Thrombosis.
    Emboli.
    Fat emboli.
    Dry gangrene.
    Toxaemia.
    Septicaemia.
    Renal failure.

Gas gangrene

The presence of dead muscle provides a medium for the growth of anaerobic organisms such as clostridia. Their presence may be suspected by extreme toxaemia, hypothermia and swelling. An X-ray shows gas bubbles in the limb. Gas gangrene has a characteristic fetid odour which the nurse can readily recognise (Chapter 2).

Complete excision of all the involved muscles is required, together with intramuscular penicillin and anti-gas gangrene serum. Amputation may be necessary. The placement of the patient in a hyperbaric oxygen chamber may raise the oxygen concentration sufficiently to prevent further multiplication of the organisms (see Glossary).

GENERAL NURSING CARE
- Nursing care is aimed at preventing further damage to the injured limb, and promoting healing by careful wound care and good nutrition.
- The limb is kept elevated at all times. This may be achieved in a number of ways:

1. For injuries which involve only the leg or foot, elevation on a Braun's[3] splint may be adequate (Fig. 63).

2. If soft tissue damage and swelling is very extensive, higher elevation can be achieved by use of balanced sliding traction on a Thomas[4] splint.

3. If the thigh is injured, a Thomas or similar splint with traction is required to provide adequate elevation.

- If there are fractures as well as soft tissue injuries, fixation following reduction may be maintained by plaster of Paris, skeletal traction or external fixation using a Hoffman[5] or Day[6] frame.

- When any soft tissue injury accompanies a fracture, the risk of bone infection is so great that internal fixation is deferred until all soft tissue wounds have healed.

- If there are circumferential wounds, as frequently occurs in degloving or crush injuries, whether there are fractures present or not, skeletal traction may be preferred to provide elevation; for example a Steinmann pin through the calcaneum provides a suitable fixing point for applying traction to elevate the whole lower limb. The whole circumference of the limb is then accessible for wound care.

- If any form of traction is necessary, it is discontinued as soon as possible and substituted by a Braun's splint. This enables the patient to get up in a wheelchair.

- Care is taken to keep the leg elevated whilst transferring from bed to wheelchair. The Braun's splint is supported on the wheelchair with a firm leg board, to which it is fixed with adhesive tape or bandage to prevent it slipping off.

- If both legs require elevation, the weight of bilateral leg boards and Braun's splints may unbalance the wheelchair, making it liable to tip forward. Sandbags can be attached to the back of the wheelchair to correct this imbalance.

- Obviously for any patient who has to spend many weeks or months in hospital with a leg injury, early mobilisation in a wheelchair is a great morale booster. With a little improvisa-

[3] Dr Heinrich Braun, 1862–1934. Anaesthetist, Leipzig, Germany.
[4] Hugh Owen Thomas, 1834–1891. Orthopaedic Surgeon, Liverpool.
[5] Dr Raoul Hoffman (1938), Surgeon, Switzerland.
[6] Brian Day, Orthopaedic Surgeon, London.

tion, wheelchairs can be adapted in many ways to achieve this. If some form of external fixation, such as a Hoffman frame, is in situ, this can be used to maintain leg elevation in a wheelchair. A bed cradle is securely attached to a leg board and the Hoffman splint is then tied to the cradle. Elevation in this way removes all pressure from the soft tissues.

- Adapting wheelchairs can be time-consuming. Once the wheelchair has been prepared with leg boards and Braun's splints, it is preferable to leave the apparatus intact, and have duplicate Braun's splints and other apparatus on the patient's bed.
- Wound care is carried out as described in Chapter 2.
- If skin grafting is used, the nursing care is as described in Chapter 3.
- A high-protein, high-calorie diet is given (see Chapter 2).

COMPOUND FRACTURE OF THE TIBIA

As the tibia lies so closely under the skin, fractures of this bone are frequently compound. Delayed union and osteomyelitis occur more often than with any other bone.

After orthopaedic fixation, the bone may be covered by split skin grafts if the periosteum is intact. More usually it is necessary to use a flap. Fractures of the upper two-thirds of the tibia may be covered by local muscle flaps (myocutaneous or fasciocutaneous flaps), or by cross-leg flaps (see below). Fractures of the lower one-third usually require fasciocutaneous or microvascular free flaps, or cross-leg flaps, since there is no local muscle available in this lower part of the leg.

The application of a flap may encourage bone healing by bringing in a new blood supply to the fracture site.

Cross-leg flap

PRE-OPERATIVE NURSING CARE
- If pre-operative counselling is inadequate the patient may panic during the post-anaesthetic recovery and detach the flap by pulling his legs apart.
- Explain the procedure to the patient and his relatives, and

ensure that they understand that his legs will be attached for a minimum of 3 weeks, until the flap has established an adequate blood supply over the injured area.

- Explain that having the legs fixed together will not render the patient totally immobile. After the first 2 or 3 days the flap circulation is usually reasonably stable, and the patient will have become used to the position and fixation. He is then able to move himself about in bed, with the aid of a 'monkey pole'.

- Two or three days before the operation, the planned post-operative position is tried out, to ensure that the patient can be nursed satisfactorily in the required position. If the position proves impractical, the type of flap planned may have to be reconsidered.

- Once a satisfactory position has been established, show the patient how he can move his ankles, knees and hips. Explain the importance of post-operative physiotherapy to keep his joints as mobile as possible.

- Demonstrate the post-operative position to the physiotherapist, so that she may prepare the patient for his post-operative exercises.

- Explain to the patient that when the flap circulation is stable, usually after 7 to 10 days, he will be able to get up in a wheelchair. Demonstrate how the wheelchair will be adapted, and show him how he can sit comfortably in the wheelchair with his legs in the post-operative position.

- Patients having this type of surgery usually suffer considerable discomfort for the first 7 days, mostly from cramp resulting from the fixation. The discomfort tends to increase daily at first, so the patient may become very demanding, constantly requesting minor adjustments to his position. This period can be very trying for the nurses as well as the patient, especially as the adjustments the patient requests are often so minor as to appear unnecessary. This situation must be accepted and time allowed in the nursing care plans to give the patient the extra attention he needs at this time. After 7 days the patient usually settles completely. This is normal and is not an indication that the patient has suddenly decided to give the nurses less work.

- Explain to the patient that the first week after surgery will be very uncomfortable for him, but reassure him that the next two weeks will be relatively easy to cope with. Tell him that the nurses will be sympathetic and will make every effort to make him comfortable by readjusting his position as often as necessary.

- The day before the operation, the flap is marked out by the surgeon on the donor leg with a skin pencil.
- Before the operation takes place, some surgeons prefer to make a plaster of Paris mould to support the legs. The mould is well-padded so there are no friction points. A more convenient mould can be made by a Polyvac splint which, when evacuated of air, becomes rigid.
- A skin graft will be taken from the thigh of the donor leg, to be applied to the defect created on the back of the donor calf. On the day of operation both legs are shaved from groin to ankle.
- Explain to the patient the importance of taking a high-protein, high-calorie, vitamin-enriched diet, to aid the body's healing ability.

POST-OPERATIVE NURSING CARE
- The patient's bed is positioned in the ward so his flap can be observed easily by both day and night staff.
- The legs are supported comfortably on pillows or by traction applied to the splintage, to elevate them above the level of the heart. This assists venous and lymphatic drainage.
- The patient is not left unattended until he is fully awake and aware of what he is doing.
- As he is recovering from the anaesthetic, constantly remind him not to move his legs. At the same time reassure him that all is well.
- Constant observation is necessary to ensure that the flap does not become stretched or kinked by movement of the legs.
- Ensure that the fixation remains in the correct position, and is not causing pressure liable to lead to sores.
- If the legs have been immobilised by plaster of Paris around the ankles and knees, the underside of the flap pedicle may be inspected by getting the patient to flex his thighs, thus lifting his legs off the bed.
- If the legs are supported in a plaster of Paris mould or Polyvac splint, the patient can lift his legs out of the mould, whilst they

are held firmly together, to permit dressings and physiotherapy.

- Fixation of both legs with a pin through the tibia has some advantages for ease of exposure of the operation sites and the ability to exercise the joints.
- For specific care of the flap, the graft on the donor calf and the split skin graft donor area, see Chapter 3.

Flap division

When the cross-leg flap is adequately vascularised by the recipient leg, usually at about 3 weeks from the initial operation, the patient is returned to the theatre, the flap pedicle is divided and the legs separated.

NURSING CARE
- When the legs are first separated the patient may again experience discomfort and cramp for a few days, due to the change in position. Encourage him to move his legs and stress the importance of continued physiotherapy to regain full movement of all his joints as soon as possible.
- The legs are kept elevated for a further 7 to 10 days to aid venous and lymphatic drainage.
- The flap requires frequent observation for the first few days after division, to detect haematoma formation and subsequent tension within the flap.
- Any haematoma must be treated promptly by gently 'milking' it out from between the sutures. Starting at the proximal edge of the flap, i.e. the part of the flap nearest to the incoming blood supply, a roll of cotton wool is gently but firmly rolled across the flap towards the suture line. If this fails to release the haematoma, one or two sutures are removed to allow evacuation of the stale or clotted blood. It may be necessary to open the wound by insertion of sinus forceps. The forceps are inserted into the area where the haematoma can be palpated. They are then opened gently whilst gentle but firm pressure is applied to the side of the haematoma furthest away from the forceps. Using the palm of the hand the haematoma is then 'rolled' towards the opening created by the forceps. When the haematoma has been completely drained, the wound edges

can be realigned using Steristrip. It is rarely necessary to reinsert sutures, but if required this can be done under local anaesthesia.

- Sutures from both the donor leg and the flap are removed after 7 to 14 days.
- As soon as the sutures are removed from the donor leg, the patient is allowed to start weight-bearing on this leg, wearing a graft dressing and elastic support bandage, as described previously for post-operative care following skin grafts (see Chapter 3).
- The leg with the flap is kept elevated for 7 to 14 days post-operatively. The time for commencing weight-bearing on the injured leg depends on the underlying injury which necessitated the flap repair. For example if a fractured tibia is present the patient may be transferred, following his flap repair, to the Orthopaedic Department for further treatment of his bone injury.

CHRONIC ULCERATION OF THE LEG

1. *Gravitational.* Caused by poor venous drainage and stasis of the circulation. Treatment of varicosities by elastic support and ligation of perforating veins is essential if skin grafting is to be permanently successful.

2. *Arteriosclerotic.* Due to occlusion of the arterial supply by atheroma. Endarterectomy, lumbar sympathectomy or arterial bypass may improve the arterial supply sufficiently to prevent recurrence of the ulcer after skin grafting.

3. *Diabetic.* Stabilisation of the diabetes, followed by debridement and skin grafting of the ulcer onto a bed adequately vascularised may heal the ulcer, but the loss of sensation which accompanies diabetic neuropathy renders the foot liable to repeated undetected trauma and subsequent recurrent breakdown of the ulcer.

Operative treatment of the ulcer

Most ulcers can be closed with partial-thickness skin grafts onto a prepared bed of granulation tissue. The thickness of the grafts may be built up at subsequent operations by shaving the surface and applying further grafts to the shaved surface (Hynes[7] procedure). This makes the grafted area more stable and less inclined to further ulceration. (See also 'Ulcer' in Glossary.)

NURSING CARE

- Whilst awaiting admission to hospital the patient's leg is supported by a firm elasticated stocking from toe to thigh.
- The ulcer is dressed sufficiently frequently for it to be kept clean. Eusol and paraffin dressings are satisfactory, though it may be wise to ring the changes from time to time with chlorhexidine tulle (Bactigras).
- Most leg ulcers are infected, usually with a mixed flora. Prior to admission, wound swabs are sent for culture and sensitivity. When the infective organisms have been identified, appropriate dressings are applied to eradicate infection. As the gravitational ulcer is the result of a poor blood supply, systemic antibiotics are of little value in clearing infection. See Chapter 2 for details of dressings suitable for specific infections.
- Forty-eight hours before admission, wound swabs are sent for culture and sensitivity. *Streptococcus haemolyticus* infection destroys skin grafts, so if this organism is cultured from the wound, admission is delayed until treatment has eradicated the infection.
- The patient is admitted to hospital several days before the operation for:

    1. Elevation of the leg to promote venous and lymphatic drainage and reduce oedema. (For methods of leg elevation both in bed and in a wheelchair, see general nursing care for lower limb injuries on page 181.)

    2. Intensive wound care to prepare the ulcer for skin grafting. Eusol and paraffin dressings are applied 4-hourly from 7 a.m. to 11 p.m. Daily debridement of the wound is carried out on the ward, until all dead tissue has been removed.

- The skin surrounding the ulcer is frequently covered in plaques of scaling dead epithelial cells. In normal skin dead

---

[7] Wilfred Hynes, Plastic Surgeon, Sheffield.

epithelial cells are constantly being discarded, leaving the normal healthy epithelium of the skin exposed. When the skin is covered for a long period by dressings, these dead cells cannot come away in the normal manner, and therefore tend to remain on the surface of the skin, forming plaques or scales. These dead cells provide an excellent medium for bacteria. The skin surrounding the ulcer should be washed daily with soap and water, and all dead cells removed. If the scales are very firmly adherent, massaging the skin with emulsifying ointment will help to loosen them.

- If the skin around the ulcer shows any sign of hypersensitivity to the Eusol and paraffin dressings, it can be protected by a covering of paraffin tulle.
- When the ulcer looks clean and is covered with healthy granulations it is ready for skin grafting.
- Forty-eight hours before operation, swabs are again sent for culture and sensitivity to ensure the wound has not become infected with *Streptococcus haemolyticus*.
- Pre-operative preparation and post-operative care following skin grafting are described in Chapter 3.
- In order to prevent recurrence of the ulcer the patient is advised always to wear elastic stockings, save when in bed.
- On returning home, the patient sleeps with the foot of his bed elevated on 23 cm (9 in) blocks.

FROSTBITE

Thrombosis of vessels by cold injury leads to gangrene of the toes, heel and foot. Emergency treatment consists of:

1. Rapid warming of the foot in water at 38°C (100°F). The foot is then dried, elevated, and kept at a room temperature of about 21°C (70°F).
2. Anticoagulation with heparin.
3. Intravenous dextran 40 to improve capillary circulation.

When tissue is clearly not viable, it is excised and the defect skin-grafted.

FURTHER READING

British Medical Association (1975) *The surgery of violence*. London: British Medical Association.

Converse, J.M. (Ed.) (1977) *Reconstructive plastic surgery: principles and procedures in correction, reconstruction and transplantation*, 2nd edn. Philadelphia: W.B. Saunders.

12　Lymphoedema

APPLIED ANATOMY AND PHYSIOLOGY

The lymphatics are responsible for collecting and returning back into the vascular circulation proteins which have leaked out of the capillaries. They are channels which, like veins, contain valves; they are compressed by the action of the surrounding muscles and drain into many collecting trunks which deliver lymph into the thoracic duct, and thence into the internal jugular vein in the neck.

Failure to return proteins from a limb results in oedema (Fig. 64). This is followed by replacement of the oedema by fibrotic scar tissue, scaling and thickening of the skin, and recurrent episodes of cellulitis and lymphangitis.

CAUSES OF LYMPHOEDEMA

1. Developmental causes:
   (a) Failure of development of lymphatics – aplasia (5%).
   (b) Development of small and few lymphatics – hypoplasia (87%).
   (c) Development of wide tortuous lymphatics whose valves are incompetent – hyperplasia (8%).
Developmental lymphoedema occurs twice as commonly in females as in males.
2. Secondary causes:
   (a) Blockage of lymphatics, for example by filaria parasites (elephantiasis).
   (a) Destruction of lymph nodes by surgical block dissection, radiotherapy or carcinomatous deposits.

CONSERVATIVE MANAGEMENT

At the earliest sign of lymphoedema, the limb is compressed with elasticated stockings. The patient is encouraged to elevate the leg in bed at night to enhance drainage. Infections are treated with long-term antibiotics. If these out-patient methods fail to control

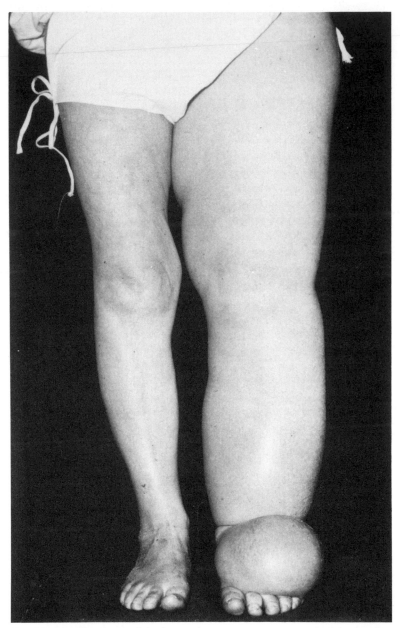

Fig. 64. *Lymphoedema of the leg.*

the swelling, in-patient bed rest and compression with Flowtron stockings is started (Fig. 65).

LYMPHANGIOGRAPHY

To visualise the superficial lymphatics, 1 to 2 ml of 10% patent blue violet dye is injected into a web space between the toes or fingers with a fine needle. The dye is taken up in the lymphatics, which appear as green–blue streaks under the skin. If required, the lymphatics shown up thus may be cannulated with a 30 gauge needle and 5 ml of radio-opaque substance (Lipiodol Ultra Fluid) injected by an electric infusion pump through a fine polythene catheter. Radiography now demonstrates the deeper lymphatics and the lymph nodes of the limb, groin and, after 12 to 24 hours, the abdomen.

OPERATIONS

Gross degrees of swelling require excision of lymphoedematous tissue through long incisions up the sides of the limb.

1. *Excisional operations.* A long incision is made from the foot to the knee or thigh on the medial side of the leg. The skin is undermined and the fat is excised down to the muscle. The skin is resutured over suction drains. After several months, the procedure may be repeated on the lateral side of the calf.

2. *Skin grafting operations.* Skin and fat are removed from the entire circumference of the foot and calf. Using a Gibson–Ross dermatome, the skin is removed from the excised tissue and applied to the fascia of the leg as a graft.

3. *Buried skin flap operation (Thompson's procedure).* A strip of skin is shaved with a skin grafting knife from the foot to the knee on the lateral side of the leg (Fig. 66). Immediately anterior to this strip, the skin is incised. The posterior flap (under the shaved skin) is thinned of fat. As much lymphoedematous fat as has been exposed is removed from the wound.

The long posterior flap of shaved skin is now rolled inwards and sutured down adjacent to the posterior tibial artery and vein between the muscles. The anterior skin is sutured to the posterior skin by overlapping.

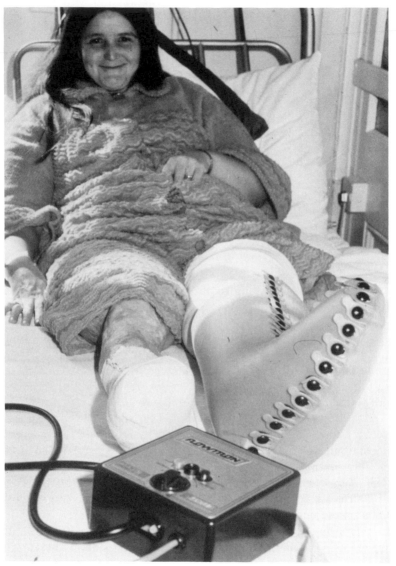

Fig. 65. *Intermittent compression stocking.*

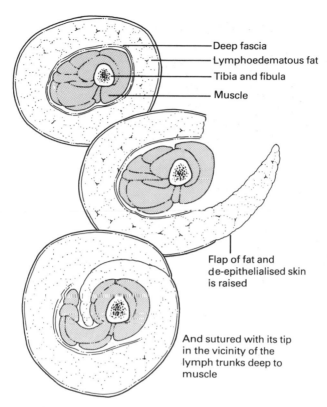

Deep fascia
Lymphoedematous fat
Tibia and fibula
Muscle

Flap of fat and
de-epithelialised skin
is raised

And sutured with its tip
in the vicinity of the
lymph trunks deep to
muscle

Fig. 66. *Burned dermis flap operation (Thompson's method).*

The fat drains its lymph into the lymphatics accompanying the posterior tibial artery and vein.

4. *Lymphatico-venous anastomosis.* Using the operating microscope, 5 or 6 lymphatics in the oedematous limb are anastomosed to adjacent veins (see Chapter 18).

Complications of lymphoedema operations

1. Because blood supply and lymph drainage are poor, wounds heal slowly and graft 'take' is unpredictable.

2. Prevention of haematoma and lymph collections necessitates prolonged suction drainage.

3. Wound infection and breakdown require debridement, Eusol and paraffin dressings and, if the loss is large, subsequent skin grafting.

PRE-OPERATIVE NURSING CARE

- Prior to admission any cellulitis or lymphangitis of the limb is treated with antibiotics.

- The patient is admitted to hospital about a week before the operation. This is to allow time for the oedema to be reduced as much as possible.

- From the day of admission the patient commences bed rest with high elevation of the limb. To assist further in reducing oedema a Flowtron stocking is applied. This device provides intermittent compression to the whole circumference of the foot and leg. A motor inflates the stocking with air for a few minutes, and then releases the compression. The amount of compression and the holding time can be varied. Explain the function of the apparatus to the patient, and adjust the apparatus to a compression ratio and time span that is comfortable. Over the next few hours, as the patient becomes accustomed to wearing the stocking, gradually increase the compression and time span to the maximum that the patient can tolerate without discomfort. During the next few days the compression may be further increased as the oedema subsides.

- The skin of the lymphoedematous limb is frequently thickened, covered in scaling plaques of dead epithelial cells, and dry. There are usually multiple cracks and fissures between the scales. These leak serous fluid which may be blood-stained. Obviously any treatment that improves the quality of the skin enhances the healing ability and reduces the risk of infection after surgery. Care of the skin is aimed at removing the scales and healing the fissures. According to the severity of the skin problem, the leg is soaked in the bath once or twice a day. This softens the scales, making them easier to remove, without causing damage to the underlying skin. Scrubbing the skin lightly with a soft brush and bland soap removes many of the scales quickly, but great care must be taken not to cause further trauma by over-vigorous scrubbing. Scales which do not come off easily should be left until further treatment softens and loosens them. At the end of the bath, the leg is not dried. Emulsifying ointment is massaged into the wet skin, and the leg is then left to dry.

- The skin of the leg is inspected 3 or 4 times a day, and a further application of emulsifying ointment applied if there is any sign of dryness.
- A few days of this treatment is usually sufficient to remove all the scales. By this time the oedema will be subsiding. With this combination of improved skin condition and reduced swelling, the fissures and cracks in the skin usually heal over the next few days.
- Care of the skin, including applying ointments or creams as indicated by the skin condition each day, continues throughout the patient's admission.
- If there is any sign of skin infection, wound swabs are sent for culture and sensitivity, and appropriate treatment started as soon as the organism has been identified.
- The skin on a lymphoedematous leg rarely bears any hairs, but if necessary the entire circumference of the limb is shaved on the morning of the operation.
- Ensure that the patient and his relatives understand the planned operative procedure. Reassure them that even though healing time is often prolonged, healing will be achieved, and that this type of surgery invariably results in improvement of the lymphoedema.
- Explain to the patient the importance of taking a high-protein, high-calorie, vitamin-enriched diet to aid the body's healing ability.

POST-OPERATIVE NURSING CARE
- High elevation of the limb is maintained until the wounds are healed.
- Ensure the splintage used to elevate the limb does not cause pressure or friction, bearing in mind that such poor-quality skin breaks down easily.
- Suction drains are usually in situ. There may be copious drainage and therefore drainage bottles need frequent checking and emptying. It is essential to ensure that adequate suction on the drains is maintained, as any collection of fluid within the wound leads to wound breakdown.
- Careful observation of the wound is continued until the wound

is healed. Any haematoma or collection of serous fluid within the wound will be evacuated urgently, as described in nursing care following division of cross-leg flaps (see Chapter 11).

● Specific wound care depends on the type of operation performed. For care of skin grafts or flaps see Chapter 3.

● Suture removal depends on the healing rate. Sutures should be removed when the wound is healed; if left in situ for an unnecessarily long time sutures act as foreign bodies, causing inflammation and producing infection.

● Before discharge from hospital, the patient is taught how to care for the poor-quality skin and the scars left after surgery. He is advised to continue wearing an elasticated stocking at all times except in bed, and to sleep with the foot of his bed elevated on 23 cm (9 in) blocks.

FURTHER READING

Johnson, H.D. & Pflug, J.P. (1975) *The swollen leg: causes and treatment*. London: Heinemann Medical.

Kinmouth, J.B. (1972) *The lymphatics: diseases, lymphography and surgery*. London: Edward Arnold.

13   Genito-urinary surgery

HYPOSPADIAS

Normal anatomy (Fig. 67)

The shaft of the penis consists of three elongated masses of erectile tissue — two dorsal corpora cavernosa and a ventral corpus spongiosum. These contain vascular spaces which become filled with blood during erection. At its tip the corpus spongiosum expands into a cone, the glans penis. The junction of the cone with the shaft of the penis is the corona, and is represented by a circumferential groove.

Down the middle of the corpus spongiosum runs the urethra, which conveys urine from the bladder to the external urinary meatus at the tip of the glans penis.

From the corona, the skin of the penis is folded back on itself to form the foreskin (prepuce), which overlaps the glans penis.

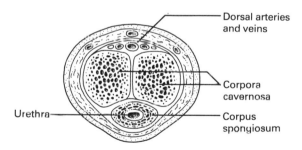

Fig. 67. *Section through the shaft of the penis showing the normal relationship of the urethra.*

Anatomy of hypospadias (Fig. 68)

The urethral opening, instead of being at the tip of the glans penis, is at some point proximal to this on the ventral surface of the penis.

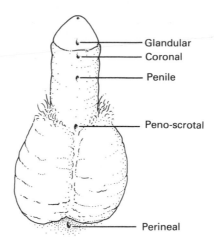

Fig. 68. *Sites of urethral openings in varying degrees of hypospadias.*

On the glans	:	glandular hypospadias.
At the corona	:	coronal hypospadias.
On the shaft	:	penile hypospadias.
At the junction of shaft and scrotum	:	peno-scrotal hypospadias.
On the perineum	:	perineal hypospadias. The appearance simulates that of the female, and may confuse sex determination at birth.

The penis is usually also curved downwards, which is especially noticeable during an erection. This chordee (*chorda* = Latin, a string) is due to the replacement of the corpus spongiosum by fibrous tissue, distal to the urethral opening on the ventral surface of the penis.

Embryological development

The development of the penis and scrotum is determined in the embryo by the testes. In the absence of the testes, the female configuration of clitoris, labia minora and labia majora dominates, but in the presence of the testes, the clitoris enlarges into the penis, the groove between the labia minora tubes into the urethra, and the labia majora swellings develop into the scrotum, into which the testes subsequently descend. Hypospadias occurs when the cells of the developing testes prematurely cease androgen production, thereby interrupting the full conversion of the external genitalia to the male form.

Incidence

Hypospadias occurs once in every 300 live male births and is usually sporadic with no familial history of the defect. It may be associated with other congenital abnormalities (especially of the kidney), undescended testes and genetic anomalies such as Klinefelter's syndrome.

NURSING CARE

- Whilst the more severe forms of this deformity are easily recognisable at birth, it is important that the midwife examines the male infant carefully in order to detect the milder glandular or coronal hypospadias, as chordee may be present even when the urethral opening is very near the tip of the penis.
- Chordee always requires surgical excision, as the downward curvature inhibits normal penile erection. This operation is usually performed at about 3 years of age. All babies born with hypospadias, whatever the degree of severity, should be referred to a surgeon.
- The downward curvature of the penis may be clearly noticeable only during erection. If the condition is not detected at birth it may remain unnoticed by the parents until the child has reached an age when development of the penis has already been affected.
- The child with glandular or coronal hypospadias is able to urinate standing up quite satisfactorily, by simply tilting the penis slightly upwards. Therefore no treatment may be required to correct the urethral opening.
- Men with uncorrected coronal hypospadias may appear to be subfertile though the sperm count is normal. This is because the seminal fluid is ejaculated below the tip of the penis, and so the sperm are not deposited in the vault of the vagina. For

this reason it may be desirable to correct the deformity, even though the patient has no problem in urinating.

- Boys with penile, peno-scrotal, or perineal hypospadias have to sit down to pass urine. To protect the boy from embarrassment when he starts school, an attempt is usually made to complete the surgery required to construct the urethra before the age of 5 years.

- The parents are seen as soon as possible after the birth by the surgeon, who explains the condition, prognosis and anticipated treatment.

- Although this is a deformity which can be kept out of sight and is, therefore, in some ways less distressing than some other congenital deformities, the parents require extensive counselling.

- Very detailed explanation of the condition may be required to convince the parents that their child is truly male, especially if the child has a perineal hypospadias.

- When one first explains to the baby's parents that he has a malformation of the penis, the common reaction is 'So he is not going to become a "normal" man.' It is, therefore, important to emphasise that following successful surgery the penis will develop to have normal function.

- Many parents express great concern about trying to explain this type of deformity to their relatives and friends. The nurse may help in this respect by offering to counsel grandparents and other close relatives herself, provided this is the parents' wish.

- Even after the parents have understood and accepted their baby's deformity, they may request that other relatives and friends are not told. The parents must be reassured of the total confidentiality of their baby's condition.

- In order to explain the child's admission to hospital, the parents often tell relatives or friends that their baby is suffering from some other more socially acceptable condition, such as a congenital hernia, undescended testicles, or that he requires circumcision. Therefore, to maintain confidentiality, the nurse needs to know what the parents have told family and friends about their child's condition.

SURGERY FOR HYPOSPADIAS

Circumcision of the neonate should not be performed, as the prepuce may be needed for the subsequent repair. Correction is usually begun at about the age of 3 years so that urethral reconstruction is completed before the child goes to school.

Two-stage repairs

Stage 1

The 'chordee' requires excision to straighten the penis before the urinary opening is brought to the tip. The defect left after excision of the 'chordee' may be closed by a local flap of penile skin or by a full-thickness skin graft. Sources of the graft are the prepuce or the hairless groin. To prevent the healing flap or graft being intermittently soiled with urine, a bladder catheter is retained through the hypospadic urinary meatus for about 10 days.

PRE-OPERATIVE NURSING CARE

- The child is admitted to hospital the day before the planned operation so that pre-operative preparation may be carried out.
- Ensure the parents understand the nature of the planned surgery, how long the child will remain in hospital, and the expected outcome of the operation.
- Tell them the child will have a urinary catheter in situ post-operatively, and explain why this is necessary.
- Explain as much to the child as he is able to understand without becoming apprehensive.
- Explain to the parents that the child will need to drink as much as possible after his operation, and advise the parents to ensure their son has an ample supply of his favourite drinks.
- On the day of operation the child is starved for the shortest time considered safe for anaesthesia.

POST-OPERATIVE NURSING CARE

- The child remains on bed rest until the catheter is removed, usually at about 10 days.
- The child should not be told that he has to stay in bed because

he has a catheter in situ, as this may encourage him to pull the catheter out!

- Every effort must be made to keep the child occupied, as a bored child will inevitably fidget and interfere with his dressings.
- This operation is usually performed at an age when it is impossible for the child to co-operate fully with his care. It is usual for children around 2 or 3 years of age to go through a 'negative period', when they appear to say 'No' to everything. This normal part of child development occurs when the child is simply trying to assert himself and is learning his own identity. Whilst this is a very trying period for the adults caring for the child, this apparent lack of co-operation must be accepted as normal, and ways found to persuade him to do what is necessary for his care.
- Both the penile and donor site wounds are kept clean and dry.
- If there are any signs of infection in either wound, swabs are sent for culture and sensitivity.
- There is frequently marked bruising and oedema of the penis for the first few post-operative days, but because of its excellent blood supply the penis tends to heal rapidly and without complications.
- Routine cleaning and care of the catheter is carried out daily.
- The urine is inspected regularly, and a specimen sent for culture and sensitivity if there is any suspicion of urinary infection, or at least twice a week.
- To reduce the risk of ascending renal infection the child is encouraged to drink as much as possible. There are many useful drinking aids for children of this age, like comic mugs and trick straws, which may entice a reluctant child to drink.
- The child's fluid intake and output is carefully recorded to ensure his intake is adequate.
- The skin sutures are removed after 5 to 7 days.
- The catheter is removed when the wounds appear to be soundly healed, usually about 10 days after surgery.
- The child is allowed up and about as soon as the catheter has been removed.
- The child is discharged home as soon as he is passing urine normally, usually the day after the catheter is removed.
- Ensure follow-up arrangements are made, and instruct the

parents to return the child to the ward if they are worried about the wound, or if the child has any problem in passing urine.

Stage 2

This operation is usually performed 6 to 12 months after the first stage.

The construction of a correctly sited urinary meatus first necessitates diversion of the urine flow, usually through a urethrostomy temporarily created in the perineum, through which a Foley[1] catheter is inserted into the bladder. Suprapubic catheterisation is an alternative. The skin of the penis is then in-turned to construct a new urinary tube (urethra) to the tip of the glans.

While the catheter is in situ, a urinary antiseptic (such as co-trimoxazole) is prescribed.

PRE-OPERATIVE NURSING CARE

● The child's pre-operative care and preparation is the same as for Stage 1.

● The fact that he is a little older makes it easier to explain all the procedures to him. The child's confidence and co-operation may be gained by acknowledging his increased maturity, and taking time to discuss his operation with him.

● Provided his nursing management was satisfactory during the first admission, the child is less apprehensive and therefore more co-operative during the second.

POST-OPERATIVE NURSING CARE

● The post-operative care is the same as for Stage 1 regarding bed rest, catheter care, fluid intake and output, and frequent observations for wound or urinary infection.

● A foam or light cotton dressing will have been applied to the penis at the end of the operation. This should be left undisturbed unless there is excessive bruising in the area suggestive of haematoma. Oedema of the glans penis and especially of the prepuce is not unusual and settles in a few days.

---

[1] Dr Frederick Foley, 1891–1966. Urologist, St Paul, USA.

- Suprapubic and perineal pain, if severe, probably indicates an irritation of the inside of the bladder by the catheter. Hot bathing, tranquillisers and hamamelis suppositories may be helpful in relieving this.
- On about the tenth post-operative day the patient is placed in the bath. Any sutures holding the catheter and dressings are cut and the Foley catheter balloon deflated. The dressings and catheter are then removed in the bath.
- The urethrostomy closes spontaneously within a few days. No dressings are required. It should be cleaned regularly and kept dry.
- Once the catheter has been removed it is important that the child is observed when he starts passing urine through his newly constructed urethra, in order to check that no urine is leaking from any fistula in the urethra.
- Do not over-emphasise the need for the child to demonstrate his ability to urinate normally, as this will cause anxiety liable to inhibit the child's natural desire to pass urine.
- If the child is mature enough to feel embarrassed at being watched when he needs to pass urine, be sympathetic and try to gain the child's confidence. The child may feel more comfortable with a male nurse or doctor, in which case his feelings should be respected, regardless of the child's age.
- If the child has previously had to sit down to pass urine, he may initially have some difficulty in urinating standing up, in which case he should be encouraged to try out his new urine passage sitting down. At the same time reassure the child that once he gets used to the new passage, he will soon learn to urinate standing up.
- If the child has real difficulty in passing urine at first, especially if he complains of pain, persuade him to relax in a warm bath, and when he appears sufficiently relaxed ask him to pass urine into the bath. This simple technique invariably succeeds, and once the child has passed urine naturally for the first time, his confidence is restored and he is unlikely to have any further problems.
- The child is discharged as soon as he has demonstrated his ability to pass urine satisfactorily, usually 24 to 48 hours after the catheter has been removed.
- If this operation has been delayed until the patient is in his

teens or older, erections and nocturnal emissions may be prevented by amyl nitrite inhalations or oral stilboestrol. In the event of an erection, the patient may be given an ethyl chloride spray to use on the penis.

One-stage repairs

When chordee is not a major factor, the first stage may be dispensed with. At the beginning of the operation, a rubber tourniquet is placed round the root of the penis. The penis is injected with normal saline to distend the tissues, and any curvature of the penis becomes apparent (Horton's[2] test). When chordee is present, techniques have been advanced to complete its removal and resiting of the urethral opening on the glans penis in one operation. The one-stage repair is suited to cases where the opening is distal on the penile shaft.

NURSING CARE

- The pre- and post-operative care and the possible post-operative complications are the same as for Stage 2 repairs.

Post-operative complications

1. *Blockage* of the catheter.
2. *Haematoma* requiring return to theatre and evacuation.
3. *Fistula.* A breakdown of the repair of the urethra results in the passing of urine through another abnormal opening in the penis, necessitating further operation at least 4 to 6 months later.
4. *Narrowing* of the new meatal opening and stricture of the urethra necessitate periodic dilatation with graduated bougies to stretch the scar.

EPISPADIAS AND BLADDER EXSTROPHY

Once in every 30 000 births, an abnormality occurs in which the roof of the penis is absent so that the urinary urethra is an open gutter (epispadias) (Fig. 69). In its most severe form (exstrophy of

---

[2] Dr Charles Horton, Professor of Plastic Surgery, Norfolk, Virginia, USA.

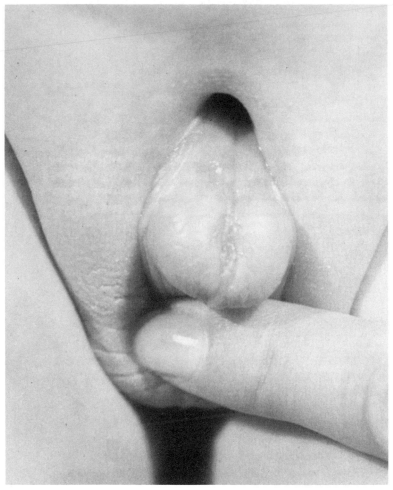

Fig. 69. *Epispadias.*

the bladder) the lower abdominal wall and pubic bones are cleft from the umbilicus to the perineum, and the anterior bladder is open; in this form both males and females may be affected. Exstrophy of the bladder leads to:

1. Maceration of the abdominal wall.

2. Repeated kidney infections, causing renal failure.
3. Bladder carcinoma after the age of 30 years.

Repair of epispadias alone involves similar principles as hypospadias (see above). Treatment is started about the age of 3 years.

When the bladder is exstrophied, two surgical methods are available:

1. Diversion of urine into an ileal loop. The ureters are drained into the ileum, which in turn drains into a bag on the abdominal wall. The bladder mucosa is removed and the bladder muscle sutured.

2. The bladder wall is mobilised and closed, after freeing the iliac and pubic bones to narrow the opening. The abdominal wall is then repaired. A catheter is left suprapubically to drain. The achievement of urinary continence is difficult, more so in boys than girls, both for epispadias and bladder exstrophy. For this reason, urinary diversion for exstrophy is more commonly performed.

NURSING CARE
- Nursing care for epispadias is the same as for hypospadias (see above)
- Plastic surgical nursing care for bladder exstrophy involves care of the flaps used to close the abdominal wall (see Chapter 3).

PEYRONIE'S[3] DISEASE

Between 40 and 60 years, a plaque of scar tissue develops in the shaft of the penis, and may calcify or ossify. Erections are painful and the penis curves. Injection of steroid early in the disease may be helpful, but excision of the plaque is later required. Vitamin E (100 mg three times a day by mouth) may relieve the pain in the penis.

[3] François de la Peyronie, 1678–1747. Physician to King Louis XIV of France.

NURSING CARE
- The principles of nursing care are similar to the care described for hypospadias (see earlier in this chapter).

CONGENITAL ABSENCE OF THE VAGINA

The vagina is represented only by a dimple in the perineum. The labia and ovaries may be normal, but the uterus and kidneys are frequently malformed. The condition is often first noticed when menstruation fails to take place at puberty. There are differences

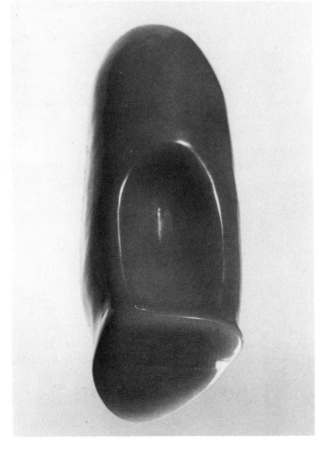

Fig. 70. *Acrylic vaginal obturator.*

of opinion as to the optimum time to operate. Many operators feel this should be delayed until marriage or regular sexual intercourse is established, to ensure regular dilatation of the constructed vagina. Others feel that regular dilatation can be satisfactorily carried out with an obturator by the patient herself.

Principles of operation

The space in the perineum in front of the rectum is dissected up to the uterus. A thick partial-thickness skin graft is draped onto a torpedo-shaped acrylic or silicone rubber obturator (Fig. 70), dermis side outwards. The obturator is slid into the dissected space and secured with sutures and a T-bandage.

When the skin graft is taken, some skin is stored in the refrigerator in case further grafting is required (see skin graft storage in Chapter 3).

After 7 days the patient is returned to theatre for a further general anaesthetic to remove the obturator and to replace it with another. When the skin grafts have attached to the walls of the cavity, usually after about 2 weeks, the obturator is removed.

Regular dilatation of the reconstructed vagina with an obturator is commenced after a further week and continued for at least 6 months. Unmarried patients will continue dilatation with the obturator twice weekly for an indefinite period.

When skin is used to line an internal cavity it gradually undergoes changes over the next 6 to 12 weeks, until it resembles mucous membrane. Therefore, after about 3 months, the mucosa of the newly constructed vagina has a normal appearance.

PRE-OPERATIVE NURSING CARE

- The patient is admitted to hospital the day before the planned operation for pre-operative and pre-anaesthetic preparation.
- Ensure the patient understands the operative procedure and that a second anaesthetic will be necessary to replace the obturator 7 days after the first operation.
- Reassure her of the confidentiality of all the staff caring for her.
- Explain that the donor site for the vaginal skin graft is usually the thigh.
- Blood transfusion may be required during or after surgery.

Explain to the patient that an intravenous infusion will be in progress when she recovers from the anaesthetic.

- Tell her she will be confined to bed until at least the day after her second anaesthetic. Explain this is necessary to prevent the obturator being displaced.
- For the first week after surgery, the patient is given a low-residue diet to confine the bowels. Explain this will prevent the skin grafts in the vagina from being displaced. On the morning of the operation the patient is given an enema, and the pubic area and the whole circumference of the thigh are shaved.
- A bladder catheter is passed and left on free drainage, using a closed circuit drainage bag system.

POST-OPERATIVE NURSING CARE
- Before collecting the patient from theatre, ascertain how much blood has been given during the operation and the intravenous regime to be continued on return to the ward. In case of post-operative haemorrhage, enquire how many more units remain in the blood bank for the patient.
- The patient is nursed in a semi-recumbent position with the foot of the bed elevated.
- The most serious post-operative complication is internal haemorrhage, which may progress unobserved because the obturator prevents the blood from leaking from the vagina. Therefore careful observations of the pulse and blood pressure are continued for 24 to 48 hours post-operatively.
- Severe pain in the lower abdomen or rectum may indicate internal haemorrhage. The doctor is notified promptly. The vaginal orifice is examined gently for any signs of blood oozing around the obturator.
- If internal haemorrhage is suspected the patient is returned to theatre immediately. Under general anaesthesia the obturator and skin graft are removed and the haematoma is evacuated. After haemostasis has been achieved, the skin graft and obturator are repositioned.
- The donor site is also observed frequently for any leakage of blood through the dressings.
- The care of the donor site is described in Chapter 3.
- The genital area is kept clean by swabbing first with sterile

cetrimide, and then with normal saline.
- If there are any signs of infection, swabs are sent for culture and sensitivity. Antibiotic therapy is commenced as soon as the organism is isolated.
- The patient remains in bed, with the foot of the bed elevated, for the first week.
- On the seventh post-operative day the patient is returned to theatre. Under general anaesthesia the obturator is removed and the skin graft examined.
- If graft 'take' is more than 80%, no further grafting is required. Another obturator is placed in the vaginal cavity, and the patient starts getting up and mobilising gently the next day.
- If graft 'take' is less than 80%, stored skin is applied to the defects before the obturator is replaced. The patient then remains in bed for a further week.
- One week after satisfactory graft 'take' has been achieved, the obturator is removed. This does not require a general anaesthetic. The procedure is carried out on the ward, using Entonox if necessary.
- After removal of the obturator, explain to the patient how to use an obturator to dilate the reconstructed vagina.
- Regular dilatation of the vagina is commenced one week after removal of the obturator.
- Ensure the patient understands the need to continue regular dilatation of the vagina twice a week. This prevents the skin grafts contracting and causing constriction of the vagina.
- The patient is discharged from hospital the day after the obturator is removed.

IMPERFORATE HYMEN

A complete septum at the base of the vagina may present at birth as a cystic swelling with mucus behind it. If undiscovered before puberty, escape of menstrual blood is prevented. The septum requires incision under a general anaesthetic. This operation is usually performed as soon as the condition is diagnosed.

ADHESION OF THE LABIA

The labia may be partly or completely fused, usually because of mild inflammation. Under general anaesthesia the labia are parted by blunt dissection, and the vestibule packed with Vaseline gauze for 4 days. This operation is usually performed at the menarche.

INTERSEX (HERMAPHRODITISM)

The individual who is hermaphrodite[4] has anatomical, hormonal and chromosomal features of both male and female, so that assignment of maleness or femaleness is not clear-cut. For social reasons, however, a decision has to be made on which gender is to be assigned to the child.

The assignment of gender will be made after reviewing the results of sex chromosome and hormonal studies (see also Chapter 4), remembering that, if it is subsequently decided that the assignment must be changed, this should be done before the child passes its second birthday.

Hermaphrodites should be clearly distinguished from transexuals. These have a clear-cut male or female anatomy, but psychologically desire to be of the opposite sex, often dressing and adopting mannerisms typical of that sex (transvestite) and seeking surgery to convert their anatomy.

In all cases, careful and close co-operation in the management of hermaphrodites is necessary between the paediatrician, endocrinologist, psychiatrist and surgeon. Many patients do not require surgery and may be managed satisfactorily with hormone treatment and psychotherapy.

Sex assignment

There are five different methods of assigning sex to an individual:

1. *Genital sex*. The long-established method of sexing the newborn baby by the presence or absence of a penis, scrotum or

---

[4] Hermaphrodite, son of Aphrodite (Venus) and Hermes (Mercury), was loved passionately by the water nymph. The gods granted the nymph's prayer that they might forever be joined into one body.

vagina. Laparotomy may be necessary to determine the presence of a uterus and ovaries.

2. *Psychological sex.* The gender role the individual pursues by way of mannerisms, dress and social behaviour.

3. *Sex of rearing.* Up to the age of 2 years a child may, without detriment, be brought up as a male or female irrespective of their true sex. After this age, alteration of gender becomes increasingly more difficult.

4. *Genetic sex.* A cell nucleus of the normal female contains two X chromosomes, that of the normal male one X and one Y chromosome (see Chapter 4). Cells used for detecting nuclear sex are taken from the buccal mucosa, vagina or skin.

5. *Hormonal sex.* The measurement of the amount of 17-keto-steroid (produced by the adrenal glands) in the urine indicates the sex of the individual.

True hermaphroditism

A rare condition in which both ovaries and testes are present in the same individual. The external genitalia appear male, but with perineal hypospadias. The child develops breasts and may menstruate. If the child is brought up as a male, treatment will involve removal of the uterus and ovaries, mastectomy, and hypospadias repair. If the child has been brought up as female, orchidectomy, reduction of the size of the phallus, and vaginal construction are carried out. This is usually more feasible than reconstruction towards the male anatomy, so early sex assignment as female is often preferable.

Female hermaphroditism

These patients have a chromosome pattern which is female. The vagina may be small or normal, while the clitoris is large and may resemble a penis. The internal genitalia are ovaries. The anomaly may be caused by administration of androgenic steroids to the mother in the first three months of pregnancy, or due to hyperplasia of the adrenal cortex.

Corticosteroids are given to suppress overactive adrenals. If these are given before the epiphyses have fused, bones continue to grow, but if untreated the girls are short-statured and attain their full size early in their teens. Surgery is performed to reconstruct the vagina and to reduce the size of the clitoris.

Male hermaphroditism

These patients have a chromosome pattern which is male. The external genitalia appear either female or ambiguous in character. The phallus is short and there is hypospadias. Some develop enlarged breasts (gynaecomastia) at puberty. The testes, which are often intra-abdominal or undescended, are sterile, and it has been suggested that because of possible carcinogenic change they should either be brought down into the hypoplastic scrotum or removed.

Most of these patients, if gender is assigned early, are better reared as females, and orchidectomy, reduction of the phallus and vaginal reconstruction performed.

NURSING CARE
● The obvious distress of the parents at being told immediately the child is born that their baby cannot be accurately determined as male or female will be treated by the nurses and doctors with all the sympathy and emotional support so clearly necessary.

● The consultations and tests required to determine the baby's sex will be arranged as a matter of urgency.

● To have to announce the birth of their baby, and at the same time tell their relatives and friends that they do not yet know if the baby is a boy or girl, is not only a difficult situation for the parents, but may be very damaging for the child's future. Whatever sex the child is eventually assigned, if there was such uncertainty at birth many lay people may never accept that the child is truly male or female.

● If the parents are not adequately counselled at the time of the birth, they may decide to assess their baby's sex themselves and accordingly announce the birth of a son or daughter. Since the appearance of the genitalia can be so misleading, the parents will not get any true indication of their child's sex by inspecting their baby, and will eventually simply guess which sex the baby is. In addition, their judgement may be affected by their preference for a boy or a girl. If the child's sex has been incorrectly announced, the parents find themselves in an even more distressing situation than one of not knowing.

● How to deal with the situation of an unsexed child at the time of the birth is obviously a difficult and controversial subject. There are many approaches to helping parents to manage this sensitive and distressing problem. One approach is to advise the parents to delay the announcement of the birth until the baby's sex has been determined. The initial delay may be explained by the father as prolonged or false labour. Sex determination usually takes 24 to 48 hours. When the father then announces the birth one or two days later, he may explain the delay by giving the reason that the baby was distressed at birth and that they waited until they were sure the baby was going to survive.

FURTHER READING

Converse, J.M. (Ed.) (1977) *Reconstructive plastic surgery: principles and procedures in correction, reconstruction and transplantation*, 2nd edn. Philadelphia: W.B. Saunders.

Fletcher, R.F. (1982) *Lecture notes on endocrinology*, 3rd edn. Oxford: Blackwell Scientific.

van der Meulen, J.C.H.M. (1964) *Hypospadias*. Kroese, Holland: H.E. Stenfert.

14   Pressure sores

Pressure sores are preventable and it is the nurse's responsibility to take the appropriate action to do this.

The most common history for patients admitted to a Plastic Surgical Unit for repair of pressure sores is some form of long-term paraplegia. Frequently the patient has been cared for at home without developing pressure sores, but develops them during admission to hospital for some acute illness (very commonly a renal infection).

Recent research[1] on patients with this type of history has shown that, of those discharged home, 35% suffered a recurrence of pressure sores within 2 years of surgery, whereas of those who were discharged to another hospital 75% suffered a recurrence. There was no association between discharge to another hospital and the severity of the illness in terms of diagnosis, number of pressure sores, or extent of paralysis. Thirty-six per cent of the patients studied were suffering from multiple sclerosis.

The implications of this information are clear. Hospital admission is strongly associated with the development of pressure sores.

In order to prevent pressure sores developing, the nurse must understand why and how they develop, how to prevent them, and what nursing aids are available. She must have the knowledge and foresight to recognise those patients at risk and provide suitably planned nursing care for each.

If we lived in space, where there is no gravity, there would be few pressure sores, since most are caused by ischaemia resulting from gravitational compression. As the ischaemic cells die, an ulcer is produced.

The pressure which produces ischaemia must be higher than the pressure in the capillaries, which in turn is dependent on the arterial blood pressure. To produce an ischaemic sore the pressure

---

[1] Berry, R.B. (1980). Late results of surgical treatment of pressure sores in paraplegics. *British Journal of Surgery, 67*, 473.

has to be maintained for a length of time; the greater the pressure, the shorter the length of time needed.

There are two types of pressure sore; one is caused by external and the other by internal pressure.

EXTERNAL PRESSURE

External pressure from the patient's bed or chair may be sufficient to cause ischaemia in the following circumstances:

1. *Immobility.* Constant or prolonged pressure on one part of the body results in permanent tissue damage. Thus paralysis, unconsciousness, immobilisation in plaster of Paris, and pain on movement in the post-operative period, which all prevent the patient shifting his position, produce prolonged pressure on the same point.

2. *Loss of sensation.* The normal response to prolonged pressure is pain. Patients with sensory loss, for example from traumatic nerve damage, loss of consciousness, disseminated sclerosis or spina bifida, do not receive the sensory sign of pain to warn them to remove the compression.

3. *Loss of muscle mass.* Wasted or paralysed muscles provide no bulk under the skin to disperse any external pressure.

Stages in development of a pressure sore caused by external pressure

1. *Erythema and swelling* in the skin. This stage is reversible if the pressure is removed early enough.

2. *Blistering* indicates death of the superficial part of the skin. The deeper layers of the skin can make good the loss by repair in 10 to 14 days, provided immediate and effective action is taken to remove all pressure from the blistered areas.

3. *Ulceration.* If the early warning signs of erythema and then blistering remain unobserved or unheeded, the full thickness of the skin becomes necrotic, exposing underlying fat or muscle.

4. *Infection.* Most pressure sores become infected, usually with a mixed flora. Infection destroys previously viable cells in the adjacent tissues. Therefore the ulcer deepens and undermines, eventually exposing bone.

5. *Bone infection* leads to formation of areas of bone death

(sequestra). If infection spreads to adjacent joints, such as the hip or ankle, septic arthritis may become chronic.

INTERNAL PRESSURE

Pressure sores which are caused by internal pressure result from:

1. *Bony prominences*. Pressure is exerted by the bony prominences of the body on the deep tissues adjacent to the bone. These deep tissues become ischaemic, producing areas of necrosis adjacent to the bone. The occiput of the skull, the spine, scapulae, sacrum, femoral trochanters and external malleoli of the ankles and the heels all provide subcutaneous points against which internal pressure may build up when the patient is lying down. When sitting, the ischial tuberosities of the buttocks are the points on which pressure is applied.

2. *Flexor spasms*. When spastic paralysis is present, such as occurs with disseminated sclerosis, the knees are pulled into flexion and the hips into flexion and adduction by involuntary muscle spasms. Because of these spasms it is very difficult for the patient to lie prone or supine on a standard hospital bed. When the patient is lying on his side, the exaggerated flexion and adduction of his knees and hips exerts additional pressure on the tissues adjacent to the trochanter of the femur, the medial condyle of the femur, and the medial malleolus of the ankle. When the patient is sitting, the spastic movement exerts additional pressure on the ischial tuberosities, sacrum and knees.

Stages in development of a pressure sore caused by internal pressure

1. Initially there may be *no outward signs* of a pressure sore developing. The skin may appear normal. Therefore the nurse must be ever conscious of the danger of this type of sore developing, and take appropriate preventive measures.

2. Later the tissues overlying the bony prominence may appear *swollen and tense*. The skin may appear shiny, of normal colour, or slightly cyanosed.

3. *Erythema* of the skin presents at a late stage in this process. The deep tissues which have necrosed suppurate, and the skin

becomes involved only when pus collects beneath it to form an abscess.

4. *Fluctuation* beneath the skin can be detected, and, if untreated, pus will eventually break through the skin.

5. *Deep tissue necrosis* is seen through the opening by which the pus has drained. The defect in the skin may be quite small initially, whilst the area of slough beneath may be very extensive.

6. Bone infection will almost certainly have been present from an early stage, and sequestra are usually present.

Some pressure sores form as a result of a combination of internal and external pressure and, therefore, the features of both types of sore may be present.

OTHER FACTORS CONTRIBUTING TO PRESSURE SORES

1. *Incontinence.* Incontinence of urine predisposes to the development of pressure sores by macerating the skin.

2. *Sweating.* Standard hospital mattresses have waterproof covers. This is necessary to prevent cross infection, but wherever the waterproof cover is in close contact with the patient's skin, sweat cannot evaporate as normal and collects beneath the patient making his skin moist with perspiration. Sweat has similar constituents to urine and is, therefore, as liable to cause maceration of the skin as urine.

3. *The condition of the skin.* Skin which is macerated and moist due to exudate and secretions ulcerates easily.

4. *Infection.* Whilst lying on any waterproof material, the patient's skin is both warm and moist. This encourages the multiplication of the bacteria normally present in the epidermis.

5. *Damaged skin.* Standard hospital draw sheets are designed for strength and durability of the material, rather than patient comfort. The twill weave used for this type of material provides strength. The type of cotton used for twill weaving is traditionally coarse, being chosen for its hard-wearing qualities. This combination of a heavily ridged weave and coarse cotton is liable to cause small friction burns to the patient's skin. Any small abrasion or fissure in the patient's skin provides a portal of entry for bacteria, which then invade and destroy the surrounding skin.

6. *Skin hypersensitivity.* In the laundering of hospital sheets,

strong detergents and harsh stain-removing additives are used. Those patients who are at risk of developing pressure sores tend to have hypersensitive skins, and frequently develop skin reactions to the traces of detergent in the hospital linen. This often results in tiny fissures in the skin, which readily become infected.

7. *The mattress*. The waterproof mattress cover tends to prevent air from entering the foam mattress. As the patient's weight gradually pushes air out of the mattress through the seams in the cover, the foam becomes compressed. The normal small movements which the patient makes do not allow time for air to re-enter the foam, so it remains flattened in the weight-bearing areas, increasing the external pressure.

PREVENTION OF PRESSURE SORES

NURSING CARE

- Every patient is carefully assessed on admission to hospital, and the degree of risk of developing pressure sores estimated.
- The skin covering all areas of the patient's body liable to develop pressure sores is kept free from urine, sweat, and any other exudate by frequent washing with a bland soap and water, followed by thorough drying.
- The value of applying talc or creams to the skin over the pressure points is questionable. Talc can cause over-dryness, whilst creams or ointments may make the skin too moist. A dry skin may benefit from a cream or ointment, but a normal skin requires no application.
- Incontinence is treated using one of the many aids available.
- Draw sheets serve very little purpose in saving on hospital laundry. If frequent soiling of the sheets is a problem, the draw sheet rarely prevents the rest of the linen beneath from becoming soiled, and so just increases the total amount of laundry. In view of the trauma draw sheets can cause to the patient's skin, their use is not recommended.
- The simplest way to overcome the problems caused by perspiration is to place a thick underblanket between the waterproof mattress cover and the bottom sheet. If standard hospital cellular blankets are used, two such blankets are required to achieve patient comfort and eliminate moist skin.

- If the patient is sweating profusely, a good-quality towelling draw sheet aids absorption of sweat away from the patient's skin. The high-grade soft cotton and the loose loop stitch weave used in this material are designed to give high absorption and a comfortable feel.

- It is not usual in the laundering of towelling to use harsh detergents or additives, since such substances destroy the natural qualities of this material, and stains on towelling tend to wash out easily with soft detergents. Therefore any patient showing a skin reaction thought to be caused by detergent may benefit from being nursed on towelling.

- The patient's linen should all be changed as often as necessary to eliminate dampness and to reduce the risk of infection.

- Common sites for pressure sores are the heels, the sacrum or buttocks, the hips, between the knees and on the point of the ankles. Pressure should be removed from these areas by altering the patient's posture at regular intervals.

- If this is not possible *the heels, ankles and knees* can be protected by various types of padding. Care must be taken that the padding itself does not cause a pressure sore. This is achieved by altering the position of the pads frequently. *The sacrum, buttocks and hips* can be protected by intermittent use of a foam ring or various cushions to alter the exact site of pressure.

- If flexion spasms of the legs are liable to cause increased internal pressure, every effort must be made to overcome them. The simplest form of treatment is to apply skin traction to the legs. If this alone is insufficient, an anti-spasmodic drug such as baclofen may be prescribed.

- If all the above measures fail to protect the patient adequately, the more expensive alternatives of special mattresses or beds must be considered (see Table 4).

- For chair-bound patients there are many types of protective cushion, ranging from the relatively cheap foam cushions to gel cushions and the rather expensive but very effective Roho cushions.

- An accurate assessment of the patient's needs must be made and the more expensive forms of treatment only used when no alternative will be effective.

Table 4. *Mattresses and beds available for pressure sore prevention.*

Type of mattress or bed	Advantages	Disadvantages
Remove the waterproof cover from the standard hospital mattress, and use the foam mattress as disposable.	The cheapest 'special' mattress Readily available The foam mattress has more 'bounce', which helps to distribute pressure more evenly Reduces the problem of perspiration causing moist skin	Impracticable for the incontinent patient or where other exudate will contaminate the mattress Not suitable for patients with infection
Ripple mattress	Relatively inexpensive Effective in altering the points of pressure frequently	The waterproof material increases the problems caused by sweating
Polyfloat mattress	Relatively inexpensive Moderately effective in distributing the pressure more evenly	The waterproof cover increases the problems caused by sweating
Net bed	Intermediate price Very effective if incontinence, sweating or other exudate is a problem Allows very easy turning of the patient by one person and with minimal disturbance to the patient Pressure is reduced because only the thin cords of the net exert any pressure	Tends to make the patient less able to help move himself Some patients, e.g. those with flexor spasms or contractures, or with leg amputation, cannot be positioned comfortably on this bed
Water bed	Distributes pressure evenly over all parts of the body in contact with the bed Very comfortable for patients with painful joints	Relatively expensive Difficult for the patient to move himself Skin tends to be moist because of sweating Difficult to move bed Some patients complain of feeling 'sea sick'

Type of mattress or bed	Advantages	Disadvantages
Astec mattress	Intermediate price The slight air flow from the sacs assists in keeping the patient's skin dry Moderately effective in distributing the pressure evenly	Airflow not adequate to keep the skin dry if sweating is profuse
Low-air-loss bed	Very effective in distributing pressure evenly Air flow very adequate in keeping the patient's skin dry Patient easily positioned in different postures and therefore suitable for patients with flexion spasms or contractures Patient's posture can be changed very easily by one person or by the patient himself The bed can be moved relatively easily	Expensive Difficult to clean; takes two people one hour to clean it efficiently Requires thorough cleaning daily if the patient has a wound or is infected
Air fluidised bed	Complete flotation effect eliminates all pressure High air flow around patient keeps skin completely dry Patient can be moved easily by one nurse Any exudate from the patient passes through the top sheet, leaving the patient dry The bed is self-sterilizing and free from odour, even if there is copious exudate or incontinence The bed can be moved Very easy to clean	Very expensive The patient tends to be reluctant to move at all, because he is never uncomfortable The sheeting covering the silicone beads may become punctured, so that the silicone beads leak If these beads get onto the floor they act like minute ball-bearings under the feet, so can be hazardous to staff and visitors Requires a piped water supply

- The cost of preventing pressure sores must be weighed against the risk to the patient's general health that pressure sores represent, and the high cost of treating established pressure sores.
- With the exception of the air fluidised bed, the use of special beds does not eliminate the need for relieving pressure by moving the patient.
- Pressure sores can kill the patient.

THE RISK TO THE PATIENT'S GENERAL HEALTH

Pressure sores lower the patient's general health, as does any wound. Wounds leak protein, so the patient may become protein-deficient unless a high-protein intake balances this loss. Infection, which is invariably present in a pressure sore, puts the patient at risk from:

1. Extensive spread of infection locally.
2. The effect of toxins produced by the local infection, producing generalised toxaemia.
3. Septicaemia, which may be life-threatening.

If surgical repair of the sore is required, the patient needs at least one lengthy general anaesthetic. In any patient whose general health is poor, general anaesthesia represents a considerable risk to the patient's life.

THE COST OF REPAIRING PRESSURE SORES

Treating pressure sores is very expensive, especially in terms of the nursing time required. The specialised equipment, such as special beds, is expensive to buy and often quite costly to run and maintain. The patient usually requires admission to the Plastic Surgical Unit for a minimum of 6 weeks. If multiple sores are present, it may be many months before they are completely healed and the patient ready for discharge. The high cost per week of keeping a patient with established sores in hospital is to be compared with the cost of the equipment to prevent sores developing.

MANAGEMENT OF THE ESTABLISHED PRESSURE SORE

Anaemia

If the oxygen-carrying power of the blood is poor, the ability of the sore to heal is reduced. Therefore if the patient is anaemic, blood transfusion is given. (For the patient in cardiac failure, packed cells are preferable.)

Nutrition

An inadequate vitamin and protein intake with low serum and tissue protein levels hinders healing. Therefore a high-protein, high-calorie diet, with vitamin and iron supplements, is taken.

Infection

Very large numbers of organisms, or selected organisms such as *Streptococcus haemolyticus*, delay healing. Therefore wound swabs are sent for culture and sensitivity and suitable dressings are applied to reduce the infection.

Wound care

Dead skin, fat and muscle is cut away down to bleeding tissue (debridement). Even for large ulcers, this may be carried out satisfactorily little by little, day by day, in the ward, especially if the area lacks sensation.

Antibiotics

Since the cause of the ulcer is avascularity, systemic antibiotics do not reach the wound. When diffuse cellulitis is present, as may occur with *Streptococcus haemolyticus* infection, intramuscular penicillin may be given. Organisms are more effectively removed by local cleaning and wound debridement than by local antibiotics, which may sensitise the skin.

Flexor spasms

Severe spasms should, if possible, be eliminated before surgery to the pressure sore is undertaken.

Skin traction to the legs provides only a temporary solution. Anti-spasmodics, such as baclofen, may not be sufficient to control the spasms adequately, and may give rise to side effects (nausea, vomiting, confusion) if taken over a long period.

The simple operation of dividing the flexor tendons of the knees and the flexor and adductor tendons of the hips (tenotomy) may provide a permanent solution. If not, injection of phenol into the space surrounding the spinal cord, carefully administered, is a satisfactory method of eliminating spasm if all chance of nerve recovery is absent. Occasionally, surgical division of the spinal cord or rhizotomy is preferable. Neither of these treatments is suitable if there is appreciable sensation or any motor function still present.

REPAIR OF PRESSURE SORES

Small wounds undergo contracture when treated adequately by general and local methods, and the edges come together to heal by secondary intention (see Chapter 2).

When large wounds have been treated and are showing signs of healing, a cover of skin, skin and fat, or skin, fat and muscle may be necessary to complete the closure.

If pressure is unlikely to be reapplied to the sore again, skin grafting may be sufficient, though grafts stand up poorly to future pressure or trauma.

Flap cover, is therefore, usually necessary. The bony point is removed with an osteotome. In the post-operative period, particular attention needs to be paid to the prevention of further pressure on the flap. Drainage is commonly used to evacuate blood and serum from beneath the flap.

The suture line and flap are usually left exposed to permit regular inspection. A penile sheath draining into a bag may prevent contamination of the wound by urine in the incontinent male patient; bladder catheterisation is required for the female.

For the complications of flap repair see Chapter 3.

NURSING CARE

- Nursing care following flap repair to a pressure sore is the same as for any flap repair (see Chapter 3).

- It may be necessary for the patient to lie in the same position for 3 to 4 weeks post-operatively. The position should be tried out pre-operatively and special aids, such as different mattresses or beds, tested until the patient can be nursed comfortably in the required position without risking development of further pressure sores.

- If the wound is very near the anus, special care must be taken to prevent faecal contamination.

FURTHER READING

Bailey, B.N. (1967) *Bed sores*. London: Edward Arnold.

15 Burn trauma

A major burn does not merely represent a very unpleasant skin wound; it constitutes a major illness. The burn injury affects all the vital systems of the body, putting the patient's life at risk from several causes. Any major burn injury is a catastrophe to the patient, both physiologically and psychologically. His family has to face the trauma of seeing their relative desperately ill as well as disfigured.

Many people have great difficulty in accepting that a patient may actually die as a result of burning, for example, only his legs. However, the whole of both lower limbs amounts to 36% of the body surface; this is a major burn which may be fatal. The fact that relatively superficial scalds can kill is also rarely appreciated by the general public. On a small baby, a burn from a cup of tea can cover sufficient of the child's body surface to cause a very extensive injury (for example 50% of the body surface), which may kill the child.

An optimistic attitude on the part of the nurse is essential to give both the patient and his relatives the emotional support they need. However, the nurse must also be realistic in her counselling of the relatives to ensure they do appreciate the gravity of the patient's illness. Initially it is the *extent* of the body surface burnt which decrees the severity of the resulting illness and the risk to the patient's life. To work out the percentage of the body surface burned see page 237. The *depth* of the burn becomes relevant only after the first 48 hours. A very approximate guide to the patient's chance of survival following a major burn is obtained by using the following formula:

100 − (the patient's age + the % body surface burned)

Thus: 100 − (60 (age) + 20(% burn)) = 100 − 80 = 20;
this patient has approximately a 20% chance of survival.

Or: 100 − (15 (age) + 20(% burn)) = 100 − 35 = 65;
this patient has approximately a 65% chance of survival.

It can readily be seen that the younger the patient, the greater is his chance of surviving a major burn. This formula does not apply to children under 10 years of age. Young children and the elderly tolerate burns badly.

Much of the illness which puts the patient's life at risk following a burn is a direct result of the inability of the skin to perform its normal function. The skin is the largest vital organ in the body, and for the nurse to understand the effects of burn injury she must first have a detailed knowledge of the anatomy and physiology of normal skin.

Anatomy of the skin

The outer layer of the skin, the epidermis, consists of squamous epithelial cells which harden and flatten as they mature. The epidermis contains no blood vessels; the cells are nourished by intracellular fluid from the dermis. The outer layer continually sheds dead cells (keratin), which are replaced from below.

The thicker, dermis layer of the skin lies beneath the epidermis. The dermis varies in thickness depending on the amount of stress or wear and tear to which it is subjected; for example the dermis of the palm and sole is thicker than that of the face. The dermis consists of fibrous connective tissue, and contains capillaries, sweat glands, sebaceous glands, nerve endings and hair follicles. The blood flow through the skin supplies nutrients to the skin, and helps to regulate the body temperature.

Functions of the skin

1. The epidermis forms a protective barrier, preventing bacteria and other organisms from entering the body tissues. When large areas of skin are lost infection may lead to bacteraemia or septicaemia.

2. The epidermis also forms a barrier to keep vital body fluids from leaking out. When large areas of skin are destroyed the resultant loss of fluid may lead to hypovolaemic shock. If the fluid loss is over-corrected by intravenous infusion, pulmonary oedema may become a severe complication.

3. The loss of fluid is accompanied by a loss of chemicals which are in solution in the fluid. This loss of chemicals produces blood

electrolyte imbalance. All the vital organs of the body rely on a correct electrolyte balance in order to function normally.

4. Body temperature is regulated by the vasodilatation or vaso-constriction of the blood vessels in the dermis. Dilatation of the blood vessels increases the blood flow through the skin, thereby increasing the amount of heat transmitted and lost through the skin. Vasoconstriction reduces the blood flow, and consequently reduces the amount of heat lost through the skin. Loss of large areas of skin, therefore, reduces this ability to adjust the body temperature.

5. The sweat glands, which are situated deep in the dermis, also help to regulate the body temperature. Perspiration is secreted onto the skin surface, where it evaporates. Evaporation requires energy in the form of heat; this natural evaporation of sweat, therefore, reduces the body temperature.

6. Since perspiration contains sodium chloride and urea, sweating helps to remove some of these products from the body. This function is reduced if very little of the skin remains intact.

7. The sebaceous glands secrete a fatty fluid through the hair follicles. This fluid helps to keep the skin soft, pliable and waterproof.

8. Nerve endings contained in the dermis are responsible for perception of pain, temperature and pressure. This sensory perception provides part of the body's defence mechanism. When these nerve endings are destroyed, sensation is lost, eliminating the protective response. Therefore patients who have required extensive skin grafting may suffer repeated trauma to the grafted areas.

SKIN REPAIR

The ability of the skin to repair itself is dependent on the depth of burn.

Superficial burns involve loss of the epidermis only. Epithelium repairs itself very efficiently by mitosis, a process which takes 7 to 10 days (see Chapter 2).

Partial-thickness burns are defined as burns involving the destruction of some of the dermis. Provided some dermal cells remain intact, these cells will regenerate and spread out over the wound until the islands of new dermal cells link up to produce complete skin cover. This process takes from 7 to 14 days, depending on the depth of dermal destruction.

Deeper partial-thickness burns may eventually heal, but do so with poor scars and by producing contractures. Such deep dermal burns require skin grafting.

Full-thickness burns involve total loss of the whole thickness of the dermis. These wounds heal only by regeneration of dermal cells from the intact dermis around the edges of the wound. Therefore large full-thickness wounds take many months to heal, or may never do so. The natural process of wound contraction reduces the size of the wound, but may also produce contracture deformities; for example if a wound overlying a joint contracts then the joint movement is restricted. Any large full-thickness skin loss requires repair by skin grafting, both to speed up wound closure and to prevent contractures.

A partial-thickness burn may be converted into full-thickness skin loss by infection or pressure. Infection may destroy those dermal cells which survive the initial injury. Pressure will also cause ischaemia and death of surviving cells. Careful debridement of the wound and a strict aseptic technique in wound care will prevent infection. In circumferential burns special beds, such as low-air-loss or air fluidised beds, are required to reduce pressure on the weight-bearing areas.

THE BURNS NURSE

Caring for the patient with a major burn injury can be very rewarding, but also very traumatic emotionally for the nurse. Major burn wounds may look horrific and smell very unpleasant. Both the appearance and smell may steadily worsen for the first few days. Added to this, the patient is extremely ill.

The gravity of the patient's illness becomes more apparent over the first few days. The patient may be on a ventilator, connected to various monitors, have several intravenous infusions in situ, be receiving nasogastric tube feeds, and have a urinary catheter. He may also require renal dialysis. In order to keep pace with such intensive treatment and the vital observations of the patient, two nurses may be needed, 24 hours a day, to 'special' the patient. The stress of caring for such a patient is obvious.

In addition to this, if the patient's face is burnt, he may be unrecognisable to his relatives, which increases their distress and the emotional support they need from the nurses.

When first caring for these patients, many nurses find they suffer nightmares and other emotional disturbances. This is not an indication that the nurse is unsuited to this type of work, but rather is a sign of the emotional support the nurse herself needs from her more experienced colleagues. A team approach to burn care is essential to the patient's well-being, but the selection of the team must take into account the emotional support that all grades of staff may need.

The severely burnt patient remains critically ill for a long time, usually many weeks and sometimes for many months. The emotional strain on the patient's family and friends, and also the staff caring for him is, therefore, both intense and prolonged.

The staff working in a Burns Unit must come to terms with a high mortality rate. Of those patients who survive a major burn, many will be disfigured. They may be physically handicapped; for example very deep burns may necessitate amputation of a limb. There may be irreparable damage to the hands, leaving the patient with limited dexterity.

The patient may undergo lengthy reconstruction procedures requiring many admissions to the Plastic Surgical Unit over a number of years. The staff of the Plastic Surgical ward to which the patient will ultimately be re-admitted should make every effort to get to know the patient and his family and, if possible, assist in his pre-convalescent care prior to the first discharge.

The patient and his family require emotional support after his initial discharge. It is very important that as many nurses as possible develop a suitable rapport with the patient and his family to enable them to offer counselling when necessary. Since the patient or a member of his family may arrive at the hospital for counselling without an appointment, the more people who are able to do this effectively, the greater the chance that someone suitable will be on duty when the need arises.

With experience, nurses working in Plastic Surgical and Burns Units become very adept at counselling such patients. It should be remembered that each nurse develops her own method of counselling according to her personality. It is unwise to try to standardise the counselling methods used. Every patient has his own personality, attitudes and objectives in life. Therefore a variety of counselling methods will more effectively meet these individual needs.

When a patient shows a preference to seek emotional support from one individual rather than another, the nurse who is not chosen must understand that human relationships are an individual and private matter. She must not show any signs of offence because she was not chosen. She can, however, help her colleague who is supporting the patient, as repeated and lengthy counselling can be very tiring emotionally for the counsellor.

THE PATIENT AND HIS FAMILY

When lay people first meet a person who is very disfigured, it is not uncommon for them to express the opinion that such people should not have been resuscitated. The nurse has a responsibility to educate the public that such people can, and do, learn to lead happy and fulfilling lives despite their social handicap.

Ex-patients from the Burns Unit can do much to help the newly burned patients, by visiting them and encouraging them during the critical phases when they may be inclined to give up the fight for life. A strongly motivated patient will do much to improve his own chance of survival. Knowing that he will ultimately be disfigured is obviously very depressing for a critically ill patient. Meeting others who have suffered what they are going through, and seeing that they can adjust and lead useful and happy lives, may make all the difference to the patient's will to survive.

Ex-patients may also help the family to prepare for the patient's rehabilitation. For example they may accompany the family on their journey to or from the hospital. In this way the family becomes accustomed to the general public's reaction to disfigurement, and can learn from the ex-patient how to cope with this before their relative is discharged.

INCIDENCE AND MORTALITY

Every year in the United Kingdom some 800 lives are lost through injury by burning. Also some 150 000 burned patients annually require out-patient and general practitioner treatment, and of the order of 15 000 need admission to hospital. Yet, since the beginning of this century, the incidence of death from burn injury has been reduced by more than half, largely due to improvements in management.

Children figure predominantly in the incidence of burn injury. Thirty per cent of domestic burn accidents happen to children under the age of 3 years.

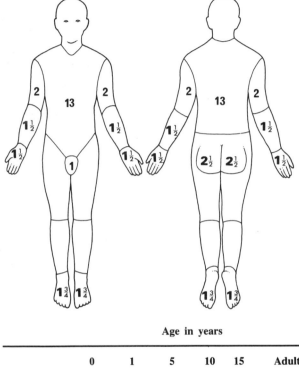

Age in years

Area	0	1	5	10	15	Adult
Head & neck	21	19	15	13	11	9
Thigh	5½	6½	8	9	9	9½
Calf	5	5	5½	6	6½	7

Fig. 71. *Percentages of different parts of the body at varying ages.*

Factors affecting mortality

1. The existence of disease prior to the burn injury, for example respiratory and cardiac disease.

2. Inhalation burns. Burns of the respiratory tract have a bad prognosis.

3. The extent of the body surface burned.

In adults, the surface area burned may be estimated using the approximation that an arm, a thigh, a calf and foot, the head and neck, the chest, the abdomen, the upper back, and the lower back and buttocks are each 9% of the body's total skin surface. For children, whose body surface distribution differs from that of adults, alternative figures are used (Fig. 71).

Electrical burns, however, defy assessment in this way, since electrical current passes along arteries and veins causing thrombosis, and along muscle producing deep tissue necrosis without necessarily causing equivalent skin loss.

Table 5. *Methods of assessing burn depth*

	Epithelial burn	Dermal burn	Full-thickness burn
Appearance	Bright pink	Red Blisters	White Charred Waxy
Sensation	Painful	Pin prick feels sharp	Anaesthetic or dulled sensation
Capillary circulation	Returns after compression	Returns after compression	Remains white
Subcutaneous veins	Patent	Patent	Thrombosed
Thermography (temperature change compared to unburned side; see Glossary)	Temperature increased	Temperature drop of more than 1°C but less than 2.5°C	Temperature drop of more than 2.5°C
Spontaneous healing time	3 to 10 days	10 to 14 days	Needs grafting

Depth of burn

The depth of a burn depends chiefly on the length of exposure to, and the temperature of, the burning agent. Burn depth is expressed as superficial (epithelial), partial-thickness (dermal) or full-thickness. Methods of assessing burn depth are given in Table 5.

BURN PREVENTION

Some 75% of burns injuries occur in domestic accidents. It is, therefore, in the home that publicity about burn prevention is likely to have its major impact. Bearing in mind the vulnerability of toddlers and crawling babies to scalds, many devastating burn injuries could be prevented by measures such as:

1. Protective grills around oven burners.
2. Avoidance of trailing flexes from electric kettles.
3. Electrical sockets fitted with automatic cut-out.
4. The proper fixation of guards to coal, electric and gas fires.
5. Care in positioning of hot liquids; for example, teapots should be stood in the centre of high tables which toddlers cannot reach.

The newspaper and television media are in a strong position to bring methods of burn prevention to the attention of the public. Suitable literature should be freely available in hospital Out-Patient Departments and general practitioners' waiting rooms.

Certain voluntary agreements between government and industry and statutory legislation have contributed to reducing the flammability of nightdresses, the safety of paraffin heaters and the fitting of fireguards. Industry's participation in prevention, by the appointment of fire officers, the insistence on the use of protective clothing and the instruction of employees in working practices designed for safety, has led to a welcome reduction in the number of burn injuries occurring at work.

FIRST AID

The ambulance should be summoned urgently, and the transport of the patient to hospital should not be delayed, since an early assessment of the burn is essential.

Flame burns

1. A patient whose clothes are on fire should be laid flat on the ground; a carpet, rug, cushion, jacket or other material to hand is used to smother the flames.

2. A room that is becoming smoke-filled should be evacuated speedily, for smoke inhalation significantly increases the morbidity of the burn injury.

3. Clothing which was previously alight and now is charred and adherent to skin is best left in place until it can be removed carefully with scissors and adequate analgesia, so as not to further damage the skin. If the clothing is still smouldering, the heat must be quenched with water.

4. Continuous dousing of the burned area in cold water will relieve pain and may also limit the depth of the burn if carried out within a few seconds of burning. Once the superficial skin has been heated and burnt, heat continues to be conducted to the deeper tissues, therefore increasing the depth of burn.

Chemical burns

1. Chemicals splashed onto the skin should be washed off with copious quantities of running water. Unless immediately available, time spent searching for the specific antidote permits unnecessary damage to the skin. Exceptions to this water treatment are burns by metallic sodium or potassium, which ignite on contact with water. Instead the metal is picked off with forceps after the wound has been covered with petroleum jelly.

2. Cement and lime become hot in contact with small quantities of water. The skin should, therefore, be doused with large quantities of water for several minutes.

Scalds

1. Clothing that has been soaked with hot fluids should be removed at once.

2. The application of cold water to areas of scald and flame burn provides good analgesia, and may limit the depth of the injury if carried out within less than a minute of the injury and continued for 10 to 15 minutes.

Electrical burns

1. A patient in contact with live electrical points should not be touched until the current has been switched off, otherwise his rescuers may also be electrocuted. If this is not possible, a non-conductor, such as a piece of dry wood, is used to lever him off the electrical appliance.

2. Electrical current may produce cardiac arrest, necessitating resuscitation by mouth to mouth respiration and external cardiac massage.

Topical agents applied to the site of injury are best avoided; they will need to be removed at the hospital (so that the burn extent and depth can be assessed), causing unnecessary discomfort. The burned part is wrapped in a cleanly laundered towel, sheet or pillow case, which is first soaked in cold water.

MINOR BURNS

Out-patient treatment is indicated for partial-thickness burns involving less than 10% of the body surface in fit patients more than 5 or less than 60 years of age, provided home conditions are satisfactory and the burn does not involve the face, feet or buttocks.

NURSING CARE

- Bacterial swabs are sent for culture and sensitivity from the burned areas, before the first dressings are applied.
- The wound is cleaned with chlorhexidene solution (0.05%).
- Dead epithelium and blisters are gently snipped away with sterile scissors.
- A simple application of tulle gras impregnated with chlorhexidine (Bactigras) is a suitable non-stick dressing, which gives antisepsis and is particularly effective against *Staphylococcus aureus* and *Streptococcus pyogenes* infections. The Bactigras is covered with gauze and cotton wool, and then bandaged.
- Unless there are signs of infection, or exudate soaks through, it is unnecessary to change the dressing more than 2 or 3 times a week. It is, however, imperative that the part should be rested as much as possible until it is healed, for example with a sling for an arm burn, or resting on a footstool for a leg burn.

Fig. 72. *Eschar removal from a partial-thickness burn.*

- Eschar is lifted off with forceps and scissors after 7 to 10 days (Fig. 72).
- Failure of the burn to heal within 10 to 14 days suggests that the burn depth is greater than partial-thickness. Conservative dressing treatment is discontinued and grafting undertaken without further delay.

MAJOR BURNS

In-patient hospital treatment is indicated for:

1. All adults with burns of more than 15% of the body surface, and all children with more than 10% of the body surface burned (excluding erythema).

2. Burns of the face, hands, feet, buttocks and perineum.

3. Burns caused by electric current.

4. Burns accompanied by inhalation of hot gases or smoke.

5. Patients who are unable to be cared for adequately at home.

6. Children who are suspected of having a non-accidental burn injury.

IMMEDIATE MANAGEMENT OF A MAJOR BURN IN THE CASUALTY DEPARTMENT

- The airway is maintained by extension of the head over a rolled towel, pharyngeal suction, or occasionally endotracheal intubation. Oxygen is given for carbon monoxide poisoning.
- Pain relief in the form of morphine is given intravenously if indicated. Morphine is contra-indicated when respiration or oxygenation are inadequate, or may become so.
- Clothing is gently removed, using scissors if necessary.
- A reliable intravenous infusion is set up. This may necessitate a cut-down to a vein, especially in babies. Adults with burns exceeding 15% of the body surface, and children with burns exceeding 10%, rapidly develop hypovolaemic shock as plasma leaks out of the circulation. Initially, pulse and blood pressure will be unaltered; changes in these indicate that shock is well established. Shock must, therefore, be anticipated, and measures taken to prevent it.
- At the time of the intravenous infusion being set up, 20 ml of blood is taken for estimation of:
  1. Haemoglobin.
  2. Packed cell volume (haematocrit).
  3. Blood grouping.
  4. Serum electrolytes.
  5. Blood urea.
  Patients who have inhaled carbon monoxide gas also have a blood sample taken for carbon monoxide levels.
- Human plasma protein fraction or dextran 110 in saline is infused at a rate dependent on the patient's weight, the surface area burnt and the clinical response. A drip burette on the intravenous line, to measure accurately the volume of fluid given, is essential, particularly with children.
- *Plasma protein fraction* contains albumin and electrolytes (52 g protein, 150 mmol sodium, 2 mmol potassium, 110 mmol chloride and 15 mmol bicarbonate per litre). *Dextran*, a sugar formed by the breakdown of sucrose into long chains of glucose molecules, is used to expand the circulating blood volume. It contains no protein but does contain 154 mmol sodium and 154 mmol chloride per litre.
- A Foley bladder catheter is inserted to enable the volume of urine produced by the patient to be measured each hour. The

urine is also tested for *specific gravity, sugar, protein* and *blood*, and its *colour* recorded. If the urine contains blood pigments, it is good practice to retain a 5 ml sample in a universal container for comparison with later specimens.

● Tetanus toxoid 0.5 ml is given intramuscularly if the patient has had previous tetanus prophylaxis, or human tetanus immunoglobulin (Humotet 250 units) if unprotected previously (see 'Immunity' in Glossary).

● Continuous optimism and quietly efficient enthusiasm by the attendant staff at this stage will help to counter the fears and anxieties of the patient.

● Arrangements are made to transfer the patient either to an Intensive Care Unit or side ward in the hospital, or to a Burns Unit.

● The wound is lightly covered with sterile cotton sheets or laid on siliconised foam for transfer.

● Burn patients travel well in the first 8 hours after burning if the above measures have first been instituted and warmth is provided by adequate sheets and blankets.

● A resuscitation kit may be required during the transfer containing:
    1. Air and oxygen cylinder.
    2. Suction pump.
    3. Airways.
    4. Laryngoscope.
    5. Anaesthetic masks.
    6. Suction catheters.
    7. Endotracheal tubes.
    8. Ambu bag.
    9. Nasogastric tube and syringes.

● If transfer to another hospital is necessary, the Casualty Officer assesses whether a doctor should accompany the patient as well as the nurse.

The first 72 hours after burning

A skin surface temperature exceeding about 50°C results in damage to the cells by destruction of protein. Very short exposure (such as an electric flash) at this temperature may permit some cell recovery, but even a short exposure above 60°C produces irreversible changes and cell death.

Immediately after burning, there is a large increase in the permeability of capillaries throughout the body which continues for about 48 hours. The capillaries, therefore, leak water, electrolytes and the smaller molecular size proteins, such as albumin, into the tissues. This results in a smaller volume of blood and plasma in the vessels to be pumped by the heart – hypovolaemic shock. The circulation through the kidneys falls, so the urine output is diminished (Fig. 73).

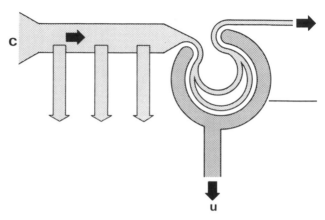

Fig. 73. *Loss of albumin, electrolytes and water from the circulation (c) reduces the renal blood flow and urine output (u).*

Because of the loss of plasma from the circulation, the circulating red cells become concentrated (a raised packed cell volume). They therefore pass less easily through the fine peripheral capillaries, producing micro-thromboses and slowing the circulation. The blood increases in viscosity. The heart pumps with increased force and rate. The blood pressure and pulse initially rise, but eventually fall as shock increases.

Red blood cells in the vicinity of the heat at the time of burning are destroyed, releasing haemoglobin. Other red cells, including transfused cells, are likely to be destroyed in the plasma of burned patients. Blood transfusion, if needed, is therefore best delayed for at least 48 hours.

When the blood contains free blood pigments, such as haemoglobin, because of massive red cell destruction, these appear in the urine and tend to block the renal tubules, leading to renal failure (Fig. 74).

In addition to the loss of plasma through the leaky capillaries into the tissues, large amounts of fluid are lost by evaporation through the burn wound. This evaporation uses energy. The rate at which fluid is lost through a partial-thickness burn diminishes as the surface hardens into a dry eschar, but through a full-thickness burn it continues at high levels, reaching a maximum about 2 weeks after burning. The application of water-impermeable dressings such as Op-Site can reduce this fluid loss significantly, thereby conserving energy.

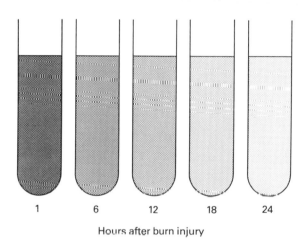

1   6   12   18   24

Hours after burn injury

Fig. 74. *Serial urine samples showing progressive reduction in haemoglobin content.*

MANAGEMENT

- The patient is weighed. Subsequent changes in weight may reflect inadequate nutrition.
- Attendants wear gowns and caps and thoroughly wash their hands before any contact is made. Those carrying haemolytic streptococci in their noses or throats are excluded from the patient. Weekly nose and throat swabs are collected from attendant staff.

- Intravenous fluid replacement with human plasma protein fraction, dextran 110 or electrolyte solutions is begun. The quantities to be given are reviewed, initially at 4-hourly intervals until 12 hours post-burn, then at 6-hourly intervals.
- The amount of fluid to be given is based on the following observations:
    1. The hourly urine output.
    2. The haemoglobin and packed cell volume (haematocrit).
    3. The pulse rate and volume, and state of capillary circulation.
    4. The rationality and clarity of the patient's mind.
    5. The lack of restlessness, thirst and sweating.
- The urine is tested and a note made of the following:
    1. Colour.
    2. pH.
    3. Specific gravity.
    4. Presence of blood.
    5. Presence of protein.
    6. Presence of sugar.
- Urine is sent for bacteriological culture twice weekly until the catheter is removed.
- In addition to the intravenous fluids, adult patients are given 100 ml (or more if tolerated) of water per hour to drink. Flavoured drinks are more acceptable to some patients and fruit juices have the advantage of containing some electrolytes. Lesser amounts are needed for children:
  0–4 years: 30 ml/hour
  5–9 years: 50 ml/hour
  10–14 years: 70 ml/hour
- If the patient is nauseated, a fine bore nasogastric tube is introduced and water given through this so long as the stomach is emptying normally. If ileus is present, the quantity of fluid which would otherwise be taken orally is added to the intravenous infusion in the form of Hartmann's[1] solution.
- Food is not usually tolerated by the patient with a large burn during the first few days, but is encouraged as soon as possible, in most cases not later than 48 hours post-burn.

[1] Dr Alexis Hartmann, b.1898. Physician, St Louis, Missouri, USA.

- Circumferential burns of the limb or chest are divided with a sterile scalpel to prevent them constricting blood flow or interfering with respiration (*escharotomy*). It may be necessary to make multiple longitudinal incisions to reduce the pressure adequately.

- Wounds are swabbed for bacteriological culture and cleaned with cetrimide 1% or chlorhexidine 0.05%. Debridement with scissors is gently carried out using an aseptic technique. Dressings of Bactigras tulle or silver sulphadiazine are applied and covered with gauze.

- Hands are bandaged with the metacarpophalangeal joints flexed to 90°, the interphalangeal joints straight and the wrist extended. This position makes joint stiffness less likely, facilitating mobility when the bandage is removed (see Fig. 53 in Chapter 10). Alternatively, hands may be mobilised immediately in clean polythene bags containing silver sulphadiazine.

- Patients with burns on the back are more easily nursed on a low-air-loss bed or air fluidised bed so as to avoid pressure on the damaged areas.

- A high room temperature (25°C) is required to reduce heat loss from the burn wound.

ELECTRICAL BURNS

Electric pylons conduct at about 32 000 volts. The domestic supply is 240 volts a.c. Electric current in the body passes along the planes of least resistance, i.e. the blood vessels, fascia and muscle. The amount of tissue destroyed is frequently far greater than is apparent from the comparatively small skin contact burn. Thrombosis of major vessels, and oedema in muscle, compressing arteries and veins, may produce ischaemic gangrene of the limbs.

The effect of the electric current on heart muscle is to cause cardiac fibrillation, arrhythmia or ischaemia, thus compromising the heart's pumping action. Electrocardiograph and serum enzyme changes (transaminase, creatinine phosphokinase and lactate dehydrogenase) are a measure of this damage.

Electric shocks exceeding 15 milliamperes produce tetanic contraction of muscles which may be sufficient to cause fractures and dislocations, for example of the cervical spine. If the respiratory muscles are involved, breathing may cease.

Renal failure after electrical injury results from the breakdown of large amounts of protein from damaged tissue, especially muscle, and the release of these breakdown products (such as myoglobin) into the renal circulation and renal tubules.

Bleeding from gastrointestinal ulcers (possibly due to stress) produces haematemesis and melaena. Burns on the abdomen may cause thrombosis of intestinal blood vessels, leading to necrosis of the bowel wall and peritonitis.

MANAGEMENT

- Estimation of the skin area burned is valueless for assessing the amount of intravenous fluid to be replaced. Enough fluid must be given to produce an adequate urine output.
- When black urine is recovered from the bladder, indicative of haemoglobulinuria or myoglobulinuria, mannitol is administered to produce a diuresis. Sodium bicarbonate may also be necessary to correct the acidosis.
- Loss of distal pulses, extreme pain or progressive cyanosis in a limb indicates muscle swelling causing pressure on major blood vessels. Immediate release of this pressure by incising through the fascia (fasciotomy) may prevent limb gangrene. When large amounts of muscle have been destroyed, their early removal, or amputation, may be life-saving. Gas gangrene threatens where dead tissue remains (see Chapters 2 and 11).
- Small wounds may be debrided as for a thermal burn (see above), and an antiseptic dressing such as chlorhexidine tulle (Bactigras) or silver sulphadiazine applied. These wounds may be excised in theatre on the fourth or fifth post-burn day and split skin grafted. Larger wounds, or wounds exposing bone or tendon, may require cover with a flap.
- Burns involving the abdominal wall are managed with a nasogastric tube through which the stomach is kept empty. Intravenous feeding is continued until it is established that there is no intra-abdominal injury.

RESPIRATORY AND INHALATION BURNS

After septicaemia, respiratory injury ranks as the commonest injures the bronchioles and alveoli, causing an outpouring of cause of death from burning. The inhalation of smoke or hot gases inflammatory exudate which prevents the exchange of oxygen and carbon dioxide in the lungs. The exudate also renders the lung susceptible to bacterial infection (bronchopneumonia). The recognition of inhalation injury is made from:

1. The history of the patient being trapped and inhaling hot gases or smoke.

2. Facial burning.

3. The presence of charred and blackened oral and nasal mucosa. Later, after several hours, stridor (due to oedema in the larynx) may develop.

4. Expectoration of blackened sputum.

5. Increasing agitation, followed by clouding of consciousness.

Treatment is aimed at:

1. Maintaining respiration until the lung damage heals.

2. Preventing secondary complications, such as bronchopneumonia.

MAINTAINING RESPIRATION

- The immediate treatment to maintain an airway is described on page 242.
- Respiratory depressants such as morphine are avoided.
- The patient is nursed sitting up, supported on pillows.
- Repeated oropharyngeal suction with a sterile catheter is essential in the presence of tracheal and bronchial exudate. After the catheter has been inserted the vacuum is applied and the catheter withdrawn.
- Frequent physiotherapy is instituted early to encourage coughing, postural drainage and deep breathing.
- Sputum specimens are sent on alternate days for bacteriological culture.
- Oxygen administered by mask is humidified.
- Viscous sputum may be liquefied by the inhalation of tyloxapol (Alevaire), nebulised water, or steam.
- Blood arterial gases are monitored at intervals by taking blood from an arterial puncture into a 2 ml syringe containing heparin. PO_2 should be maintained above 8 kPa and PCO_2 below 7.7 kPa (Kilopascal[2]).

[2] Blaise Pascal, 1623–1662. Physicist, France.

- If these measures are failing to maintain adequate oxygenation as evidenced by increasing pulse or respiration rate, restlessness and dyspnoea, endotracheal intubation is necessary. It is preferable to intubate before laryngeal oedema has occurred, by which time it may be difficult to insert a tube.
- Plastic endotracheal tubes are preferable as they have low-pressure cuffs enabling them to be left in place for many days. Periodic deflation of these cuffs is unnecessary. To do so merely permits oral debris and secretions to slip down into the trachea and bronchi.
- Use of a mechanical ventilator attached to the endotracheal tube may restore the oxygenation of the blood sufficiently. However, if mechanical ventilation fails to restore and maintain oxygenation of the blood, positive pressure ventilation is required.
- The prognosis for patients with respiratory or inhalation burns is poor, particularly when associated with large skin burns.

Dangers of mechanical ventilation

1. Over-inflation of the lung causing pneumothorax or surgical emphysema.
2. Lowering of the blood pressure and reduced cardiac output.
3. Pulmonary infection.
4. Oxygen toxicity. With high concentrations of inspired oxygen, a membrane forms across the alveolar wall preventing exchange of oxygen into the capillaries of the lung. Higher and higher concentrations of oxygen have to be given as less and less is able to be exchanged across the lung wall. Therefore the oxygen content requires very careful monitoring.
5. Accidental disconnection of the tubes or ventilator failure.

Pulmonary infection

Infection from the skin burn, the attendants or from the patient's own bacterial flora may produce tracheobronchitis or bronchopneumonia. Tracheostomy rarely improves the prognosis, since the advantages gained by easier bronchial toilet and respiration are greatly outweighed by the disadvantages of direct access to the lung of air-borne infections.

Carbon monoxide poisoning

Forced inhalation of smoke and combustion products results in carbon monoxide replacing oxygen in the haemoglobin of circulating red blood cells. The patient may appear confused. The skin may be cherry-coloured (the haemoglobin–carbon monoxide complex, carboxyhaemoglobin, is pink) even though the tissues lack oxygen. Oxygen is given by mask or, if needed, by ventilator, until the carbon monoxide has been displaced from the red cells.

Table 6. *Adequate urine output according to age*

Age	Adequate urine output
0–1 year	8–20 ml/hour
1–10 years	20–30 ml/hour
10–15 years	25–35 ml/hour
Adult	35–60 ml/hour

RENAL FAILURE

The quantity of urine produced (see Table 6) is dependent on:

1. The blood circulation being delivered to the kidneys. This is affected by hypotension and inadequate fluid replacement.

2. The level of antidiuretic hormone secreted by the pituitary gland in response to the body's need to secrete or retain fluid

3. The ability of the kidney to function efficiently in the secretion or reabsorption of electrolytes and nitrogen. This is impaired by septicaemia, shock or renal tubular necrosis.

Urine tests

1. *Blood.* Whole red blood cells in the urine usually indicate infection or trauma of the urethra, bladder or kidney. Haemoglobin or myoglobin are passed into the urine when they are in high concentration in the blood following massive red cell or muscle destruction.

2. *Protein and specific gravity.* Plasma proteins should not pass through the kidney into the urine. Their presence, therefore, usually indicates kidney (or bladder) infection, or kidney failure. The specific gravity (osmolarity) of urine rises when the amount of

protein (and other solids) in the urine increases.

A kidney unable for reasons of disease to regulate the amount of solids in the urine produces urine with a specific gravity of about 1.010 (the specific gravity of water is 1.000), which is equivalent to 300 milliosmoles/litre. Thus, a persistent specific gravity of 1.010 indicates a failing kidney.

3. *Ketones*. Ketones appear in the urine when the body is metabolising protein or fats rather than sugar, such as in diabetes mellitus, starvation or severe trauma producing a negative nitrogen balance.

4. *pH*. The acidity (pH less than 7.4) or alkalinity (pH more than 7.4) of urine may be altered to control urinary infection. *Pseudomonas aeruginosa* flourishes in an alkaline urine so giving oral ammonium chloride in sufficient dosage to make the urine acid may inhibit its growth. Urinary antiseptics such as sulphonamides require an alkaline urine to be effective; sodium citrate is used to increase the urine pH.

5. *Electrolytes*. The amount of sodium and potassium in a 24 hour collection of urine is determined in order to assess how much of these electrolytes needs to be administered to the patient.

6. *Sugar*. Sugar appears in the urine in certain stressful conditions such as a burn (pseudo-diabetes). Ketones, by contrast, are absent from the urine in pseudo-diabetes. To confirm a diagnosis of (true) diabetes mellitus, a glucose tolerance test is performed.

7. *Creatinine*. The amount of this waste product in urine is raised when nitrogen metabolism is increased. When the kidneys are failing, creatinine is not removed from the blood into the urine.

It will, therefore, be appreciated that the *ability of the kidney to retain or secrete specific substances* from the body is as important a guide to its efficiency as the *total volume of urine* produced.

Failure of renal function, despite adequate fluid replacement or the treatment of the cause (such as septicaemia or cardiogenic shock), is characterised by:

1. *Oliguria* or *anuria* (persistently small or no urine output), or output of a urine with a fixed specific gravity of 1.010.

2. *Rising blood urea* (normal value 2.3 to 6.7 mmol/l), due to failure of the kidneys to remove urea and nitrogen in adequate amounts from the circulation.

3. *Rising serum potassium* (normal value 3.5 to 5.0 mmol/l), indicating failure of the kidneys to remove potassium from the circulation. High levels of potassium cause cardiac excitability leading to cardiac arrest.

4. *Falling serum sodium* (normal value 135 to 145 mmol/l), due to the inability of the kidneys to prevent sodium leaving the body in the urine.

MANAGEMENT

- The commonest cause of renal failure in burns is a delay in instituting adequate intravenous fluid replacement in the first 48 hours post-burn. Oliguria should, therefore, be treated by rapid intravenous infusion.

- When oliguria persists, and there is haemoglobin or myoglobin in the urine, mannitol (1 g/kg body weight) is given intravenously. A 15% solution is given in 30 minutes and repeated once after 4 hours if no diuresis occurs.

- If there is no diuresis after the second dose, the planned intravenous replacement regime is continued up to 48 hours after burn injury. Thereafter intravenous fluid replacement is continued to make good the fluid lost by evaporation from the burn, and the metabolic requirements of sweating and respiration.

- High serum potassium levels may be reduced by intravenous insulin and hypertonic glucose infusion. Alternatively Resonium A may be given as an enema.

- Failure of the kidneys to respond to these measures will necessitate haemodialysis.

Haemodialysis

The patient's radial artery (or other suitable vessel) is cannulated and his blood passed through the artificial kidney before being returned to a vein. In the artificial kidney, the patient's blood is passed across a semi-permeable cellophane membrane, on the other side of which is a balanced electrolyte solution. This solution contains those substances which are required in the blood but not those which are in excess (Fig. 75). The electrolytes and urea pass across the membrane, slowly equalising their concentrations on each side of it.

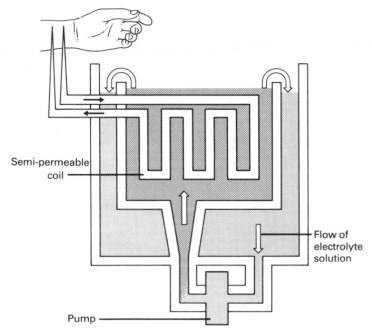

Fig. 75. *Haemodialysis.*

NURSING CARE

- Accurate intake and output charts are kept.
- Strict aseptic techniques are necessary since these patients are particularly susceptible to infection.
- The blood pressure is taken every 5 minutes.
- The pulse and respiration are recorded every 30 minutes.
- The use of a monitor will allow frequent recording of 'vital signs' without disturbing the patient.

Complications:

1. *Convulsions* occasionally occur, more commonly in children, when the flow through the dialysis machine removes urea too rapidly. A slower removal rate is selected.

2. *Hypotension* results from too-rapid fluid removal, or from a blood transfusion reaction (see below).

3. *Hypertension* may also result from too-rapid fluid removal if

the hypertensive agent, renin, is released from the kidneys.

4. *Fever*, *headache*, *backache* and *shivering* may be due to:

(a) A blood transfusion reaction. The transfusion is stopped and the remainder of the blood kept for analysis. The patient is treated with antibiotics, hydrocortisone and vasopressors.

(b) A reaction to the materials in the dialysis machine, or contamination of the machine.

5. *Bleeding*. Since blood emerging from the artery is heparinised before entering the dialysis machine, inadequate reversal with protamine before reintroduction into the vein may result in bleeding.

Peritoneal dialysis

Instead of using haemodialysis, the peritoneum may be used as the semi-permeable membrane. With strict aseptic technique, a peritoneal cannula is inserted through unburnt abdominal skin below the umbilicus. (The bladder will have already been catheterised and emptied.)

The electrolyte solution, warmed to 37°C, is slowly run into the abdominal cavity, together with an antibiotic, and then allowed to drain out by gravity. The amount drained out must be equal to, or greater than, the amount run in, and careful input and output measurements are obligatory.

Complications:

1. *Abdominal pain* is usually caused by the infusion being made too rapidly or under too high a pressure.

2. *Dehydration or electrolyte imbalance*. To treat this the patient is given increased amounts of oral fluids. If severe, the imbalance is corrected by intravenous fluid replacement.

3. *Peritonitis*. Although rare when the dialysis is properly administered, the return of a cloudy peritoneal fluid, the presence of abdominal pain and a fever require a sample to be sent for bacteriological culture, the addition of another antibiotic to the dialysis fluid and consideration to be given to discontinuing the dialysis temporarily.

4. *Peritoneal tube blockage*. If the fluid cannot be run into the peritoneum readily without resort to high pressures, or if it does not flow out again, omentum has probably wrapped around the tip

of the catheter. This may be dislodged by giving 5 to 20 ml of castor oil by mouth. More usually the tube requires to be resited.

5. *Spread of hepatitis B*. A patient who carries the hepatitis B (Australia) antigen virus in his blood will also do so in his peritoneal fluid. Dialysis fluid is disposed of without opening the container. Any staff member who sustains a skin prick or cut should receive immunoglobulin antiserum intramuscularly at once.

THE BURN WOUND

Infection of the burn wound remains a serious complication until the wound has healed spontaneously or has been successfully skin grafted. Frequent monitoring of the wound surface by bacteriological swabbing is imperative. Micro-organisms may be introduced to the wound from:

1. *The patient's own flora*, especially from the nose, throat and rectum. Swabs for bacterial culture are taken from the wounds, nose, throat and rectum on admission and every few days thereafter.

2. *The attendants*. Regular nose, throat and hand swabs are taken for bacteriological culture from staff engaged in treating burns patients. Those with haemolytic streptococci should be diverted to other work. Those with staphylococci in their noses are treated with an anti-bacterial agent such as chlorhexidine and neomycin (Naseptin). Masks are worn when dressing wounds.

No burn wound should be touched by the attendant's hands unless absolutely necessary, and then only with sterile gloves covering hands washed with chlorhexidine. Dressings are done by the 'no touch' technique, in which sterile instruments are used as an extension of the fingers. The attendant's clothes are covered with a gown kept in the patient's individual room, and the attendant's hair should remain well covered.

3. *Other patients*. Infection may be carried by air from one patient to another. The number of organisms counted in the air of the dressing room after wound dressing is markedly reduced when the air is changed by ventilation systems. Where there is no such air change system, there is a progressive rise in bacterial counts after each dressing change.

4. *Fomites*, such as communal eating utensils, washing bowls, bedpans and baths, in which organisms may lurk. Washing bowls are used by one patient only. Eating utensils should be washed in a dishwasher, which will sterilise them. Bedpans, baths and showers are sterilised before use. Disposable plastic liners in baths will reduce cross-infection. Many Burns Units consider that the dangers of cross-infection from baths outweigh their advantages, and therefore limit their use to those patients with healed wounds who require hydrotherapy to encourage joint mobilisation.

Topical antiseptic agents

The use of antiseptic agents on the wound is no substitute for aseptic wound care and attention to prevention of contamination. Topical antiseptic agents are most effective when organism counts on the wound are low, but many have undesirable as well as desirable effects.

Chlorhexidine 0.05% is bactericidal to a wide range of organisms, and is virtually without complications. Very rarely, skin reactions have been reported. It is conveniently incorporated into Vaseline gauze as a dressing (Bactigras) which is non-adherent to the wound.

Silver sulphadiazine 1%, a combination of silver nitrate with a sulphonamide, is bacteriostatic to a wide spectrum of bacteria but especially to *Pseudomonas aeruginosa*. However, reports have appeared suggesting some organisms are becoming resistant. It is produced as a cream which is applied with sterile gloves at least every 24 hours, after which it loses its efficacy. A light dressing may be used to cover it, or it may be incorporated into a polythene bag, in which a burned hand can be mobilised under direct vision.

Separation of the eschar is delayed by sulphadiazine, and surgical removal of the resultant soggy eschar is more difficult than for a dry eschar.

Silver nitrate 0.5% is bacteriostatic and widely effective. Oxidisation of the silver results in a black wound, and the absorption of water from the solution into the circulation produces low serum sodium, potassium and calcium concentrations, which can lead to convulsions if not corrected. The solution is applied onto a pad of open mesh gauze every 2 hours, and the dressings changed once or twice daily.

Mafenide cream (Sulfamylon) 8.5% is chiefly useful against *Pseudomonas aeruginosa*, but is painful when applied to partial-thickness burns. Some 10% of patients develop skin rashes. It may be applied under a single gauze dressing which is changed once or twice a day, usually in a bath. It is said to delay epithelial regeneration.

Phenoxyethanol 2.2% solution has antibacterial activity. It is particularly effective against *Pseudomonas aeruginosa*.

Topical antibiotic agents such as gentamicin, neomycin and polymyxin, are not recommended as they are liable to produce resistant organisms, and some cause skin reactions.

The periodic changing from one topical agent to another is a useful ploy to delay emergence of resistant organisms.

WOUND CARE

Three basic methods of wound care are practised:

1. *Exposed (open)*. Areas difficult to dress, such as the face and ears, are most easily left exposed to the air. Exudate is removed frequently using sterile saline. The patient requires nursing in a room on his own so the wound does not become contaminated from others. A dry wound inhibits bacterial growth, but it also delays epithelial healing. Therefore this method has largely been replaced by the semi-open or closed methods.

2. *Semi-open*. The wound is covered with a topical agent or biological dressing. A few layers of gauze may be applied to hold the agent in place.

3. *Closed*. Over Bactigras tulle, silver sulphadiazine or silver nitrate, many layers of gauze and wool cover the wound, and dressings are changed daily or on alternate days. The wound is kept warm and moist by the dressings, conditions which encourage bacterial proliferation. Dressing changes are time-consuming and may be uncomfortable for the patient. However, dressings may enable the patient to be more mobile.

Chemical debridement

Chemical debridement, using topical enzymes such as Travase, has been disappointing.

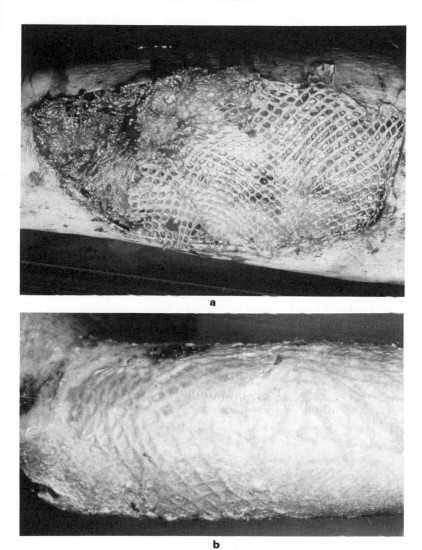

Fig. 76. *(a) Recently applied meshed skin, (b) produces a reticulated scar.*

SURGICAL EXCISION AND GRAFTING

When the patient's condition is stable and the burn wound relatively free of pathogenic bacteria, the eschar of a full-thickness burn is excised down to healthy tissue and covered with a skin graft (see Chapter 3).

At least two nurses should be scrubbed, three if the burn is extensive. Two separate surgical trolleys are set, one for the escharectomy, the other for the removal of the skin grafts. Under general anaesthesia the eschar is removed using scissors, a skin graft knife or a scalpel, down to bleeding tissue (tangential excision). Blood loss can be large, and deft assistance is necessary to reduce operating time to a minimum.

Skin grafts are removed from unburnt areas. Some will be meshed on the skin mesher (Fig. 9, Chapter 3) to expand the area which can be covered. However, since meshed skin heals with a reticulated (chicken wire) appearance, its use is confined to regions where appearance is less important, such as the back and the trunk (Fig. 76). The remainder of the skin graft is spread onto tulle gras. The edges of the tulle gras not covered by skin are trimmed to conform exactly to the shape of the graft.

The grafts are applied to the burned areas either in sheets or as postage stamp sized pieces, around the sides of which haematoma and serum can escape. A second layer of tulle gras is placed on the first to immobilise the grafts. Gauze dressings are applied and covered with bandages. Joints are immobilised either with splints, bulky padding or plaster of Paris.

The patient frequently passes from one critical phase to a more stable condition, only to re-enter a critical phase again when the skin grafting operations necessary to achieve wound healing are carried out.

For the patient with extensive burns it may not be possible to cover the entire wound with skin autografts at one operation. If more than 30% of the body surface requires grafting, there is insufficient 'intact' donor skin to achieve total skin cover in one operation (see Chapter 3). Each time skin is taken from healed and applied to unhealed areas, the total extent of skin loss is increased. For example, if the patient has a 60% burn and 20% of his intact skin is removed for grafting, the total area of skin loss becomes 80%. The patient's general condition will, therefore, deteriorate until some healing takes place.

The donor sites take from 7 to 10 days to heal and the grafts take from 5 to 7 days to become stable. Burns of large extent may not be wholly excised in preparation for skin grafting, because of the unacceptable amounts of blood loss and prolonged operating times which would be involved. In such instances, excision and grafting of small areas will be carried out at weekly or fortnightly intervals, thus allowing time between each operation for the donor sites to heal. The same donor site can be re-cropped after 10 to 14 days.

CARE OF SPECIAL AREAS

The face

Burns are most readily treated by the semi-open method, applying a topical agent without dressings. Frequent cleaning with saline is necessary, particularly in the beard area. The beard is clipped with scissors since hair retains bacteria. Crusting within the nostrils is removed with a moistened cotton bud. Intra-oral burning is treated with frequent antiseptic mouth-washes such as thymol.

Eyelids

Burns of the eyelids cause them to retract, so that the cornea cannot be covered by the lids. The cornea, therefore, dries out and ulcerates. Corneal ulceration causes corneal scarring which may result in blindness. Chloramphenicol eye ointment is instilled every 4 hours to prevent the eye drying out. Eye pads may abrade and damage the cornea. At an early stage, the patient is taken to theatre for eyelid grafting to permit eye closure. The eyelids are cleaned with saline.

Hands

The hand may be splinted by enclosing it in a boxing glove dressing (see Chapter 10). Attention is paid to immobilising the fingers with the metacarpophalangeal joints fully flexed and the interphalangeal joints straight; the thumb is fully abducted with generous padding between it and the index finger (Fig. 53). Dressings are changed daily. The hand is elevated.

An alternative is the 'hand bag' treatment. The hand is placed in a polythene bag containing silver sulphadiazine, and the bag is lightly bandaged onto the forearm. The hand is elevated. The patient, with the physiotherapist's supervision, can actively move his fingers through their full range of movement.

In full-thickness burns of the hands, grafting is performed to enable early healing and mobilisation.

NUTRITION

In extensive burns, as with any other major injury, the patient enters a catabolic phase of metabolism, characterised by loss of weight. From the third post-burn day, the intake of a *high-calorie, high protein* diet is mandatory. The greater the amount of sepsis, the higher are the nutritional requirements (see Appendix).

The dietician calculates the patient's requirements and orders the preparation of diets, which must be appealing and palatable. An adult with a burn covering 50% of the body surface requires about 5000 kcal (21 000 kJ) and 35 g of nitrogen per day. *Iron* and *vitamin* supplements, particularly of ascorbic acid, are given. These large intakes are unlikely to be achieved by the usual three daily meals. Therefore supplementary feeds will normally be necessary to maintain an adequate intake.

The required daily intake of calories and nitrogen (protein) is calculated from Sutherland and Batchelor's[3] charts, taking into consideration the patient's weight and percentage body surface burned (see Appendix). When oral feeding fails to provide adequate intake, a nasogastric fine bore (1 mm) tube of PVC or silicone-coated polyurethane is inserted using a guide wire in the lumen of the tube. These can be kept in situ for several weeks, and do not cause oesophageal ulceration. Oral feeding can continue, supplemented by feeds through the tube.

When the patient is unconscious or drowsy, the position of the end of the tube must be confirmed by listening for bubbling with a stethoscope over the epigastrium as 20 ml of air is injected down the tube. The tube is fitted with a reversed luer fitting so it cannot inadvertently be connected to the intravenous drip.

The amount of feed given is controlled by an electronic roller pump. An electronic eye counts the drips and automatically alters the flow to maintain a pre-set volume. Less accurately, the nurse controls the drops by a mini-drip burette. There are approximate-

[3] A. Sutherland and A.D.R. Batchelor, Plastic Surgeons, Edinburgh.

ly 16 drops in 1 ml. The volume given should be checked every 30 minutes.

To avoid *diarrhoea* or *nausea*, the volume of the feed needs to be built up slowly over 3 or 4 days to the required total. Diarrhoea and occasionally septicaemia have also been reported due to contamination of the feed. The same aseptic care is therefore required for giving feeds as is used for intravenous drips. There are several proprietary feeds on the market useful for burned patients including Clinifeed, Ensure Plus, Triosorbon and Vivonex. Since each differs from the others in their composition, it is as well to use one or two only and to become conversant with those.

The patient takes the tube feed sitting up. Although feeding may continue for several hours using a gravity or pump lead, it is advisable to discontinue at night. Loose stools may necessitate dilution of the feed, or the administration of kaolin or codeine phosphate.

Melaena or haematemesis indicates intestinal ulceration (Curling's[4] ulcer). Gross haemorrhage requires blood transfusion and oral antacids.

MOBILISATION AND POSITIONING

The natural tendency of a burn scar is to shorten. This produces contracture (Fig. 77), pulling in the adjacent skin or resulting in a joint deformity. The amount of contracture can be lessened by:

1. *Early mobilisation*. The patient puts the joint through a full range of movements from the beginning of the healing phase. This method has widespread application in burns of the hand. Other joints may be fully exercised under the supervision of the physiotherapist and occupational therapist and in the hydrotherapy bath. The nurse ensures that, in accordance with his prescribed regime, the patient is encouraged to carry out his own daily toilet and use eating utensils.

2. *Splinting*. When joints have been splinted to retain a functional position while skin healing is taking place, these splints are carefully removed, washed and replaced at the time of dressing changes. Care must be taken to ensure the splint does not cause a

---

[4] Thomas Curling, 1811–1888. Surgeon, The London Hospital, London.

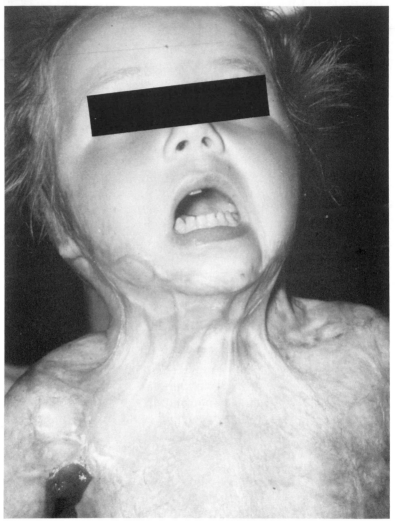

Fig. 77. *Neck burn contracture.*

pressure sore. (See Chapter 10 for methods of splinting.)

3. *Positioning* the patient's limbs and head (without splintage) may reduce contracture. In general, joints should be positioned in extension, since flexor muscles are, on the whole, stronger than

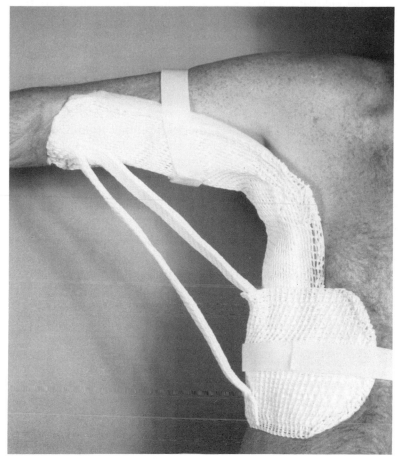

Fig. 78. *Axillary splintage for a burn contracture.*

extensors, and extension deformity is more easily overcome than flexion deformity. (The main exception to this rule is the metacarpophalangeal joints of the hand, which are immobilised in a position of flexion.) Thus, pillows are not placed behind the head in anterior neck burns, nor behind the knees in popliteal fossa burns. Arms are nursed abducted in burns of the axilla (Fig. 78). A footboard is placed beneath the sole to prevent foot-drop.

The patient who succeeds in using his own resources to feed himself and carry out his daily toilet gains satisfaction from such achievements. The nurse is uniquely in a position to encourage him in this, as well as to provide the emotional support he needs.

NON-ACCIDENTAL INJURY

In a number of reported series, between 2 and 6% of children admitted to Burns Units have injuries resulting from abuse by a parent or guardian. The diagnosis should be suspected when:

1. The history given by the parent is not compatible with the situation or extent of the burn, or if details of the history are lacking.

2. There is delay between the time of the injury and medical attention being sought.

3. The history of the burn varies each time it is recounted by the parent.

4. There are signs of previous injury, such as scars, fractures and old haematomas, for which there is no satisfactory explanation.

5. Burns involve the buttocks and perineum, both feet in a 'stocking' distribution or both hands in a 'glove' distribution.

6. Cigarette stub burns are present.

7. Several different surfaces of the body are burned.

8. The child is excessively withdrawn.

9. The parent either shows lack of concern or appears to be depressive.

MANAGEMENT

- The child is admitted to hospital if non-accidental injury is suspected. Complete records are kept, which must be adequate if they are later to be used for legal investigation. Photographs of the injuries are taken at the time of admission. The body is X-rayed for evidence of previous fractures (skeletal survey), and a bleeding tendency is excluded by blood tests.
- The nurse needs to show understanding and tact towards both parent and child. An accusatory attitude is unhelpful.
- If the parent demands to take the child home before the

investigation is complete and a course of action decided on, a magistrate's order to keep the child in hospital will be sought.

- The psychiatrist and social worker are involved in the management at an early stage. When healed, some children can be discharged back into their home under the close supervision of the social services and general practitioner. For some a period 'in care', away from home, may be necessary and, in criminal cases, the child may be removed permanently from the parents.

REHABILITATION

The aim is for the patient to regain both his *mental* and his *physical* independence. The foundations for the achievement of this aim must be laid as soon as the patient enters the ward, for an optimistic outlook at this stage will affect the patient's concept of his recovery, both then and in the future. The patient must be encouraged to do what he can for himself, even though the nurse may be able to do it more quickly. The balance between cajoling and sympathy will vary from patient to patient.

The patient who finds himself passive at the centre of a team, all of whom are doing different things to him and for him, succeeds less well in achieving independence than one who sees himself as making a major contribution to his own rehabilitation.

Kindness and realism are the keys to the nurse's approach. A close involvement of the spouse or other relative with a supportive personality is invaluable.

Once the skin is healed and the major complications passed, visits outside the ward, and eventually outside the hospital, are arranged at increasing frequencies. The occupational therapist, social worker, re-employment officer, general practitioner and district nurse are all involved in the transfer from hospital to home, and the return to work.

FURTHER READING

Artz, C.P., Moncrief, J.A. & Pruitt, B.A. (1979) *Burns: a team approach.* Philadephia: W.B. Saunders.

Calnan, J.S. (Ed.) (1976) *Recent advances in plastic surgery*, Vol. 1. Edinburgh: Churchill Livingstone.

Cameron, S. (1981) *Kidney disease – the facts.* London: Oxford University Press.

Cason, J.S. (1981) *Treatment of burns.* London: Chapman & Hall.

Feller, I. & Archambeault, C. (1973) *Nursing the burned patient*. San Paolo, Michigan, USA: National Institute for Burn Medicine.

Hummel, R.P. (Ed.) (1982) *Clinical burn therapy*. Bristol: John Wright.

Kyle, J. (Ed.) (1977) *Pye's surgical handicraft*, 12th edn. Bristol: John Wright.

McLaren, D.S. (1981) *Nutrition and its disorder*, 3rd edn. Edinburgh: Churchill Livingstone.

Muir, I.K.F. & Barclay, T.L. (1974) *Burns and their treatment*. London: Lloyd-Luke.

Wagner, M.W. (Ed.) (1981) *Care of the burn-injured patient*. London: Croom Helm.

Willatts, S.M. (1982) *Lecture notes on fluid and electrolyte balance*. Oxford: Blackwell Scientific.

16 Skin lesions and tumours

Some 30% of the work in Plastic Surgery is generated by the treatment of tumours, most of which are tumours of the skin. The remainder may be sited anywhere in the body, but often it is the involvement of the bones or tissues of the head and neck – which require reconstruction after excision of the tumour – that necessitates referral to a Plastic Surgeon.

To understand the nursing needs of patients who are receiving treatment for tumours, the nurse must know what types of tumour exist, which are benign and which are malignant, their appearance and their prognosis.

The dermatologist will manage many of the benign lesions without recourse to the surgeon, and this section will, therefore, deal only with those lesions more likely to come to the view of the Plastic Surgical nurse.

BENIGN LESIONS

Chondrodermatitis nodularis helicis

A painful inflammatory nodule of the cartilage and skin of the pinna which responds only to excision of the full thickness of the ear.

Cutis hyperelastica (Ehlers–Danlos[1] syndrome)

The skin is highly distensible and elastic, and the patient is 'double-jointed'. Because the blood vessels are fragile, haematomas and poor wound healing are common if surgery is undertaken. The sufferers are often circus attractions because of the contortions they can perform. The disease is inherited as an autosomal dominant trait.

---

[1] Edvard Ehlers, 1863–1937. Dermatologist, Germany; Henri Danlos, 1844–1912. Dermatologist, Paris.

Cutis laxa

Loosely lying folds of skin of the eyelids, cheeks, ears, breasts and abdomen produce an appearance of premature ageing. The elastic fibres of the dermis are deficient. Defects of the elastic tissue of the heart and lungs cause cardio-respiratory difficulties at operation. The disease is inherited as an autosomal recessive trait.

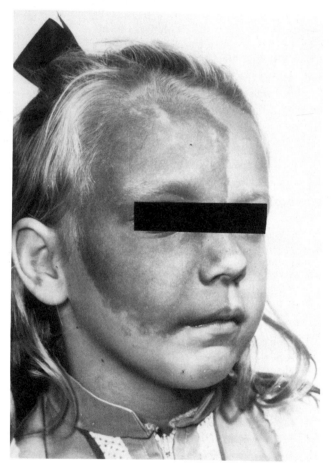

Fig. 79. *Capillary haemangioma.*

Haemangiomas

1. *Capillary haemangioma (port-wine stain).* A flat, barely palpable, red stain caused by dilated capillaries in the dermis, often in the distribution of one or more of the branches of the trigeminal (fifth cranial) nerve (Fig. 79). Associated haemangiomas in the meninges (which may be calcified) may cause epileptic fits (Sturge-Weber[2] syndrome). The stain is present at birth and persists into adult life.

Treatment. Small lesions may be excised. Large lesions are amenable to cosmetic camouflage make-up (such as Covermark), supervised by a trained cosmetician to obtain colour tone balanced with the patient's own skin. Some early results suggest that production of thrombosis in the dilated capillaries by shining an argon laser beam onto the stain may be beneficial. Tattooing the lesion with white titanium dioxide may render it less conspicuous.

2. *Cavernous haemangioma (strawberry mark).* These red lesions are raised above the surface of the skin, and consist of embryonic capillaries (Fig. 80). Unlike the port-wine stain, they usually appear within a few weeks of birth and the majority have spontaneously faded by the age of 8 years. Intervening infection may cause earlier resolution. Intralesional injection of prednisolone may shrink some lesions.

Indications for excision include:
  (a) Persistence after 8 years.
  (b) Obstruction of the eye, mouth or nose.
  (c) Recurrent nose bleeds.
  (d) Purpura and low platelet counts (thrombocytopenia).

3. *Arterio-venous fistula.* This is a direct connection between an artery and a vein, without any intervening capillaries, usually producing a pulsatile swelling. If close to the patient's ear, he will hear a bruit.

Causes include:
  (a) Congenital.

---

[2] Dr W.A. Sturge, 1850–1919. Royal Free Hospital, London; Dr F.P. Weber, 1863–1962. Physician, German Hospital, London.

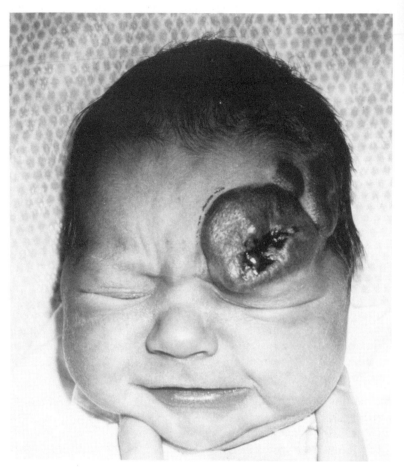

Fig. 80. *Cavernous haemangioma.*

(b) Stab or gunshot wounds passing through an artery and a vein.

An arterio-venous fistula may lead to:
1. Enlargement of the part concerned, i.e. local gigantism.
2. If large, tachycardia and cardiac failure due to the large amounts of blood flowing through the fistula.
3. Non-healing ulceration distal to the fistula caused by a lack of adequate blood supply.

Investigation includes an arteriogram, which outlines the arterial input and venous drainage.

Treatment. Small lesions are totally excised, with ligation of the feeding vessels. Most, however, are too large for this and require multiple ligation of the arteries. Ligation may need to be repeated.

If the radiologist, at the time of arteriography, is able to pass a catheter along the artery to the fistula, injection of an embolus of muscle or Sterispon down the catheter into the fistula causes it to thrombose (selective embolisation).

4. *Glomus tumour*. An exquisitely painful pink nodule, often found around the finger nail or ears. It consists of vascular channels, muscle and nerve fibres. Complete excision is curative.

Histiocytoma (dermatofibroma, sclerosing angioma)

This usually presents as a pinkish patch or nodule in the skin of the legs or arms, consisting of blood vessels and fibrous tissue in varying proportions.

Hyperhidrosis axillae

A pathologically excessive degree of axillary sweating causes clothes to be ruined and severe social embarrassment. Causative factors such as tumours secreting thyroxine are excluded prior to excision of the sweating area. This is mapped out before operation by painting the axilla with iodine, drying the area and then applying starch powder. Where sweating occurs the starch turns a blue colour. Medical treatment with aluminium hexahydrate 20% paint and anti-perspirants is tried before resorting to surgery.

Hidradenitis suppurativa

Recurrent abscesses in the axillae and groins produce sinuses which intermittently discharge pus. Antibiotic cover is given prior to excision of the whole of the offending region, which is then covered with a split skin graft.

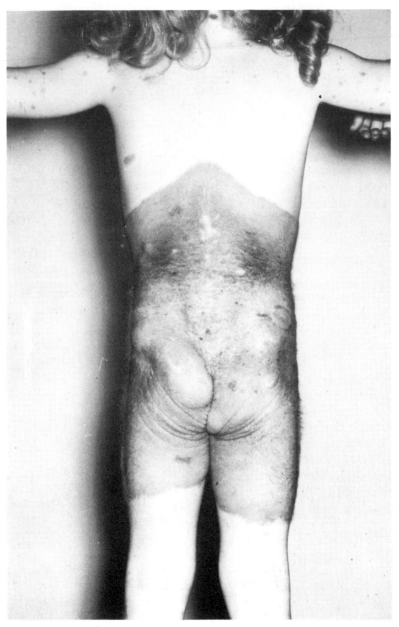

Fig. 81. *Giant melanotic naevus.*

Juvenile melanoma

A benign tumour, commonly in children, appears as a reddish-brown nodule. It may bleed and crust. Its importance lies in its histological similarities with malignant melanoma, with which it may be confused.

Leukoplakia

Patches of white on the lips or mucosa of the mouth, which may be caused by a response to sunlight, tobacco, broken or ill-fitting dentures, or syphilis. About 10% of patients with leukoplakic patches subsequently develop carcinoma in the patch. Management requires biopsy for histological examination, followed by removal of the irritant, excision, curettage, electrocautery or cryotherapy.

Naevi

1. *Blue naevus*. A dark blue or black shiny circular lesion (or lesions) which appears in childhood and does not thereafter alter. It consists of cells containing melanin pigment.

2. *Giant naevus*. Large areas of the skin such as the trunk or whole limbs are covered with pigmented skin lesions (Fig. 81). These become thick and greasy. There is a significant risk of change to malignant melanoma. Excision requires large areas to be skin grafted, and this may be impossible if the lesion is extensive. There is some evidence that the pigment cells may be abolished if the skin is deeply dermabraded within the first 2 months of life.

3. *Pigmented naevus*. A benign skin lesion containing cells which arise from the basal layers of the epidermis of the skin. If most of these naevus cells are at the border between the dermis and epidermis, the naevus is 'junctional', if most are in the dermis, 'intradermal', and if there is spread in the epidermis and dermis, 'compound'.

In adults, 'junctional' naevi have a rare tendency to malignant change, so any recent change in size, bleeding, or inflammation should be followed by excision for histological examination.

4. *Verrucous naevus*. A congenital warty lesion, often linear, with light brown pigmentation, which persists until excised.

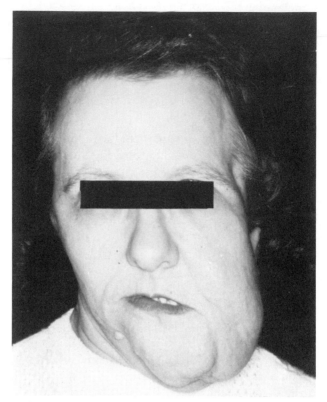

Fig. 82. *Neurofibromatosis.*

Neurofibromatosis (von Recklinghausen's disease)

This condition is inherited as an autosomal dominant disease. Multiple neurofibromatous nodules in the skin with coffee-coloured skin patches usually appear around puberty, and continue to enlarge slowly (Fig. 82). Neurofibromas in the skull may produce palsies, fits and mental retardation. Occasionally malignant change has been reported. Nodules causing symptoms are excised but usually they are too widespread for all to be removed.

Pyogenic granuloma

A rapidly growing lesion which bleeds easily and occurs most commonly on the face and hands. Having reached 1 to 2 cm in diameter, it remains the same size or regresses. Excision or curettage is usually curative.

Ranula

A mucous cyst arising in the mucosa of the mouth.

Rhinophyma

A sebaceous thickening of the skin of the nose, produced by hyperplasia of the sebaceous glands. Later, the underlying fibrous tissue and nose cartilage undergo hypertrophy. Rarely, a basal cell carcinoma may lurk in one of the skin crevices. Treatment consists of shaving off the thickened tissue in layers until a more normal size of nose is achieved.

Sebaceous or epidermoid cyst (Wen)

This tumour lies just beneath the skin and may have a small pin-hole opening at its summit. It arises from the hair sheath, and contains a thick waxy substance which, if released by cyst rupture, causes a chronic inflammatory reaction. Implantation of epidermis into the dermis by a penetrating injury such as a needle prick may give rise to a cyst. In babies, a dermoid at the external angle of the eyebrow is due to epidermis developing within the dermis.

Treatment. Acute inflammation of the cyst may require incision and drainage. The cyst may then abort, or the residual wall may require removal when the inflammation has settled. Unsightly, uninfected cysts may be excised through a small skin incision.

The sebaceous cyst may be confused with the rarer *pilomatrixoma* (benign calcifying epithelioma of Malherbe), a benign nodule of hair, or with the *trichoepithelioma*, which occurs chiefly on the cheeks or lips, and incomplete removal of which leads to recurrence. In order to confirm a diagnosis, these tumours should be sent for histological examination.

Seborrheic keratosis (basal cell papilloma)

This is a light or deep brown pigmented warty lesion, sometimes on a stalk. Occasionally it may cause confusion with nodular malignant melanoma. Treatment consists of curettage or excision.

Solar keratosis

Fair skin exposed to prolonged sunlight is liable to develop areas of thickening and reddening which may later develop into skin carcinoma. A generous, or even complete, biopsy is required for histological examination. Benign keratosis may then be treated by cryotherapy, cautery, or excision. Large areas may respond to topical applications of 5-fluorouracil cream.

Spider naevus

A haemangioma with a central supplying arteriole which fans out horizontally in the dermis to form a small red flare in the skin. Electrodiathermy of the arteriole thromboses the lesion. Some appear for the first time during pregnancy and disappear after delivery.

Verruca vulgaris (wart)

A tumour caused by a virus which can be found in the nucleus of epidermal cells. The tumour is commonest on the fingers, especially at sites of picking or nail biting, and is transmitted by indirect or direct contact. Acuminate warts (soft pink lesions), occurring mainly around the anus and genitalia, may rarely become malignant.

Treatment may include:
1. Liquid nitrogen or carbon dioxide snow application.
2. Currettage.
3. Electrodiathermy.
4. Salicylic acid plaster 40%.
5. Podophyllin resin paint.
6. Silver nitrate.

NURSING CARE
- Members of the public often ask a nurse for advice about warts, moles and other common skin tumours. In the light of

experience and knowledge of the nature of tumours, some general advice on such matters can be offered. However, it must be made clear when offering advice that it is not the nurse's role to diagnose, and that the person should seek the advice of his doctor for a positive diagnosis, as it can be very difficult to differentiate between various types of tumour. It is very important that a correct diagnosis be made, so that effective treatment may be carried out for those tumours with a poor prognosis.

● The patient who is receiving treatment for any type of tumour is invariably anxious. It may be difficult to convince the patient who has a benign lesion with an excellent prognosis that he has nothing to worry about. It is very easy when busy coping with the problems of those patients whose prognosis is poor, to dismiss such unnecessary anxiety lightly. Time spent on explanation is just as essential to that patient as the nursing time spent on patients with more serious problems.

● The over-anxious patient will be reassured if he feels his natural fears are understood, even though they may be groundless.

MALIGNANT TUMOURS

These lesions spread locally or disseminate to distant organs via the lymphatics or blood stream to produce metastases. Causative factors include:

1. *Sunlight*. The ultra-violet spectrum (which produces the bronzing of the skin which Europeans seek as a sign of health) produces keratoses and cancers of exposed skin. Since more skin is being exposed these days, it is to be expected that more skin cancers will occur. Exposure over prolonged periods seems to be necessary.

2. *Age*. Because prolonged exposure is necessary skin cancers are uncommon under the age of 40 years. Certain occupations, such as farming, are prone to such tumours, perhaps because of the time spent outdoors.

3. *Skin pigmentation*. Blondes and redheads have a higher incidence of skin cancer than brunettes; negroes are rarely affected.

4. *Radiation*. Victims of nuclear fall-out, miscalculated

radiotherapy and workers with radioactive isotopes are at risk of skin cancer. For this reason, radiotherapy is no longer used for benign lesions such as keloids and ringworm of the scalp.

5. *Heredity*. Inheritance of the multiple basal cell naevus syndrome (Gorlin's[3] syndrome) as an autosomal dominant trait renders the individual liable to cysts of the mandible, scoliosis, abnormalities of the ribs, and skin naevi, of which some may become basal cell carcinomas. Xeroderma pigmentosum, an autosomal recessive trait, renders the child likely to produce multiple skin cancers when exposed to sunlight.

6. *Chronic irritants*. Burn scars and ulcers which repeatedly break down are liable to malignant change after many years (Marjolin's ulcer). Sinuses from chronic osteomyelitis may eventually undergo malignant change.

7. *Chemicals*. Oils, tars and paraffin products induce skin cancers among workers exposed to these substances. Arsenic (found in, for example, Fowler's[4] solution) induces keratoses and cancers on the palms and soles.

Bowen's[5] disease

A brownish scaly thickening appears in the dermis. The condition is pre-malignant and eventually progresses to carcinoma.

Basal cell carcinoma ('rodent ulcer')

The carcinoma destroys local tissue by spreading within, and deep to, the skin. It tends to follow tissue planes, such as along the walls of the orbit, where spread is delayed for a while by more solid structures such as the dura mater and bone, though eventually it will erode these too. It does not metastasise. Three main clinical types are recognised. In ascending order of malignancy, and therefore in ascending order of recurrence after inadequate excision, these are:

1. Nodular type.
2. Ulcerating type (Fig. 83).
3. Diffuse invasive (morpheic) type.

[3] R.J. Gorlin, Professor of Pathology, Minnesota, USA.
[4] Thomas Fowler, 1736–1801. Physician, England.
[5] John Bowen, 1857–1941. Professor of Dermatology, Boston, Massachusetts, USA.

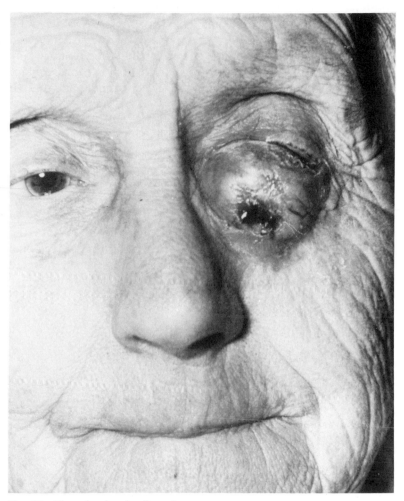

Fig. 83. *Ulcerating basal cell carcinoma.*

Treatment by excision or radiotherapy gives a cure rate of 90% over 5 years. The 10% of recurrences after radiotherapy, however, are very much more difficult to manage. Because the tissues have been irradiated, they respond poorly to healing after surgery and probably will not nourish a skin graft. For the small nodular types, curettage, cryotherapy and electrodesiccation may be curative.

Because basal cell carcinoma does not metastasise it rarely causes death unless it erodes into a major blood vessel or the brain. However, it will continue to invade and erode tissue locally if radiotherapy fails to produce a cure, or if excision is inadequate. A small percentage of these tumours are very resilient and tend to recur even after radical excision.

Untreated or inadequately treated basal cell carcinoma can erode away very extensive areas, for example the whole cheek and orbit. Fortunately with better education and improved medical care, such extensive lesions are rarely seen.

Squamous cell carcinoma ('epithelioma')

A more rapid local spread is followed by penetration into the lymphatics and the appearance of tumour cells in the regional draining lymph nodes. Eventually, the blood stream is invaded with dissemination of metastatic lesions to the bones and lungs. Prognosis depends on:

1. The size of the lesion.

2. The degree to which the cells resemble normal epithelial skin cells.

3. Whether the lymphatics have been invaded.

4. The speed of growth.

5. The site of the lesion (whether a wide margin can be taken at excision).

6. The patient's age (the younger the patient, the worse is the prognosis).

The principles of treatment are:

1. In the absence of palpable lymph nodes, the carcinoma is excised adequately and the patient carefully followed up at the Out-Patient Clinic.

2. In the presence of palpable lymph nodes at the time of primary excision, the nodes, the intervening tissue and the carcinoma are all excised together (en bloc).

3. Later appearance of lymph gland invasion necessitates regional block excision of the glands.

For large diffuse carcinomas, X-radiation may be given pre-operatively to reduce the size of the lesion, to render it resectable and to reduce the likelihood of disseminating carcinoma cells during the dissection.

Keratoacanthoma

A rapidly growing nodule which may reach 5 cm diameter in 3 months, ulcerate and then regress equally rapidly. It probably arises from a hair follicle. Histologically, it closely resembles a squamous cell carcinoma, but is self-healing, leaving behind a scar.

Sarcoma

Malignancy arising in fat, connective tissue, muscle and blood vessels, produces liposarcoma, fibrosarcoma, myosarcoma, or angiosarcoma respectively. Spread is usually by the blood stream to produce distant metastases in lung, bone, brain or liver. Dermatofibrosarcoma, however, tends to remain localised in the skin but, despite wide excision, has a high tendency to local recurrence; skin grafting the defect is therefore preferable to attempting to close the defect by direct suture.

Malignant melanoma

This tumour is increasing in frequency. It has an incidence of about 18 per million males and 26 per million females in England. The Scots and Irish are particularly prone. Exposure to sunlight is a predominant causative factor. Annual mortality rates in Britain are about 10 per million of the population. However, the mortality depends significantly on the type of melanoma, its size, and whether it has invaded into the lymphatics. The types of malignant melanoma are:

1. *Lentigo maligna (Hutchinson's[6] freckle)* (20% of cases). This normally occurs on the face or hands of elderly people. The flat brown patch slowly enlarges over several years. Alteration to a more malignant phase is marked by the development of nodules within the patch.

2. *Superficial spreading malignant melanoma* (40% of cases). A

[6] Jonathan Hutchinson, 1828–1913. Surgeon, The London Hospital, London.

thickened plaque of brown or black pigmented skin, occurring most commonly on the trunk or leg.

3. *Nodular malignant melanoma* (40% of cases). Occurs on the trunk, head or neck. Males are twice as commonly affected as females. The nodule may bleed and ulcerate. Spread to the lymphatics occurs early. Satellite nodules may arise a few centimetres from the main lesions, indicating lymphatic involvement.

Survival rates are given in Table 7.

Table 7. *Survival rates for malignant melanoma*

Type	% surviving 5 to 7 years	
Lentigo maligna	55–80	
Superficial spreading	46	208 cases
Nodular	27	

Data are taken from Clark, W.H., Goldman, L.I. & Mastrangelo, M.J. (1979) *Human malignant melanoma.* New York: Grune & Stratton.

Treatment. Early excision, with a wide enough margin of skin and fat to include possibly involved lymphatics, is desirable. The defect is closed with a skin graft. This is taken from another limb to prevent the possibility of seeding malignant cells onto the donor site.

When lymph nodes draining the affected lesion become enlarged, block dissection is performed.

Incurable disease with widespread skin deposits may be improved by injection of each lesion with BCG vaccine to stop bleeding and infection. Intravenous chemotherapy with dimethyl-triazeno-imidazole-carboxamide (DTIC) may cause temporary regression of the tumour, as may intra-arterial perfusion of the affected limb with phenylalanine nitrogen mustard, but these treatments are liable to produce anaemia, nausea and vomiting, loss of hair, and fever.

NURSING CARE FOR PATIENTS UNDERGOING RADICAL EXCISION OF MALIGNANT TUMOURS

- The patient who is seen in the Out-Patient Department with what looks like a small skin lesion (such as a mole which has suddenly appeared or changed in character, suggesting malignant melanoma) will be extremely alarmed when he is told that he requires urgent admission to hospital for radical excision of a malignant tumour.

- If the patient is initially very shocked to learn that the lesion is something very serious, he may not take in what the doctor says to him when explaining the surgery he requires.

- When the patient is subsequently admitted to hospital, ensure he understands the extent of the surgery he will be undergoing.

- In order not to alarm an already anxious patient further, continuity of information is essential. Before the patient is admitted to hospital ensure that what the doctor has already told the patient, and how much information the doctor wishes the patient to be given about his condition, is known.

- The fact that Plastic Surgery so often involves the skin has an advantage in teaching staff since, unlike internal surgery, the operative procedure can be seen. Whilst this is advantageous in teaching, and sometimes in explaining things to the patient, it can be a great disadvantage in that the patient can see what has been done, causing him anxiety.

- Very wide and deep excisions may be necessary for small skin lesions which are malignant. Unless well prepared the patient will be alarmed when he sees the extent of the excision.

- Some very large and deep excisions may be satisfactorily closed by split skin grafts. To the patient the wound will at first appear to be an enormous hole. Warn the patient before his operation that the wound will appear very large and that there will be a cavity.

- Reassure him that as the graft 'takes' the wound appearance will improve daily. Explain that the wound will contract over the course of the next 6 to 12 months, so that eventually it will not look so large. Explain that the cavity will gradually fill out over the first 3 to 6 months, until the contour is restored to near normal.

- Care of skin grafts is described in Chapter 3.

- When the wound cannot be closed satisfactorily by skin grafts, skin flaps will be required (see Chapter 3).
- After-care arrangements for any patient receiving treatment for a pre-malignant or malignant disease include instructions to the patient to telephone the hospital for an urgent appointment should the wound change in appearance or if any other signs suggesting recurrence of the disease occur.

FURTHER READING

Milton, G.W (1977) *Malignant melanoma of the skin and mucous membranes*. Edinburgh: Churchill Livingstone.

Norman, A.P. (1971) *Congenital abnormalities in infancy*. Oxford: Blackwell Scientific.

Rook, A. & Wilkinson, D.S (1979) *Textbook of dermatology*, 3rd edn. Oxford: Blackwell Scientific.

17 Cancer of the head and neck

'It is the duty to tranquillise the temper, to beget cheerfulness and to impart confidence of recovery.'
Sir Astley Cooper, 1768–1841. Surgeon, Guy's Hospital, London.

With increasing understanding of the behaviour of these tumours and the multitude of treatments available, malignant disease of the head and neck is now managed by several disciplines acting together; the term 'oncologist' (Greek = 'tumour studier') has become fashionable in the past 10 years. The disciplines involved include ablative surgery, reconstructive surgery, radiotherapy, immunotherapy, chemotherapy (for drug treatments) and rehabilitation. It is now the aim of surgery to ensure that ablation of the tumour and reconstruction of the tissues are performed at one operation.

Before any treatment is undertaken the extent of the tumour is carefully assessed.

Staging of the tumour

The size and degree of metastatic spread of tumours are described by a shorthand method, the TNM system (T = tumour size, N = lymph node involvement, M = evidence of metastases in distant sites such as bone, lung or brain).

T1	Tumour measures up to 2 cm diameter.
T2	Tumour measures between 2 and 4 cm diameter.
T3	Tumour measures more than 4 cm diameter.
T4	Tumour is invading into nearby bone, muscle or skin.
N0	Nodes not involved.
N1	Nodes involved on the same side of the neck as the tumour, and moveable.
N2	Nodes involved on both sides or opposite side of the neck, and moveable.

N3   Nodes fixed to adjacent tissues on one or both sides of the neck.

M0   No distant metastatic deposits detected.
M1   Distant metastatic deposits are present.

This staging determines how extensive the treatment requires to be. The staging also gives some indication as to the probable prognosis of the disease. Survival rates are given in Table 8.

Table 8. *Survival rates for head and neck cancer*

Site	Approximate 5 year survival of patients	
	No lymph nodes present	Lymph nodes involved
Lip	80%	30%
Cheek	70%	20%
Mouth	60%	20%
Tongue	50%	20%
Larynx	50%	25%
Tonsil	30%	10%
Nasopharynx	25%	5%

Data are taken from Cocke, W.M., McShane, R.H. & Silverton, J.S. (1979) *Essentials of Plastic Surgery*, Boston: Little, Brown & Co.

THE MULTIDISCIPLINARY TEAM

In treating patients with tumours a team approach, with excellent communication between all those involved in the patient's care, is essential. The relationships between all staff must be such that they can communicate freely with one another as well as with the patient.

If the patient is to receive the best care available, many decisions must be made about his treatment such as:

1. The exact type of treatment which is most beneficial to the patient. This takes into account all the forms of treatment available, the patient's age, motivation and family situation.

2. The order in which treatment will be given. If more than one type of treatment is necessary, for example radiotherapy, surgery and chemotherapy, the order in which the treatment is given is dependent on the nature and position of the tumour, and the complications that one therapist's treatment may cause for another.

3. How much the patient is to be told about his disease and prognosis. This decision takes into account all that is known about the patient, both physiologically and psychologically. If information is withheld from the patient initially, a decision must be taken as to when he will be given further information.

Every member of the caring team may be able to contribute some information which will help in making the right decisions for each patient. Different members of the team will glean various pieces of information from the patient about his particular anxieties. All aspects of the patient's attitude to his disease must be assessed in order to know how best to help him.

The ward team

The worried patient often asks various questions of all grades of staff on the ward, often repeating the same question to different members of the team in a search for reassurance. Therefore, continuity in the information given to the patient is essential. This can only be achieved if all members of the ward staff are adequately trained and correctly informed about what they should and should not say to the patient.

Feedback of information to the Ward Sister from both day and night staff is vital if she is to carry out her role as co-ordinator. Good communication with the medical staff is also important, as the doctor–nurse relationship can be as important in making the correct decisions as the patient–nurse relationship.

The patient's family

The patient's next of kin will be informed of the patient's disease, the treatment he requires, and his prognosis. They then decide what information they wish to be passed on to the rest of the family. The patient's wishes and those of his nearest relative are respected when answering questions from the rest of the family.

GENERAL PRE-OPERATIVE PREPARATION

Protein deficiencies, anaemia and weight loss due to poor nutrition are corrected before major resection operations are undertaken. Fine bore nasogastric tube feeding may be necessary if swallowing is not possible. Attention should be given to dental hygiene. Since many of these patients are elderly, chest physiotherapy is commenced if the patient has emphysema or chronic bronchitis.

If a tracheostomy is to be performed, careful explanation is given as to whether this is permanent or temporary.

Tracheostomy

Whenever post-operative difficulties with the airway are anticipated, such as with major facial reconstructions, tracheostomy is performed. Tracheostomy may also be carried out before resection operations on the tongue, the mandible, the oesophagus or the larynx.

ORAL CARCINOMA

In Europe, oral carcinoma accounts for 5% of all cancers. Oral carcinoma, usually squamous cell carcinoma but less commonly malignant melanoma, occurs on the tongue, oral mucosa, tonsil and palate. The carcinoma may extend to involve the mandible, and metastasises via the lymphatics to the cervical lymph nodes. Carcinoma of the lip tends to spread more slowly and has a better prognosis. Predisposing factors include:

1. Smoking.
2. Syphilis.
3. Leukoplakia.
4. Alcoholic cirrhosis.
5. Dental caries.
6. Tobacco chewing.
7. Ill-fitting dentures.
8. Iron deficiency anaemia.

Tumour removal

For small carcinomas, excision and suture of the adjacent mucosa to close the defect may eradicate the tumour. For most, however, such small excisions are inadequate and skin graft or flap reconstruction is necessary.

1. *Intra-oral skin grafts.* Defects resulting from excision of cancers which have not penetrated deeply into muscle may be split skin grafted. The graft is held in position by:

(a) A bolus of foam held in place by tie-over stitches.

(b) A denture. Before operation a dental plate is made. (If the patient already has a denture, this is brought to the operating theatre.) The excised defect is measured. Dental compound or gutta percha, both of which soften in hot water, is then moulded to conform to the defect and fixed to the denture. The denture is inserted into the mouth to support the skin graft.

(c) Inserting multiple stitches through the centre and edges of the graft, like a quilted eiderdown.

2. *Intra-oral skin flaps.* Skin flaps may be used for reconstruction after:

(a) Extensive excisions.

(b) Excisions removing the cheek as well as the muscle and mucosa of the mouth.

(c) Excisions exposing bones such as the mandible or the maxilla.

(d) Excisions including the mandible and the maxilla.

It may be necessary to use two flaps, one to reconstruct the skin of the cheek, the other to reconstruct the mucosa inside the mouth.

Forehead (temporal) flap. The forehead skin and dermo-fat is cut above the eyebrows, across one of the temples and along the hair line, leaving it attached by the superficial temporal artery of the other temple. This long, narrow flap is turned down directly onto the cheek or passed through a tunnel made in the cheek into the mouth. A split skin graft is applied to the forehead (Fig. 84).

Delto-pectoral flap (Fig. 85). This long flap is nourished by branches from the internal mammary artery behind the sternum. It extends from the sternum towards the point of the shoulder, and may be made longer by extending it round the shoulder as a random pattern flap. The shoulder end of the flap is brought up to the cheek or passed through an incision made below the mandible into the mouth. A skin graft is applied to the shoulder. The pedicle

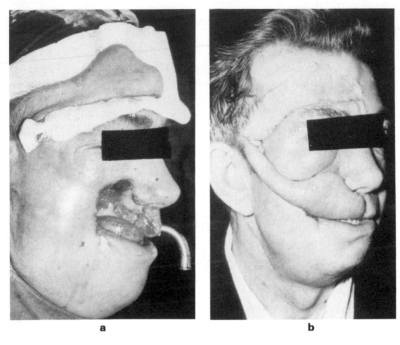

Fig. 84. *(a) and (b) The forehead flap.*

of the flap is sutured into a tube so the raw area is not exposed to infection. After 3 weeks the part of the pedicle outside the mouth not required for reconstruction is cut and returned to the chest.

A comparison of the disadvantages of forehead and delto-pectoral flaps is given in Table 9.

Table 9. *A comparison of the disadvantages of forehead and delto-pectoral flaps*

Forehead flap	Delto-pectoral flap
Scarring on the forehead.	Stiffness of the shoulder.
Less skin available than with the delto-pectoral flap.	Higher incidence of fistula into the mouth.

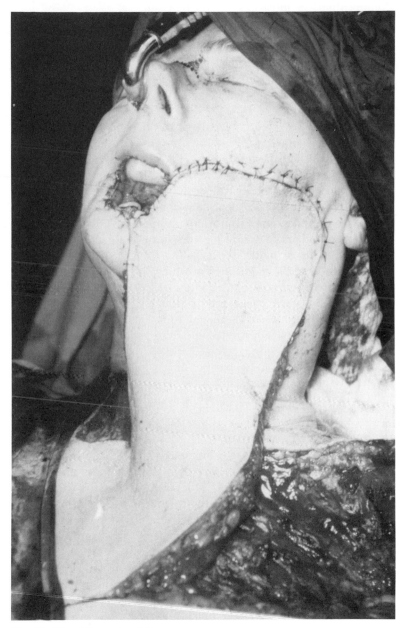

Fig. 85. *The delto-pectoral flap.*

Complications of intra-oral reconstruction

1. *Fistula*. The loss of saliva from the mouth through a fistula onto the cheek or neck more commonly occurs when the operation has followed irradiation, or if flap necrosis has occurred. Small fistulae heal spontaneously if kept clean and free of saliva. Nasogastric feeding may be necessary to prevent food particles entering the fistula.

2. *Flap necrosis*. Death of part of the flap inside the mouth is usually the result of kinking or tension on the flap. This is particularly likely if the flap is stretched over a prosthesis or bone graft used to replace an excised mandible. Immediate replacement of the mandible is, therefore, now carried out less frequently. Dragging of the delto-pectoral flap, causing tension, needs to be rectified by appropriate support or strapping.

3. *Nerve injuries*. To remove the tumour adequately, nerves may have to be divided:

   (a) Excision of the mandible (in which the alveolar nerve runs) produces numbness of the chin.

   (b) Excision of the cheek may produce facial palsy and anaesthesia of the face.

   (c) Excision of part of the tongue may produce paralysis of the remainder.

   (d) Block dissection of lymph nodes in the neck produces paralysis of the trapezius muscle of the shoulder (causing drooping and winging of the scapula).

PRE-OPERATIVE NURSING CARE

- The patient is admitted to hospital at least 2 days before the planned surgery, so that pre-operative and pre-anaesthetic preparation can be carried out.
- The patient may be nursed in an Intensive Care Unit for the first few days post-operatively. The staff who will nurse the patient after surgery visit the patient pre-operatively and explain his post-operative nursing care to him.
- If possible the patient and his relatives are shown the Intensive Care Unit and what equipment will be around him when he recovers from the anaesthetic.
- Ensure the patient understands the operative procedure. If more than one operation is necessary to complete his recon-

struction, ensure the patient is aware of the various stages of his surgery and the anticipated length of his stay in hospital.

- Explain to the patient and his relatives how he will look after each stage of his surgery.

- If the patient will be facially disfigured after his operation, appropriate counselling of the patient and his family is commenced on the first day of his admission to hospital, and continued until after his discharge home.

- If the patient or his family are very apprehensive, it may be helpful to ask an ex-patient who has undergone similar surgery and is emotionally stable to visit the patient and his family, either before he undergoes surgery or during the post-operative period.

- When skin is used inside the mouth as part of the reconstruction, the skin cells undergo change until they look like mucous membrane cells. This process takes from 6 to 12 weeks. During this period the patient suffers an unpleasant taste in his mouth and halitosis. Explain this to the patient, and reassure him that these symptoms are temporary.

- Explain that, post-operatively, no food or fluid can be taken orally, and that nasogastric feeds will be commenced a few hours after surgery.

- Explain that blood transfusion is usually required, and that an intravenous infusion will be in progress when he recovers from the anaesthetic.

- To maintain a free airway and reduce oedema, the patient is sat up in bed as soon as possible after surgery. Ask the patient to try to remain in the position he finds himself when recovering from his anaesthetic.

- Following surgery the patient may have difficulty in speaking. Show him how to use the nurse call system. If no such system is available, give the patient a hand bell to summon the nurse. Show the patient what aids will be available to him when he is unable to speak, such as a word bracelet, picture/word card, and pencil and paper attached to a reading stand.

- Reassure the patient that he will not be left unattended until he is confident in his own ability to cope with his post-operative problems.

- If a tracheostomy is planned, explain this to the patient. Explain to him that caring for the tracheostomy is a simple procedure, and that when the tracheostomy is no longer required it will close spontaneously on removal of the tube.

- If tracheostomy is not planned, reassure the patient that he will not suffer any breathing difficulties. Explain that he will be able to breathe very well through his nose and mouth.

- Show him the electrical suction apparatus, and explain how it is used to remove secretions from the mouth if necessary.

- Tell the patient that, should he feel sick, he should inform a nurse immediately so she may aspirate his nasogastric tube and administer an anti-emetic if necessary. Explain that should he vomit this will not present any problems. (It is not desirable for the patient to vomit as this may dislodge the grafts or flaps, but to tell the patient this may cause undue anxiety which could produce nausea.)

- If split skin grafts are to be used either to re-line the mouth or to close the defects created by the raising of flaps, tell the patient which donor site is to be used, and explain the post-operative care of the donor site (this is explained in Chapter 3)

- When dealing with the patient, appear calm, confident and optimistic.

- If a tracheostomy has not been performed before the patient is returned from theatre have at hand:
    1. An electric sucker.
    2. An ample supply of soft rubber, round-tipped catheters.
    3. A pair of tongue forceps.
    4. A mouth gag.
    5. An airway of suitable size for the patient.
    6. Sponge-holding forceps loaded with gauze swabs.
    7. Emergency intubation equipment.

- If a tracheostomy has been performed prepare:
    1. An electric sucker.
    2. An ample supply of oral and tracheal suction catheters.
    3. A mouth gag. ⎫
    4. A pair of tongue forceps. ⎬ These may be needed to inspect the grafts or flaps inside the mouth.
    5. Tracheal dilators.
    6. A replacement tracheostomy tube.
    7. Sponge-holding forceps loaded with gauze swabs.

- Do not clutter the patient's bedside area with any unnecessary equipment. Emergency sets, such as intubation and tracheostomy packs, should be positioned conveniently near, but not beside, the bed.

- In case of cardiac arrest, ensure there is sufficient space around the bed, and that equipment is positioned so the resuscitation team will have easy access to the patient.

POST-OPERATIVE NURSING CARE

- Blood transfusion is usually commenced in theatre. Before returning the patient to the ward enquire how much blood has been given during the operation, and what intravenous regime is required during the post-operative period.
- In case of post-operative haemorrhage, ascertain how much blood remains in the bank for this patient.
- The patient is not left unattended until both he and the nurse are confident in his ability to cope with his post-operative problems. This is usually at least 48 hours after surgery.
- The patient may initially be nursed on his side, with his head in the best position to maintain a free airway.
- As soon as the blood pressure is stable the patient is gradually sat up in bed, adding one pillow at a time. Check the blood pressure 10 minutes after each pillow is added. If the blood pressure falls, but remains at or above 100 mmHg systolic, no more pillows are added until the blood pressure rises to 110 mmHg. If the blood pressure falls to below 100 mmHg the pillow is removed until the blood pressure returns to 110 mmHg.
- Frequent observation of the pulse and blood pressure is continued until both have remained stable for 6 hours. Four-hourly recordings are then continued for a further 24 hours.
- Mouth toilet is commenced as soon as possible. Various methods of administering mouth-washes are described on page 323.
- Avoid using oral suction if possible. Encourage the patient to lean forward to allow secretions to drain out of the mouth by gravity. However, do not delay in using suction if there is any danger of the patient inhaling the secretions.
- If suction is necessary, introduce the catheter along the side of the mouth, as far away from the operation site as possible (see also Chapter 19).

- Intra-oral haemorrhage may proceed unobserved if the semi-conscious patient keeps swallowing the blood. Therefore, careful observation for repeated swallowing is essential during the immediate post-operative period and when the patient is asleep.
- In the event of a rapid fall in blood pressure or post-operative haemorrhage, do not raise the foot of the bed, as this will increase the pressure in the operation site and may predispose to, or increase, haemorrhage. Summon the doctor urgently. Immediate administration of drugs to raise the blood pressure, rapid blood transfusion or return of the patient to theatre for haemostasis may be necessary.
- Nasogastric feeding is commenced 12 to 24 hours after surgery. For feeding requirements see Chapter 19.
- For post-operative care of grafts and flaps see Chapter 3.
- Gradual mobilisation of the patient is commenced as soon as possible after surgery, usually on the first post-operative day.
- The patient should not be discouraged from looking in a mirror if he wishes to do so. First explain his appearance to him, then, when he is looking in the mirror, explain the details of his surgery such as what tissue has been moved and to where. Be prepared for the patient to faint, but do not suggest this to him. Be optimistic and reassure him that he will see a great improvement over the next few weeks.
- Before any lay person visits the patient ensure they understand the patient's appearance. Stay near the new visitor for a short time in case he faints, but do not suggest that he may do so.

RADICAL NECK DISSECTION

Spread of tumour to the lymph nodes in the neck requires removal en bloc of these nodes together with the oral tumour. The block of tissue removed extends from the mandible above to the clavicle below, and from the midline of the neck anteriorly to the border of the trapezius muscle posteriorly.

Because of the extensive undermining of the skin flaps and the volume of tissue excised, suction drainage is usually employed for at least 48 hours post-operatively. Too high a suction pressure, however, may dislodge clots resulting in bleeding from vessel ends.

Complications

1. *Haemorrhage*. Hand pressure is applied to reduce bleeding until the patient can be taken back to theatre and the vessel or vessels ligated.

2. *Airway obstruction*. An endotracheal tube may be left in the nostril post-operatively until the patient is fully awake. If this becomes blocked, the blockage is relieved by a suction catheter. If there is no endotracheal tube or tracheostomy, the suction catheter is introduced either through the mouth or the nose to clear the pharynx.

3. *Difficulty with swallowing*. This usually improves, but may necessitate taking food in small amounts or, occasionally, temporary nasogastric feeding.

4. *Sweating and pain in the cheek* after eating (Frey's[1] syndrome), caused by damage to the nerve supplying the skin around the ear.

5. *Leakage of lymph*, if persistent, probably indicates that the ligature on the thoracic duct (on the left side of the neck) has been dislodged and requires re-ligation.

PRE-OPERATIVE NURSING CARE
- This operation may be performed at the same time as radical excision of the primary tumour.
- Pre-operative nursing care is similar to the pre-operative care described for oral carcinoma.

POST-OPERATIVE NURSING CARE
- The following care is carried out as described for oral carcinoma (see above):
    1. Blood transfusion and any other intravenous infusions necessary.
    2. Observation of pulse and blood pressure. (The patient is sat up in bed as soon as the blood pressure is stable.)
    3. Oral and endotracheal suction.
    4. Observations and action for post-operative haemorrhage.
    5. Mobilisation of the patient.

---

[1] Lucja Fréy, 1889–1944. Physician, Warsaw, Poland.

- Suction on the drains is maintained by reliable electric suckers which give a continuous but gentle suction, such as Roberts pumps. Two or three drains may be in situ. All or some of these drains may require suction via a pump. Therefore, before returning the patient from theatre, ensure clear instructions have been given as to which drains are to have suction applied and at what pressure.

- Frequent observation of the pumps is maintained to ensure the pressures remain stable. Too low a suction pressure may lead to haematoma formation. Too high a suction pressure may provoke post-operative haemorrhage.

- Haematoma beneath the thin skin flaps, which are raised to allow access to the neck glands, may result in flap death (see Chapter 3).

- Swelling of the neck beneath the wound suggests haematoma formation. However, this may be difficult to detect since the natural contour of the neck is altered by the removal of the neck glands. Therefore careful observations of the neck contour should be made immediately after the operation. It is then possible to compare its future appearance with the initial observations. For this reason it is very important that, when handing over the patient's care to another nurse, the appearance of the neck immediately after the operation is described.

- If haematoma formation is suspected, summon the doctor urgently. It may be necessary to return the patient to theatre for haemostasis or repositioning of the drains.

- If post-operative haemorrhage occurs, immediately apply hand pressure to the wound. The doctor is summoned urgently and pressure on the wound is continued until the patient is returned to theatre for haemostasis.

- Haemorrhage from the blood vessels of the neck can be massive and very rapid. In the event of massive haemorrhage:
  1. Summon another nurse urgently. At the same time apply firm hand pressure to the bleeding site.
  2. Speed up the intravenous infusion to the maximum rate. If an infusion pump is in situ, increase the infusion rate to match the rate of blood loss.
  3. The second nurse:
     (a) Calls a doctor urgently.
     (b) Notifies the surgical team to prepare the theatre for

emergency haemostasis.
(c) Arranges for all remaining blood in the bank for this patient to be brought to the ward immediately.
(d) Returns to the patient and commences pumping the intravenous infusion with a Martin's pump or, if an infusion pump is in situ, ensures that the rate of flow equals the amount of blood loss.

4. Commence blood transfusion as soon as the blood arrives.
5. Return the patient to theatre as soon as help arrives.
6. Check how much blood is available for the patient, as massive transfusion may be life-saving. If necessary, uncross-matched blood is obtained (the patient's blood group will be known). In a dire emergency any blood in the bank of the correct group, or of group O negative, may be used.

- The patient remains in hospital until there is no risk of secondary haemorrhage, usually 10 to 14 days.
- Drains are removed 24 hours after the last drainage.
- Sutures are removed after 7 to 14 days.

PAROTID TUMOURS

Eighty per cent of parotid tumours are *benign mixed salivary tumours (pleomorphic adenomas)*, but these are liable to recur locally if inadequately excised. For most adenomas, suprafacial parotidectomy is necessary, removing all that part of the gland superficial to the facial nerve (which runs through the middle of the parotid gland).

Carcinoma of the parotid makes up about 0.5% of all malignant tumours. It spreads locally through the gland and metastasises to the cervical lymph nodes. Total removal of the gland (which necessitates removing the facial nerve) is necessary for cure. The nerve is reconstructed using a nerve graft (see Chapter 3), and temporary protection is given to the cornea of the eye by performing a lateral tarsorrhaphy, until there is sufficient recovery of the nerve. Lateral tarsorrhaphy involves suturing together the outer one-third of the upper and lower eyelids, so that the paralysed lids cover sufficient of the cornea to prevent it drying out.

If the carcinoma has invaded the masseter muscle, part of the mandible is removed to ensure clearance of the tumour. Radical neck dissection is performed for cervical lymph node metastases. Drainage of the wound is usually employed.

Complications of Parotidectomy

1. *Facial palsy*. Accidental division of the facial nerve during the operation of suprafacial parotidectomy for a benign tumour is repaired at the time of operation. Spontaneous recovery of facial muscles can be anticipated after a few months. Temporary paralysis of facial muscles of 2 to 4 months duration may occur if the nerve has been damaged but not divided.

Division of the facial nerve during total parotidectomy for carcinoma, if not repairable, leaves the patient with a permanent palsy. This possibility will have been explained to the patient before operation.

2. *Frey's syndrome* (see page 299) consists of sweating and flushing of the skin in front of the ear, and is due to damage to the auriculotemporal nerve.

3. *Fistula*. Leakage of saliva from remnants of the parotid gland onto the cheek usually ceases spontaneously. A small dose of irradiation will dry up the secretion if the fistula does not close.

4. *Facial tic*. Inappropriate involuntary movements of the facial muscles after facial nerve division may be due to the nerve regenerating into the wrong muscles. Further section of the nerve may be necessary if the symptoms are sufficiently severe.

NURSING CARE
● Nursing care is the same as for radical neck dissection (see above).

RECONSTRUCTION OF THE OESOPHAGUS AND PHARYNX

Carcinoma of the oesophagus and pharynx usually presents with difficulty in swallowing when the tumour is well advanced. For the reconstructive surgeon, the problem is to form a channel through which food can be passed from the mouth to the stomach after the pharynx or oesophagus has been removed by the ablative surgeon.

Less commonly, oesophageal reconstruction is required follow-

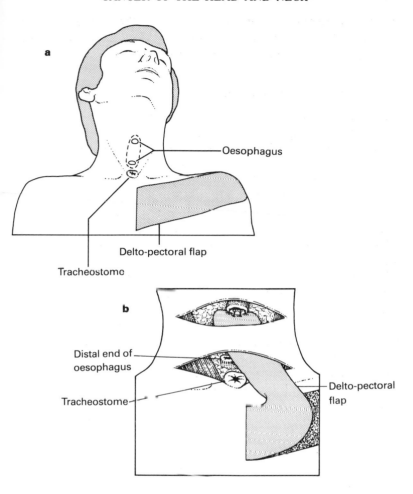

Fig. 86. *(a) and (b) Oesophageal reconstruction using the delto-pectoral flap.*

ing stricture due to the swallowing of chemicals, or following congenital failure of formation. The methods of reconstruction may be considered under three headings:

1. Repair using local tissue.
2. Repair using stomach, small or large intestine, brought up to

the neck on a vascular pedicle or nourished by free micro-vascular anastomosis of vessels.

3. Repair using distant skin flaps turned into a tube (pectoralis major or delto-pectoral flap).

1. *Local tissue.* Skin flaps from the neck may be inturned to form a tube or, if part of the circumference of the oesophagus or pharynx remains, to complete the remainder of the circumference. The tube (with the skin innermost) is then covered either with a skin graft or by advancing skin from either side to the middle of the neck.

This method cannot be used if the skin of the neck has previously been irradiated, or if there are inappropriately placed operation scars.

2. *The stomach or intestine,* brought up into the chest on its arterial pedicle, has been used particularly for reconstruction of the lower two-thirds of the oesophagus. Higher reconstructions stretch the arterial pedicle, making vascular failure more likely.

The 'free transfer' of a segment of intestine, anastomosing its vessels to vessels in the neck, is an attractive idea. Unfortunately, there is a significant failure rate. Also the patient is subjected to an intra-abdominal as well as a neck (and possibly thoracic) operation.

3. *The delto-pectoral flap,* extended onto the upper arm by a 'delay' if necessary, is raised and formed into a tube, with the skin innermost. The shoulder end is threaded beneath the skin of the neck and sutured to the upper remnant of the oesophagus (Fig. 86). Three to four weeks later the middle of the tube is opened and sutured to the lower oesophageal remnant. At each stage suction drainage is employed, and radical neck dissection, if necessary, may be carried out with the first stage. Tracheostomy is performed either at or before the first stage. (See also myocutaneous flaps in Chapter 3.)

Pre-operative preparation of the patient

Tube feeding with a high calorie diet to ensure the patient is gaining weight and the correction of anaemia and hypovitaminosis are essential to successful surgery.

Complications

1. *Fistula.* Unless very small, breakdown of the suture line at the junction of the oesophageal remnant with the skin tube or grafted intestine necessitates resuture.

2. *Stricture* at the upper or lower suture sites may be dilated using graduated bougies. If this is unsuccessful, resection and resuture of the anastomosis, possibly bringing in further tissue, may be needed. Recurrence of the carcinoma must first be excluded by biopsy.

3. *Haemorrhage.* Primary haemorrhage resulting from slippage of an arterial ligature will lead to a large loss of blood through the drains or the rapid formation of a haematoma swelling. Hand pressure is maintained over the wound until the patient is returned to theatre.

Reactionary haemorrhage occurs 7 to 10 days post-operatively, and is due to the dissolving of a blood clot, often by infection. It is sometimes possible to deal with this by a combination of wound aspiration and compression.

4. *Carotid artery rupture* is caused by infection eroding through the wall of the vessel, particularly if the artery is exposed or adjacent to a necrotic flap. Immediate digital pressure on the carotid artery (the position of which should be identified and marked on the skin in the immediate post-operative period), together with rapid transfusion, may be life-saving.

NURSING CARE
- Pre- and post-operative nursing care involves a combination of the care described for oral carcinoma and radical neck dissection.

CANCRUM ORIS

Diets deficient in protein contribute to infection and ulceration of the gums, extending to involve the cheeks often in their entire thickness, a condition known as cancrum oris. Patients on immunosuppressive and cytotoxic drugs are particularly at risk from this type of fulminating widespread infection. After high-protein diets and vitamin supplements have corrected the deficiencies, reconstruction of the cheeks can be carried out.

GENERAL NURSING CARE

When caring for a patient who is undergoing major reconstruction of the head and neck region the nurse must constantly be aware of the following:

- Failure of a flap will probably result in the patient's death.
- Death due to flap failure will not occur for some days or even weeks after surgery. Therefore the urgency of a situation may be overlooked if the danger signs are not recognised.
- Constant observation of a patient to whom nothing untoward is happening can become tedious and appear pointless to the inexperienced.
- Good nursing care relies on observation of the patient's appearance. When constantly attending to the patient, slight changes in his appearance may pass unnoticed. Over a long period of time many small changes may proceed unheeded, not through neglect or inexperience, but because powers of observation are reduced by constant contact with the patient. When caring for such a patient, make a conscious effort to look away from the patient for a short time and then, before looking again, try to remember exactly how the patient looked at the start of the shift. If in doubt, call another nurse who also saw the patient a few hours ago.

When a patient is being 'specialed' following this type of surgery, at least one other nurse should be present at the hand-over from one shift to the next. This second nurse should then make her own observations of the patient. Thereafter she only goes back to the patient about once an hour, to allow a more objective assessment of any changes in the patient's appearance. The nurse who is 'specialing' the patient should be relieved frequently for short breaks to reduce fatigue and increase her powers of observation.

FACIAL PROSTHESES

In those for whom reconstructive surgery with biological tissue is inappropriate, for example some elderly patients, acrylic, silicone or other artificial tissue may be used to camouflage a defect. Facial prostheses may be appropriate after removal of extensive carcinoma, burns or trauma.

An accurate impression of the face and the defect to be camouflaged is made by moulds. From these, a cast is made on which the prosthesist can plan and sculpt the final prosthesis. Once the shape has been made, it is necessary to tint the prosthesis to match the patient's own skin colour. Various methods are used to keep the prosthesis in position on the face. Glues may be necessary, or the prosthesis (such as a nose) may be mounted onto a spectacle frame.

CARE OF THE PROSTHESIS

- The area covered by the prosthesis should be kept meticulously clean by gentle bathing.
- If the prosthesis rubs, excoriating the skin, it should be returned to be modified by the prosthesist.
- Make-up may be used to mask the junction of the skin with the prosthesis.
- The prosthesis may be washed in lukewarm water and cleansed gently with a non-medicated soap. Excessive rubbing may damage the paint.

FURTHER READING

Anderson, R. & Hoopes, J.E. (1975) *Symposium of malignancies of the head and neck*. St Louis: C.V. Mosby.

Batsakis, J.G. (1979) *Tumors of the head and neck*, 2nd edn. Baltimore: Williams & Wilkins.

Conley, J.J. (1979) *Complications of head and neck surgery*. Philadelphia: W.B. Saunders.

Roberts, A.C. (1971) *Facial prostheses*. London: Henry Kimpton.

Stell, P.M. & Maran, A.G.D. (1979) *Head and neck surgery*, 2nd edn. Philadelphia: J.B. Lippincott.

18 Microsurgery

'In surgery, eyes first and most, fingers next and little, tongue last and least.'
Sir George Humphrey, 1820–1896. English surgeon.

The use of the microscope in the operating theatre has made possible the anastomosis of blood vessels of 1 mm diameter or less, and the repair of individual nerve bundles.

For suturing larger blood vessels, lenses mounted on a spectacle frame, magnifying 2.5 to 4 times, are useful. For smaller vessels, magnification of 10 to 20 times is necessary, which is possible only by means of the microscope. Binocular vision for both the operator and his assistant is incorporated into the microscope, and an additional observation eyepiece is used by the assisting nurse. For clinical work, the microscope should also be fitted with zoom magnification and automatic focusing.

Although replantation of severed limbs has been the main subject of the media's attention to microsurgery, the operating microscope has been used in many other surgical techniques. For example 'free tissue transfer' (free flap) has made possible the transplantation of tissue from one part of the body to another in one operation, whereas previously 2 or more operations were required, with about 3 weeks between each stage. The periods between each stage of the well-known methods of tissue transfer, such as the tube pedicle or cross-leg flap, are often very uncomfortable for the patient. Therefore microsurgery is a great advance in reconstructive surgery.

There are limitations and complications in the use of microsurgery for the following reasons:

1. The operating time is very lengthy (5 to 24 hours). If a general anaesthetic is required, the long anaesthesia time precludes all but the healthiest patients.

2. The long time spent in one position on the operating table leads to the development of deep vein thrombosis and pressure sores during surgery. Flowtron stockings may be used to prevent thrombosis of the calf veins, and ripple mattresses have been tried

for the prevention of pressure sores. Unfortunately neither of these devices has yet solved this problem. This is because the movement that this apparatus produces in the patient, although minimal to the naked eye, is magnified under the operating microscope. This may make a very difficult and tedious operative procedure an impossible one. So far the only reliable method of preventing both deep vein thrombosis and pressure sores is to stop operating whilst the calves and pressure areas are gently massaged. This increases the anaesthesia time and may present technical difficulties to the surgeon, who has to choose the moment to stop operating.

3. Because the techniques are new, nurses lack experience in recognising complications. This is something which only time, and communication between those working in this speciality, will correct.

NURSING CARE

- Although microsurgery has been the subject of much publicity over the past few years, this is still one of the newest specialities. Therefore, nursing care for these patients is still being developed and its value assessed. New techniques continue to develop rapidly.
- As with any new speciality, the provision of a high standard of nursing care relies on the nurse understanding the anatomy, physiology and surgical techniques involved, and the use of that knowledge, together with her own common sense, to assess the patient's needs.
- Massive oedema following limb replantation or free flap is a common problem. Warn the patient of this occurrence. The oedema subsides slowly over the first few post-operative weeks.
- Gross oedema makes observation of the limb or flap for circulatory problems more difficult.

MICROVASCULAR SURGERY

Replantation surgery

A limb or digit which has been amputated may be revascularised by anastomosis of the amputated part's arteries and veins to vessels in the stump. Successful revascularisation is more likely following a clean cut. A crushing injury to the amputated part devitalises the tissue and makes successful revascularisation less likely.

From the moment the part has been severed, the lack of blood supply causes increasing degrees of tissue death. Some tissue, such as muscle, deteriorates rapidly, whilst other, such as bone, does so more slowly. The time at which irreversible changes have taken place can be lengthened by cooling the amputated part.

As soon as the amputated part has been received in the Casualty Department, it should, therefore, be placed in a clean plastic bag which is surrounded by ice. It is transported in this manner, with the patient, to the hospital at which the replantation is to be carried out.

Bleeding vessels in the amputation stump should not be clamped as this damages them. The limb is elevated and bandaged sufficiently firmly to contain the bleeding. If blood loss is appreciable, intravenous fluid replacement with dextran 110 or plasma is started prior to transfer, but repeated failed attempts in the Casualty Department to institute a drip prolongs the time for which the amputated part is ischaemic, and lessens the likelihood of successful replantation.

Pre-operative preparation. Once hypovolaemic shock has been corrected, the patient is taken to the theatre. General anaesthesia, or brachial block anaesthesia for upper limb replantation, is appropriate.

Operative principles. One surgeon cleans and prepares the amputated part while another cleans and prepares the stump, identifying and tagging tendons, vessels and nerves with a suture.

Bone fixation. After assessing pre-operative X-rays and inspecting the limb, a few centimetres of bone may need to be resected to facilitate the blood vessel anastomoses. The bone ends are united by appropriate plates, intramedullary pins or interosseus wires.

Tendon repair. Extensor and flexor tendons are repaired with 4/0 or 5/0 nylon or similar synthetic material.

Vessel and nerve repair. The operating microscope is now moved into position above the vessels to be repaired. The surgeon, his assistant and the nurse are comfortably seated. The tagged arteries are again identified, and the orifices irrigated with warm heparin–saline solution (20 i.u./ml) to remove thrombi. The heparin–saline solution is drawn up in a 10 ml syringe to which a hypodermic needle is attached. The artery ends are prepared by peeling back the outer adventitial layer of the wall for a few millimetres, and the two ends brought into approximation using a suitable clamp (such as the O'Brien[1] or Acland[2] clamp). The ends are sutured using 10/0 nylon and the clamp removed. The anastomosis is flushed with warm Ringer lactate solution. If it is not possible to approximate the ends of the artery without tension, a length of vein is removed from some suitable site, and inserted as a graft between the ends of the artery.

The veins are repaired next in a similar manner, and nerve suture is then carried out before the microscope is moved away. The skin is closed so that there is no compression over the site of the anastomoses, if necessary applying partial-thickness skin grafts to any skin defect.

PRE-OPERATIVE NURSING CARE

● Speed is essential in all dealings with the patient about to undergo replantation surgery to reduce 'ischaemia time' (i.e. the length of time that the amputated part is starved of a blood supply). The shorter the ischaemia time, the greater the chance of a successful replantation. If the severed part has been adequately cooled, replantation may be successful up to 12 hours after the injury. If the part has been at room temperature, operation must be performed within 5 hours.

● As soon as notification is received of the pending admission, the operating team prepares for emergency surgery. Two surgical teams may work side by side, one preparing the amputated part and the other preparing the replantation site. This greatly reduces the operating time.

● As soon as the patient arrives on the ward, the amputated part and the stump are examined by the surgeon, who then decides if replantation is feasible. If a replant is to be attempted, the amputated part is taken straight to theatre for preparation.

● The patient is then prepared and transferred to theatre as quickly as possible.

---

[1] Bernard O'Brien, Plastic Surgeon, Melbourne, Australia.
[2] Robert Acland, Surgeon, Louisville, Kentucky, USA.

- No specific pre-operative preparation is required.
- It may be possible to perform the surgery under regional block anaesthesia. The patient is given a sedative by intravenous injection prior to induction of anaesthesia.
- If general anaesthesia is required and the patient has recently eaten or had a drink, a nasogastric tube may be passed to aspirate the stomach contents before induction of anaesthesia.
- If the patient's relatives have accompanied him to the hospital they will naturally be very anxious. Explain to them that a speedy transfer to theatre is essential if the limb is to be replanted successfully. Tell them that the surgeon will explain the prognosis in more detail following surgery.
- As soon as time permits, inform the relatives of the patient's condition. Be reassuring, optimistic, but realistic. Explain that the surgery is an attempt to replant the limb. Reassure them that it is the patient's limb and not his life which is at risk. Explain that if the surgeons feel the operation is putting the patient's life at risk, the attempted replant is discontinued.
- Explain to the relatives that the surgery will take many hours. Encourage them to leave the hospital, and arrange to telephone them as soon as you have any more news. Ensure that they have the hospital and ward telephone number before they leave.
- For the first few hours after surgery the patient looks unwell and may be surrounded by technical equipment. It is, therefore, preferable for the relatives to delay visiting the patient until he looks fitter. Be sympathetic to their distress, but remain firm in your advice to them to wait at home for news.
- Because of the long anaesthetic time and the close observations required post-operatively, the patient is nursed in the Intensive Care Unit. Notify the Unit of the pending admission, so they may prepare to receive him.

POST-OPERATIVE NURSING CARE
- Blood transfusion is usually given during surgery. Before collecting the patient from theatre enquire how much blood has been given and what intravenous regime is required for the post-operative period.
- In case of post-operative haemorrhage, also enquire how

much blood remains in the bank for this patient.

● General nursing care is the same as for any patient who has undergone prolonged anaesthesia.

● The patient is given no food or drink for up to 24 hours after surgery in case failing circulation in the replanted limb necessitates urgent return to theatre.

● Minimal dressings are applied so the circulation can be inspected easily and compression of the anastomosis be avoided. The limb is elevated a little above the horizontal to assist venous and lymphatic drainage (for methods of elevation see Chapters 10 and 11). However, high elevation may reduce arterial flow.

Table 10. *Mode of action and side effects of drugs used in replantation surgery*

Drug	Mode of action	Side effects
Aspirin (acetylsalicylic acid)	Inhibits aggregation of blood platelets, which initiate a clot	Gastro-intestinal bleeding Bronchospasm (asthma-like symptoms) Skin rashes
Dipyridamole (Persantin)	Inhibits aggregation of blood platelets and dilates small blood vessels	Exacerbates headache and hypotension Nausea Diarrhoea
Dextran 40 (glucose polymer) in sodium chloride 0.9%	Improves blood flow in capillaries by expanding vascular volume and reducing red blood cell clumping	Congestive heart failure Anaphylaxis (stridor, oedema and shock) especially in asthmatic patients Interferes with blood cross-matching reactions
Heparin	Inhibits thrombin clot formation and stickiness of blood platelets	Bleeding, e.g. from a peptic ulcer Skin rashes

● Aspirin 600 mg twice daily and dipyridamole (Persantin) 100 mg three times a day orally, and dextran 40, 500 ml in 12 hours intravenously, may be prescribed to discourage thrombosis of the anastomosis and encourage blood flow. The mode of action and side effects of the drugs used are given in Table 10. An antibiotic may be given prophylactically.

- The following observations are made, initially at 30 minute, and later at hourly, intervals.

1. *Colour*. A red or purple dusky colour of the replanted part indicates a poor venous return and may be improved by elevating the limb higher or by removing haematomas if present. More severe degrees of venous congestion may be improved by the application of a leech to encourage bleeding. (The leech bite injects an anticoagulant, hirudin.) A pale white colour indicates that the arterial anastomosis is inadequate. Arterial inflow may be improved by loosening all the dressings, and allowing the limb to hang down or be horizontal.

2. *Capillary release test*. An estimate of the capillary circulation can be made from the speed at which the colour returns to the nail bed when the nail is compressed momentarily and then released.

3. *Tissue tension*. By gently pressing on the skin, a feeling of resistance can be appreciated. The more blood there is present in the tissue, the greater will be this resistance. Limbs or flaps which have an inadequate arterial input have little or no tissue tension. Those with poor venous drainage feel turgid.

- Any blood clot around the wound is very gently cleaned away with a saline-soaked gauze or a cotton bud, so that it does not constrict the limb or digit.
- Failure of conservative measures to improve the circulation in the replanted part necessitates a return to the theatre for exploration of the anastomosis.
- Because of the numerous blood vessel anastomoses, post-operative haemorrhage is likely to occur. If a small artery starts spurting blood, elevate the limb but do not apply digital pressure, as this may cause further damage, not only to that artery, but also to other vessels lying close to it. Summon the doctor urgently and prepare to return the patient to theatre immediately for repair of the leaking artery.

● If massive haemorrhage occurs, apply a tourniquet to the most proximal part of the stump possible. Try not to exert any pressure within the operative field (if vein grafts have been used to repair the damaged blood vessels, some of the anastomoses may lie some distance from either side of the wound). Summon the doctor urgently and prepare to return the patient to theatre immediately for haemostasis.

Free tissue transfer

The ability to move skin, muscle, bone or nerve from one part of the body to a distant site, and to restore the blood supply of that tissue by anastomosis of arteries and veins at the new site, makes possible in one operation the reconstruction of tissues which might otherwise take several staged operations by transfer of flaps.

The following tissues may be moved by free tissue transfer:

1. *Single free flap transfer*.
   (a) Skin and fat, for example from the groin.
   (b) Bone, for example using the fibula to reconstruct un-united tibial fractures.
   (c) Muscle, for example from the arm to the face in facial paralysis.
   (d) Nerve, for example to repair large gaps between damaged nerve ends.

2. *Compound free flap transfer*:
   (a) Skin, fat and muscle (myocutaneous flap), for example latissimus dorsi from the back.
   (b) Nerve and blood vessel (neuro-vascular flap), for example innervated dorsalis pedis flap from the foot.
   (c) Bone and skin (osteo-cutaneous flap), for example rib and chest skin for mandibular reconstruction.
   (d) Toe-to-hand transfer for reconstruction of the thumb.

Complications include:

1. *Vascular failure*. The incidence of total loss of the transferred tissue due to vascular failure varies from 8 to 25% of patients. In 20 to 40% of patients re-exploration of a failing circulation is required.

2. *Complications due to the prolonged anaesthesia*, such as bronchopneumonia, deep vein thrombosis and pressure sores.

PRE-OPERATIVE NURSING CARE
- Pre-operative nursing care is similar to the care described for other types of skin flap (see Chapter 3).

POST-OPERATIVE NURSING CARE
- Post-operative nursing care is similar to that for limb and digital replantation. Anti-thrombotic drugs are not needed.

Technical aids to clinical observation of flaps and replants

1. *Photoplethysmography*. A probe attached to the flap surface transmits infra-red light into the tissues. Reflected light is picked up by a detector in the centre of the probe. The flow of blood in the subdermal plexus of capillaries alters the amount of light which is reflected, and this is recorded on a moving chart. The wave form indicates whether there is venous congestion or arterial obstruction.

2. *Doppler ultrasound*. High frequency sound waves transmitted from a probe on the skin are reflected back to the receiver in the probe at a different frequency. The frequency depends on the rate of blood flow in the vessel being investigated.

3. *Laser Doppler*. Moving blood cells in the dermal capillaries alter the frequency of a laser beam shone onto the skin from a probe. In the absence of flow, the frequency is unaffected. This method does not distinguish between arterial and venous obstruction.

4. *Skin temperature*. A fall in skin temperature below 30 °C has been considered an indication to return the patient to theatre for re-exploration of the flap.

MICROLYMPHATIC SURGERY

To bypass obstruction of lymphatics caused by radiotherapy, scarring or lymph node block dissection, lymphatic vessels distal to the obstruction have been anastomosed to veins using the operating microscope (see Chapter 12).

PRE-OPERATIVE NURSING CARE

- The patient is admitted to hospital several days before operation for:
  1. Elevation of the limb.
  2. Compression of the limb with intermittent inflation (Flowtron) stockings.

  These two procedures reduce the amount of fluid in the limb, rendering the tissues less turgid.
- Attention is given to weeping or ulcerated areas.
- See also pre-operative nursing care for lymphoedema in Chapter 12.

POST-OPERATIVE NURSING CARE

- The limb is elevated above the level of the heart. This is continued at night by the patient on his return home.
- Initially the limb is compressed by intermittent inflation stockings for 2 to 3 days. This is followed by repeated firm bandaging or elasticated support, which is continued indefinitely.
- The wound, which is closed by direct closure, requires routine care.

MICRONEUROSURGERY

To obtain perfect re-innervation of a hand whose nerve has been cut, it would be necessary for axons in the proximal stump of the nerve to be aligned with the endoneurial tubes in the distal part, in which the axons lay before injury (see page 169). With the thousands of axons present in the nerve, this is impossible in practice. The nearest approximation feasible at present is to line up corresponding bundles (Fig. 87). This requires a microscope able to magnify about 10 times. One 10/0 suture is placed in each bundle.

Repair of the outer epineurium is sufficient for digital nerves which contain only 2 or 3 bundles. For this, operating spectacles, which magnify 2 to 4 times, are used. Three or four 6/0 sutures are placed into the epineurial sheath.

If there is a gap of more than about 3 cm between the cut nerve ends, it is necessary to insert a length of nerve graft taken from an unessential nerve, such as the sural nerve of the calf or the lateral

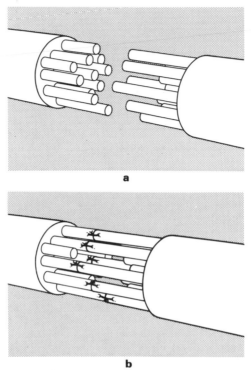

Fig. 87. *(a) A cut nerve showing bundles awaiting suture. (b) A bundle (perineurial) repair completed.*

cutaneous nerve of the thigh. In the event of the diameter of the nerve to be repaired being greater than the diameter of the graft, a *cable* of 2 or 3 strands of the nerve graft will be sutured into the gap to make up for the discrepancy in size.

In a successful repair, the axons in the proximal stump grow across the suture line into the distal nerve at a rate of about 1 mm per day. Thus, following a successful repair of the median nerve of the wrist, sensation at the tip of the finger would be regained after 6 to 9 months.

If nerve repair is delayed for several months after the injury it may still be possible to regain some sensation. However, return of muscle function is less certain. Muscle begins to degenerate from the moment the nerve is cut, and the longer re-innervation is delayed, the poorer the eventual muscle function will be. The optimum time for repair is, therefore, within 3 to 4 weeks of the injury.

NURSING CARE

- Nursing care is the same as for nerve grafts (see Chapter 3).

MICROSURGERY INSTRUMENTATION

Relatively few instruments are needed on the operating tray for repair of nerves or suture of vessels. The following is a working set:

2	no. 7 needle holding forceps
2	no. 5a vessel stretching forceps
2	no. 5 jeweller's forceps
1	Vannas spring scissors
1	Weiss scissors (SAS, 11 and 15 cm)
1	Waldermar scissors (Link)
1	needle holder (14 cm)
1	clamp applying forceps, size 3a
1	Hutchinson small forceps
10	Scovell clamps (assorted sizes)
10	Acland clamps (assorted sizes)
2	O'Brien clamps (assorted sizes)

Yellow and green background material of soft plastic
10/0 Supramid sutures on a 4 mm ($\frac{3}{8}$ in) circle needle

1	bipolar coagulator

FURTHER READING

Jackson, I.T. (Ed.) (1981) *Recent advances in plastic surgery*, Vol. 2. Edinburgh: Churchill Livingstone.

O'Brien, B. McC. (1977) *Microvascular reconstructive surgery*. Edinburgh: Churchill Livingstone.

Shaw, W.W. (Ed.) (1983) *Clinics in plastic surgery*, Vol. 10, 1. Philadelphia: W.B. Saunders.

19 Maxillo-facial trauma

The facial skeleton consists of:

1. The *mandible*, which carries the lower teeth and articulates with the skull deep to the parotid glands at the temporo-mandibular joints.
2. The *maxilla*, which carries the upper teeth, projects backwards into part of the roof of the mouth, and forms the medial part of the cheeks.
3. The *nasal bones*, which are attached to the front of the upper part of the maxilla.
4. The *malar* (or zygomatic) bones, which form the lower and lateral parts of the orbits of the eyes and the 'prominence' of the cheeks. The maxilla and malars together make up the middle third of the face.

Fractures are commonly caused by direct blows on the face, such as dashboard injuries or from missiles. Soft tissue lacerations occur from windscreens and knife blade assaults.

EMERGENCY CARE
Maintenance of the airway

Loose teeth, broken dentures or any other loose debris in the mouth are removed immediately on admission to hospital to prevent their inhalation into the trachea. The patient, provided he is conscious, is sat up with his head propped forward. If unconscious, he is lain prone with his face turned to one side. Oropharyngeal suction is used as required and tracheostomy equipment is made available.

For fractures of the maxilla, two fingers inserted into the mouth and hooked behind the hard palate may re-establish an airway. A fractured mandible can be supported by a barrel bandage, which helps prevent respiratory obstruction due to loss of tongue control.

Repeated mouth toilet is required for intraoral injuries until definitive treatment is begun.

Haemorrhage

Bleeding into the tissues results in swelling, which may cause respiratory obstruction. If the skin or mucosa of the mouth or nose is lacerated, blood may be apparent. Correct positioning of the patient prevents blood entering the pharynx. Ligation of the vessel, local pressure on the bleeding point or packing with gauze controls the loss. Persistent bleeding from the nose may be controlled by the introduction of a Foley catheter into the nostril, with inflation of the balloon.

Cerebrospinal rhinorrhoea

A watery fluid (cerebrospinal fluid) dripping from the nose, sometimes blood-tinged, indicates a fracture of the thin bone (cribriform plate) separating the nose from the dura surrounding the brain. Cerebrospinal fluid may be identified by the fact that it gives a positive Dextrostix reaction. Meningitis may develop, especially if the tear is large and is not repaired urgently by the neurosurgeon. This is usually done with a sheet of fascia placed over the cribriform plate.

Eye damage

Diplopia (double vision) may indicate an orbital fracture or intra-orbital bleeding, which interferes with movements of the eye muscles or displaces the globe.

Damage to the cornea may be rendered more visible by instilling fluorescein drops 1% into the eye. To dilate the pupil to permit ophthalmoscopic examination of the retina, tropicamide 0.5% (which has a duration of action of 3 hours) is instilled.

When periorbital oedema has closed the eye, examination of the globe becomes difficult and a Desmarres[1] retractor is useful for holding open the lids. If oedema has closed the eye so firmly that the normal tear production cannot drain away, the collection of fluid beneath the eyelids may cause sufficient back pressure to cause permanent damage to the eye. Therefore the eyelids should

[1] Louis-Auguste Desmarres, 1810–1882. Ophthalmologist, Paris.

be opened every half-hour, to allow drainage of any fluid that has collected.

SOFT TISSUE FACIAL INJURY

Because of its generous blood supply, wounds of the face usually heal readily. The amount of eventual scarring is reduced by judicious debridement and wound cleaning. Blood is irrigated away with saline and devitalised tissue is excised. Foreign material such as hair, road dirt and glass fragments is removed. Skin tattooed with dirt is gently scrubbed to remove all particles. Failure to do this at the time of injury leaves a permanently grey scar – a 'traumatic tattoo'.

When part of the nose, ear or lip has been amputated and the missing part is brought to the hospital, it may be possible to replace and revascularise it by resuturing the vessels under the operating microscope. If primary repair is not possible, ear cartilage is banked under the skin of the abdominal wall for use at a later date.

Human bites (more often in anger than in love!) have a reputation for severe infection. Thorough cleaning and removal of devitalised tissue is mandatory.

GENERAL NURSING CARE

- Soft tissue injuries to the face, although not life-threatening, are obviously very distressing to the patient and his relatives. Whilst it is important to try and allay the patient's anxiety, it is essential that any information given is accurate. Be sympathetic and optimistic. Explain that wherever there has been an injury there will always be a scar, and that repair by Plastic Surgery is aimed at reducing the scarring as far as possible.
- In the light of past experience of Plastic Surgical techniques, explain how scars can be camouflaged and to what extent their appearance can be improved by surgery. If inexperienced, it is better not to offer further reassurance than to raise false hopes.
- Eventually the patient must learn to live with the final result of his injury, and this will be more readily achieved if, from the outset, the patient's expectations are low rather than high.
- It is a very important part of the nurse's role to help the

patient and his relatives come to terms with his changed appearance. Careful counselling will be needed, often over a long period of time, and continuing after his discharge from hospital.

- A positive attitude throughout his care enhances the patient's confidence in his new self-image.

PRE-OPERATIVE NURSING CARE

- To reduce the amount of oedema and the risk of inhalation injury, the patient is kept sitting as upright as possible, unless this is contra-indicated by the presence of other injuries.
- Because of its excellent blood supply, even small facial wounds tend to bleed copiously and therefore look horrific to the patient and his relatives. All blood is cleaned away as quickly as possible and suitable dressings applied to control any further bleeding. All blood-stained clothing is removed as soon as possible.
- If a facial wound is gaping widely or if large portions of tissue such as the lip or part of the nose are severely displaced, the tissues can be carefully brought into alignment and tethered in place temporarily with Steristrips. This may make the patient more comfortable and his relatives less anxious during the time the patient is being transferred to the Plastic Surgical Unit, and whilst he is waiting to go to theatre.
- If there is any intra-oral injury, mouth toilet is commenced on admission to hospital. The mouth is cleaned in various ways according to the injury. If blood clots have formed and are adherent to injured tissue, for example over a tooth socket where a tooth has been knocked out or loosened, removing these clots provokes fresh bleeding. The patient is advised not to try pushing these clots out with his tongue.
- Loose clots in the mouth may be removed by gentle swabbing with cotton buds soaked in thymol. If the intra-oral damage is not severe, mouth-washes may be given. The patient is advised not to swallow any of the mouth-wash solution, and not to swill the solution around his mouth too vigorously as this may loosen adherent clots.
- The type of cup or beaker used to administer the mouth-wash depends on the injury. If the lips are not damaged and the patient is sitting up, an ordinary cup may be best, as the spout on

a beaker may knock against loosened teeth or damaged gums. If the lips are not damaged but the patient cannot sit up, a drinking straw is used. If the muscles encircling the lips are damaged, then use of a drinking straw will cause these muscles to pull on the wound. A beaker with a feeding spout should be used instead, with the nurse guiding the positioning of the spout. If the injuries to the mouth are very severe, or the patient is not able to assist in his mouth toilet, a Higginson's syringe may be used to gently irrigate the mouth.

POST-OPERATIVE NURSING CARE

- In order to reduce facial and intra-oral oedema, the patient is sat up in bed as soon as possible after surgery by gradually increasing the number of pillows supporting him, according to the stability of his blood pressure recordings.
- Blood pressure is recorded every 15 minutes, then every 30 minutes, reducing to 4-hourly as the blood pressure becomes stable.
- Facial wounds are usually left exposed. The suture lines are kept clean by swabbing with gauze soaked in saline.
- If dressings have been applied, careful observation is maintained for any signs of haemorrhage or haematoma formation.
- Severe pain beneath the dressings may indicate a haematoma, so the dressings are removed and the wound inspected. If a haematoma is present it may be possible to 'milk' this out through the suture line, or one or two sutures may have to be removed to allow it to drain. If sutures have to be removed, once the haematoma has been drained and all bleeding has ceased, the application of Steristrips may be sufficient to hold the skin edges together or the sutures may need to be reinserted under local anaesthesia.
- Mouth care is continued until the intra-oral wounds are healed, usually after 7 to 10 days.
- A soft diet is given until the patient can chew comfortably and there is no further risk of the movement involved in chewing causing post-operative bleeding.
- The patient is usually allowed up and about on the first post-operative day, unless other injuries contra-indicate this. The patient is advised not to bend head down and to continue sleeping with his head on a high pillow for 7 to 10 days to help minimise oedema.

- Superficial facial sutures are removed after 2 to 4 days. Early suture removal helps to reduce stitch marks, which add to the ultimate scarring. In order to support the delicate wound, Steristrips are applied and left in place for a further 3 to 5 days.

- If tension sutures have been used, these are removed after 7 to 10 days.

- If there is any sign of infection, wound swabs are sent for culture and sensitivity, and appropriate antibiotic therapy is commenced as soon as the organism has been identified.

- As soon as possible after surgery the patient is encouraged to look in a mirror – usually on the first post-operative day. Remain with the patient when he first views his injury, and offer both sympathy and reassurance.

- It is important that the patient sees his injured face as early as possible. He then sees daily improvement, which helps him to come to terms with his disfigurement. Provided he has been counselled adequately, so his expectations of his final appearance are not too high, he will view the final result as good. He will always compare the scars with how he looked when he first saw himself.

- If disfigurement is severe the patient is first encouraged to socialise on the ward. He is then urged to go out into the hospital grounds so he may experience other people's reactions to his disfigurement whilst he is still an in-patient. Counselling is offered tactfully and only when it appears appropriate. Over-stressing the need for counselling may only make the patient more self-conscious.

- If possible, before discharge the patient is encouraged to go out of the sheltered atmosphere of the hospital for a few hours, preferably accompanied by his relatives. For example the patient may make a trip into the local town to shop, or to visit the local pub. This enables both the patient and his relatives to become accustomed to the general public's reaction to his appearance.

NASAL FRACTURES

Fractures are caused by:

1. A sideways force, striking the prominent nose and displacing it laterally.

2. A frontal force, splaying the nose backwards against the maxilla. If the force is sufficiently strong, it splays the facial bones, forcing the orbits of the eyes apart (traumatic hypertelorism).

Fractures of the nasal bones with displacement require manipulation using Walsham[2] forceps under general anaesthesia within 3 or 4 days of the injury. Thereafter the fracture becomes increasingly sticky and difficult to reduce. Asch[3] forceps are used to straighten a buckled septum. A haematoma of the nasal septum is incised and released at the same time. The nostrils are packed with Vaseline gauze. A plaster of Paris splint is applied for a fortnight to the outside of the nose to reduce oedema, protect it from knocks, and steady the bones.

NURSING CARE
- Nursing care for nasal fractures is the same as for corrective rhinoplasty (Chapter 20).

COMPLICATED NASAL FRACTURES

Fractures of the nasal and intra-orbital (ethmoid) bones may require open reduction and fixation with wires. If the nasolacrimal (tear) duct has also been lacerated, a nylon suture around which the duct can heal is placed through the lacrimal punctum and brought out in the nose to restore continuity. Comminuted fragments of nasal bones can be held in position with soft padded lead plates placed on either side of the nose and secured with wires passing through the nose.

NURSING CARE
- Nursing care of the nasal fracture is the same as for corrective rhinoplasty (Chapter 20).
- If the nasolacrimal duct has been repaired, the eye and eyelids are kept clean by gentle irrigation and swabbing with sterile saline.
- Care must be taken that the external end of the nylon suture does not rub against the eye, causing ulceration of the conjunctiva or cornea.

---

[2] William Walsham, 1847–1903. Surgeon, St Bartholomew's Hospital, London.
[3] Morris Asch, 1833–1902. Surgeon, New York, USA.

- The end of the suture is usually tethered to the skin below the eye using Steristrip. This fixation may need to be reapplied frequently if the eye is watering copiously.
- An antibiotic eye ointment (such as chloramphenicol 1%) is instilled 4-hourly. This both protects the eye if swelling of the lids has caused ectropion and reduces the risk of infection.
- The nylon suture is removed after 10 to 21 days, depending on the severity of the injury.
- If lead plates are used, care must be taken to clean the areas around the plates thoroughly, to reduce the risk of infection.
- If any signs of infection are present, wound swabs are sent for culture and sensitivity and appropriate antibiotic therapy is commenced when the organism has been identified.
- If post-operative swelling is severe, oedematous tissue may push against the lead plates causing pressure sores. Oedema may be reduced by applying ice packs, but if this fails to reduce the pressure adequately it may be necessary to bend the edges of the plates away from the surrounding tissue until the oedema subsides.
- The lead plates are usually removed after 10 to 14 days. Using small, sharp-pointed wire cutters, the wire is cut where it passes over one of the plates. The other plate is then lifted away, drawing the cut ends of the wire through the nose. This procedure is uncomfortable for the patient, but no more painful than removal of any deep suture.

MALAR (ZYGOMA) FRACTURES

Fractures which can be stabilised in their correct position using friction against the adjacent bone require no fixation. The fracture can be reduced by manipulation through an incision in the hairline using a Bristow's[4] elevator as a lever under the zygomatic bone (Fig. 88).

Fractures which cannot be stabilised in this manner require open reduction and fixation with 0.35 mm stainless steel wire through drill holes at the temple and/or below the orbit.

Blunt blows on the eye (for example caused by a cricket ball)

[4] Walter Bristow, 1882–1947. Orthopaedic Surgeon, St Thomas' Hospital, London.

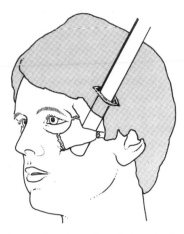

Fig. 88. *Elevation of fractured malar with a Bristow's elevator.*

force the bone of the floor of the orbit downwards into the maxillary antrum – a 'blow-out' fracture. Double vision is common. Such fractures can be managed in two ways:

1. The fracture is elevated through an incision either in the cheek or just inside the lower eyelid. If a hole remains in the orbital floor, a sheet of silicone, Teflon, bone or cartilage is slipped over the hole to prevent the eye dropping down into it and the eye muscles becoming stuck to the fracture.

2. The maxillary antrum is opened through an incision into the maxilla above the canine tooth (Caldwell–Luc[5] incision). It is packed with ribbon gauze soaked in Whitehead's[6] Varnish to push up the floor of the orbit from below. The pack can be removed after about 2 weeks when the fracture is stable.

Management

The patient may be admitted to hospital for reduction of the

---

[5] George Caldwell, 1866–1946. ENT Surgeon, New York, USA; Henri Luc, 1855–1925. ENT Surgeon, Paris.

[6] Walter Whitehead, 1840–1913. Surgeon, Manchester Royal Infirmary.

fracture either immediately or a few days after the injury. The optimum time for reduction depends on the exact nature of the fracture and the degree of soft tissue swelling.

Simple fractures of the cheek bone, with no fracture of the orbital floor, are reduced by elevation of the fractured area into its correct position. No fixation is required to hold it in place if the fracture is stable. Operation is deferred if there is gross swelling because it is then impossible to feel whether the bones are aligned correctly.

For the uncomplicated malar fracture which is accompanied by severe soft tissue oedema and bruising, it is preferable to defer reduction for a few days until the swelling is beginning to resolve. The thin and rather fragile malar bone heals very quickly, so after a few days the fractured bone has already become slightly 'tacky'. When the fractured area is then elevated into position, this slight 'tackiness' assists in holding the fractured bone in place. The soft tissue swelling will be resolving, and therefore will not put undue pressure on the fractured area. If reduction is delayed for more than 5 days, the early callus formation makes reduction more difficult.

For fractures which require open reduction, operation is usually performed within 24 hours of the injury, provided there is no gross swelling.

Proptosis (bulging of the eye) may result from the soft tissues around the eye bleeding into the orbital tissues. Incision of the soft tissues beneath the eye may be required to evacuate the haemato ma and relieve the tension which is pushing the eye forward. This is performed if the proptosis is increasing.

When the fractured malar is accompanied by a blow out fracture, the soft tissues of the orbital floor swell and push the fracture fragments downwards. Initially the swelling of the sub-orbital tissues may be sufficient to hold the eye up in its correct position. In this case there may be little or no disturbance of vision until the swelling subsides and the eye drops downwards. Even minimal displacement of the eye in this way causes double vision. The displacement of the eye may be very obvious, but only careful and regular checking of the patient's vision will reveal small amounts of displacement. Reduction of orbital fractures is therefore always undertaken urgently.

If there is severe or sustained pressure, for example from

oedema, on the sub-orbital fat (the pad of fat on which the eyeball normally rests), fat necrosis occurs. The fat then liquefies and is absorbed. Sub-orbital fat does not repair itself and so the eyeball remains displaced downwards and double vision is permanent. This condition can sometimes be corrected by replacing the sub-orbital fat with a silicone or autogenous implant.

PRE-OPERATIVE NURSING CARE

- Pre-operative nursing care is aimed at reassuring the patient, but where the eye is, or may become, involved, care must be taken not to raise false hopes concerning the future vision or appearance of the eye.
- An eye which is obviously displaced downwards is quite disfiguring. Spectacles may correct the double vision and if the patient is self-conscious about the displaced eye, tinted glasses may be used.
- Explain to the patient that he will be sat up in bed as soon as possible after surgery to reduce oedema. Ask him to try to stay in the position he finds himself in when he wakes up.
- Tell him not to touch the injured cheek, as any pressure on the elevated fracture may displace it again.

POST-OPERATIVE NURSING CARE

- The area of the fracture is usually clearly marked in ink with a large X to remind all staff and the patient not to touch the injured area, even for normal washing.
- As the patient is recovering from the anaesthetic, remind him not to touch his injured cheek.
- Ensure the patient does not turn onto his injured side until he is fully conscious and aware of what he is doing.
- Gradually sit the patient up as soon as possible. Check the blood pressure every 15 minutes. If the blood pressure remains stable increase the number of pillows supporting the patient one at a time. If the blood pressure rises rapidly, add 2 or 3 pillows at once. A rapid rise in blood pressure may increase the oedema of the injured area and the risk of post-operative bleeding.
- Continue to check the blood pressure every 15 minutes until the patient has been sitting as upright as possible, with his blood pressure remaining stable, for one hour. Reduce the

frequency of the recordings to every 30 minutes until the blood pressure has remained stable for a further 2 hours, then gradually reduce to 4-hourly recordings.

- Observe the eye for the rare complication of proptosis. Should this occur, urgent treatment is required to relieve the pressure within the orbit.

- If swelling of the eyelids causes ectropion, the eye is protected from corneal ulceration by instilling a bland eye ointment such as soft paraffin every 4 hours. Explain to the patient that the ointment will make his vision blurred for about 20 minutes.

- Before instilling the eye ointment check the patient's vision. Any changes in vision are promptly reported to the doctor, as they may denote displacement of the eye.

- Keep the suture lines clean by gentle swabbing with sterile saline.

- If there is any sign of infection, wound swabs are sent for culture and sensitivity, and appropriate antibiotic therapy commenced as soon as the organism has been identified.

- The patient is usually allowed up and about from the first post-operative day. Advise him not to bend his head down, and to continue sleeping with his head on a high pillow for 7 to 10 days to minimise oedema.

- A soft diet is given for 7 to 14 days, as chewing is uncomfortable for the patient and may increase the oedema.

- Sutures are removed after 2 to 7 days, depending on where they are sited.

- If a Caldwell–Luc incision has been used, as soon as the patient is fully conscious he is told not to touch the pack inside his mouth.

- The antrum pack is just visible through the incision above the gum. Check that the pack remains firmly in place. If the end of the packing becomes loose and protrudes into the mouth the loose packing may be reinserted or the part of the pack protruding may be cut off.

- Mouth hygiene is commenced immediately after surgery, using gentle mouth-washes. The patient is instructed not to swill the solution around his mouth too vigorously as this may loosen or dislodge the pack.

- The antrum pack is removed after 14 to 21 days. This procedure is uncomfortable for the patient, but not usually painful. The patient is sat up in bed or on a couch (in case he faints) and his head is firmly supported. The upper lip is then retracted with the fingers and the end of the pack gripped firmly with a pair of artery forceps. The pack is then pulled firmly and continuously downwards. Up to 1 m of ribbon gauze may have been packed into the antrum. It may require considerable pressure to start the pack moving.

● Having reassured the patient, present a confident and unhesitant attitude throughout the procedure. As the pack is coming away it may both feel and sound as if tiny splinters of bone are coming with it. This is of no consequence. As soon as the pack begins to move, continue to pull it downwards firmly so the whole pack comes away quickly and in one continuous movement. Talk to the patient, or have a radio on, throughout the pack removal. This will cover any unpleasant sounds caused by the packing.

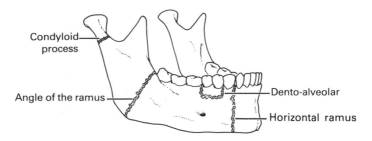

Fig. 89. *The more common sites of mandibular fracture.*

MANDIBULAR FRACTURES

'You are old,' said the youth, 'and your jaws are too weak
For anything tougher than suet.
Yet you finished the goose, with the bones and the beak;
Pray, how do you manage to do it?'
Lewis Carroll, 1832–1898. Lecturer in Mathematics, Oxford.

Fractures occur as a result of direct violence or where the mandible has been weakened by tumour, old age or disease. The more common sites of fracture are (Fig. 89):

1. The alveolus.
2. The condyloid process.
3. The angle of the jaw.
4. The horizontal ramus.

The objectives of treatment are to realign the dental occlusion and to stabilise the bone until healed. These objectives may be achieved by *dental* or *interosseus* fixation.

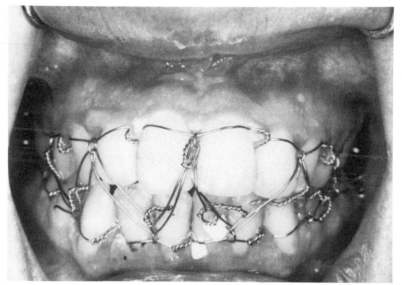

Fig. 90. *Mandibular fixation with dental eyelet wires.*

Dental fixation

1. *Eyelet wiring* (Fig. 90). Gauge 22 to 28 stainless steel wire is twisted around a nail or similar instrument with a diameter of about 3 mm, producing an eyelet. The ends of the wire are twisted round the necks of adjacent teeth on the maxilla and the mandible. About 4 eyelet wires are required on the mandibular and 4 on the maxillary teeth. The upper and lower jaw teeth are brought into their proper occlusion and the opposing eyelets are wired together, closing the mouth.

2. *The arch bar* (Fig. 91). When only a few teeth remain, a bar

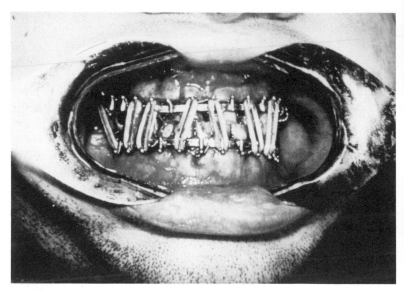

Fig. 91. *Mandibular fixation with arch bars.*

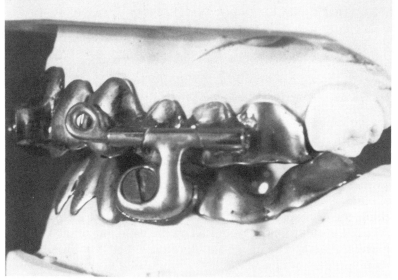

Fig. 92. *Mandibular fixation with dental cap splints.*

of malleable silver may be wired to those teeth that are available. If there are no teeth, the bar may be held onto the gum with wires around the mandible or round the floor of the nostril on the maxilla. The bar has hooks or loops on it, through which rubber bands or wire can be passed to close the mouth in the correct alignment.

3. *Dental cap splints* (Fig. 92). Impressions of the teeth are taken with alginate or dental compound in dental trays. These are converted into dental models in plaster of Paris. Metal splints of silver–copper alloy are made in the dental laboratory to conform to the teeth on the model and fitted with hooks or locking plates. The splints are cemented onto the teeth with black copper cement and the jaws locked together by rubber bands or a locking plate. When the patient has no teeth but has a denture, the cap splint can be made to fit the teeth on the denture.

4. *Gunning*[7] *splints*. For edentulous patients, a cast is taken of the gums and acrylic splints made to fit them. These Gunning splints can be wired to the mandible and maxilla and then rubber banded or wired together. A gap is usually left in the front of a Gunning splint through which the patient can feed easily. Since accurate alignment of the bones is less necessary when the teeth are absent, it may be sufficient to keep the jaws closed on the splints with a barrel bandage.

Interosseus fixation

The fracture is exposed, reduced and a vitallium plate is applied, held by screws or a wire through drill holes. Fixation splints can usually be removed after 4 to 6 weeks when the fracture has stabilised.

PRE-OPERATIVE NURSING CARE
- The patient is admitted for reduction and fixation of the fractured mandible immediately following injury.
- Keep the patient sitting upright to ensure a free airway is maintained.

---

[7] Thomas Gunning, 1813–1889. Dentist, New York, USA. Published a description of oral splints in 1866.

- A barrel bandage to support the jaw may make the patient more comfortable.
- Reassure the patient that his fractured jaw can be successfully repaired. Explain that some type of fixation will be required for 4 to 6 weeks until the fracture is united.
- Explain what type of fixation is being planned. Describe the apparatus to him and how he will look after surgery.
- Strong reassurance and a positive attitude is required to convince the patient that he will be able to breathe satisfactorily and to take an adequate liquid diet with his teeth locked together.
- The pre-operative counselling of the patient is probably the most important part of his nursing care. A patient who is frightened by the prospect of having his teeth locked together will panic during recovery from the anaesthetic. This may result in attempts to tamper with the fixation, over-ventilation or vomiting. The nervous patient may experience a feeling of claustrophobia. If counselling fails to calm the patient, adequate sedation is essential until the patient becomes accustomed to the appliance.
- Demonstrate how easy it is to breathe, talk and drink with the teeth firmly closed. Explain to the patient that, should he feel sick after the anaesthetic, he will promptly be given effective medication to overcome the nausea. However, in case he does vomit, explain to him that if fluid can be taken in with the teeth clenched, it can as easily be expelled. If necessary, demonstrate this to the patient.
- Explain that a nasal airway may be in place for the first 24 hours to ensure he can breathe freely through his nose, without needing to concentrate on doing so.
- The patient may be nursed in the Intensive Care Unit for the first 24 hours, as constant observation of the patient is necessary to ensure the maintenance of a free airway. If this is planned, explain to the patient that this is not because he will be dangerously ill, but simply to assist the nursing staff.
- Wherever possible, the nurse who will care for the patient immediately after the operation should meet him pre-operatively and assist in his counselling.
- If eyelet wiring or Gunning splints are to be used, the operation is usually carried out within a day or two of injury.

- If an arch bar or cap splints are to be used, the preparation of these usually takes between 24 and 48 hours. The operation is therefore delayed until the splints are ready and have been tested for a comfortable fit.
- Whilst awaiting surgery the patient is fed with liquidised food. An electric liquidiser satisfactorily liquidises any normal meal, provided some extra fluid, such as gravy or milk, is added. The amount of fluid added should not be so great as to make the liquidised meal too large.
- Liquidised food tends to come out of the liquidiser as a nondescript coloured liquid. The meal is more palatable if the patient is shown his meal served on a plate before it is liquidised. This practice also gives the patient the opportunity to indicate the size of meal he normally takes. Care in presentation of the liquidised meal is as important as for any meal.
- A feeding beaker with a spout is the easiest way for the patient to take the meal at first, but as soon as he is able to manage a normal cup or mug he should be encouraged to do so, as this may make the meal appear more palatable.

POST-OPERATIVE NURSING CARE
- The patient is taken to the recovery ward lying on his side.
- A stitch may have been inserted into the tongue, by which it can be held forward.
- Do not leave the patient unattended until he is fully conscious, aware of his surroundings and confident that he is not going to choke.
- The patient is sat up in bed as soon as possible, by gradually increasing the number of pillows supporting him, provided his blood pressure remains stable (as described for malar fractures).
- Constant reassurance is required until the patient is fully awake and confident.
- As he is waking up, gently remind him not to try to open his mouth.
- If the patient vomits, immediately instruct the patient to blow the vomit out between his teeth. Use high pressure suction to remove vomit from his mouth and nose. Instruct the patient to breathe through his nose, and allow time between suction for

him to draw breath. Remain calm and reassure the patient that the vomit can be adequately cleared from his mouth with his co-operation.

- Should the patient panic and inhale vomit, immediate release of the fixation is life-saving. Therefore always have at hand a suitable device to unlock the jaws. Should this be necessary the fixation can be relatively easily reapplied after the emergency is over.
- On collecting the patient from the theatre ask what type of locking device is in place and how to release it.
- If eyelet wiring alone is holding the fixation, a small sharp-pointed *wire cutter* is needed. Only the downward (or vertical) wires need cutting to release the jaw.
- Rubber band fixation requires only a pair of *sharp pointed scissors* to release the jaw.
- If a split pin is holding a locking plate, a pair of small *artery forceps* is required to pull the split pins out.
- If screws have been used, either a suitably-sized *screwdriver* or *universal dental spanner* is needed to release the jaw.
- Before the patient returns from theatre place all the above instruments at the bedside. As soon as it is known which of these instruments is required, all surplus instruments should be removed. Leaving an assortment of 'unlocking' instruments beside the patient may cause confusion in an emergency.
- In case of an emergency arising from respiratory obstruction, also have at hand:
    1. Tongue forceps.
    2. A mouth gag.
    3. An airway.
    4. Gauze swabs loaded onto long artery forceps.
    5. An electric sucker with a range of suction catheters.
- Appear calm and confident in order to reassure the patient.
- The patient may at first be reluctant to swallow even his normal saliva. Gentle suction may be required to keep the airway free. If the splintage has been designed so there is a gap at the front, or if a missing tooth provides a gap, a soft blunt-tipped rubber suction tube can readily be inserted. If no such gap exists, the suction tube is inserted gently along the side of the teeth to the natural gap at the back of the teeth.
- When suction is required for any purpose, occlude the suction

tube by pinching it while it is being inserted. The occlusion is then released so that suction is applied only as the tube is withdrawn. If suction is applied when introducing the tube, the open end of the tube is drawn onto the mucosa, making the tube stick temporarily. This makes introducing the tube to the correct site more difficult and may traumatise the mucosa.

- As soon as the patient is able, encourage him to swallow his saliva. If this proves difficult, instruct him to blow the secretions out through the gaps at the back of and between his teeth.

- If a nasal airway is in place, it is sucked out as required to keep it completely clear.

- The nasal airway may become encrusted with secretions which stick to the inside of the tube, making suction ineffective in clearing the airway. This may be overcome by using a humidifier. A closed circuit system of humidification is most effective. If hard or tenacious secretions remain, squirting 1 to 2 ml of sterile saline down the tube immediately prior to suction may clear the airway.

- If the patient complains of nausea, an anti-emetic drug is given by intramuscular injection.

- If the patient becomes very anxious, sedation may be required until he gains confidence. To obviate the danger of respiratory obstruction, no hypnotics are administered when the jaws are locked together.

- Within 24 hours the patient is usually coping calmly, without respiratory distress. The nasal airway is then removed and oral fluids commenced.

- If the patient has been nursed in the Intensive Care Unit, he is returned to the ward when he has taken his first feed without complication.

- Oral hygiene is commenced on the first post-operative day. A very soft toothbrush or cotton buds are used to keep the teeth and splints thoroughly clean. Splints may be cleaned with a powder made up of 4 parts of precipitated chalk, 4 parts sodium bicarbonate and 1 part sodium chloride. Saline washes alone are used for cleaning dental compound. Thymol or sodium bicarbonate mouth-washes are used after every meal to clean the inside of the mouth. These may be administered via a drinking straw at first, later graduating to a normal cup.

- If there is intra-oral swelling or the patient is unable to use a mouth-wash, a dental syringe may be used to irrigate the mouth.
- The mucosa of the lips and cheeks is inspected daily to ensure the intra-oral apparatus is not rubbing and causing ulceration. If the apparatus is causing trauma, it can be covered with soft dental ribbon wax to relieve the pressure.
- If there is any sign of infection, wound swabs are sent for culture and sensitivity, and appropriate antibiotic therapy is commenced as soon as the organism has been identified.
- A liquidised diet is given as described in the pre-operative nursing care.
- It may be difficult to maintain body weight on a liquid-only diet. Supplementary feeding, for example Ensure Plus or Clinifeed is given between meals to maintain adequate nutrition (see Table 11). Accurate fluid and diet charts are mandatory. (See Appendix.)

Table 11. *Recommended normal daily intake*

	Fluid	Calories	Carbohydrate	Fat	Protein
Adult	2500 ml	2400 kcal	400 g	60 g	70 g
Child 12 years	1800 ml	2500 kcal	400 g	60 g	70 g
Child 1 to 3 years	750 ml	1200 kcal	180 g	40 g	40 g

Data are taken from Ministry of Agriculture, Fish and Food. (1981) *Manual of nutrition: Reference book 342.* London: H.M.S.O.

- The patient is allowed up and about from the first post-operative day. Advise him not to bend his head down and to continue sleeping in a sitting position for 7 to 10 days in order to reduce oedema.
- The patient is discharged home when:
    1. He is managing his own mouth care adequately.
    2. He has learnt to care for his fixation apparatus and is confident in coping with this.
    3. He is taking an adequate diet, understands how to prepare his foods and knows what his daily requirements are.

- The patient should be told during the first post-operative day what factors will decide his discharge date, as this encourages him to learn to manage his own care as quickly as possible.
- It may be necessary to lend the patient an electric liquidiser. If so, the social worker is told of this as soon as possible (preferably on the day the patient is admitted).
- After-care arrangements are made for the patient to have the dental apparatus inspected regularly and to check on his oral hygiene and weight (usually weekly).
- The dental fixation is removed when the fracture is united, usually after about 4 to 6 weeks. The patient's dental bite is then inspected to ensure good occlusion. Some filing of teeth may be required for adjustment.

Complications

1. Delayed bone union (beyond 8 weeks).
2. Malunion with bad occlusion of the teeth.
3. Failure of bony union.
4. Loss of bone (probably necessitating bone grafting).

MAXILLARY FRACTURES

The maxilla tends to fracture along certain planes and at the alveolus (Fig. 93), as described by René Le Fort[8] in 1901.

A maxillary fracture often needs to be disimpacted under general anaesthesia using Rowe's[9] disimpaction forceps. To maintain an airway, a flanged Magill's[10] nasal tube may be inserted into the nostril. The tubes are maintained free of blood and secretions using a polythene tube sucker. Since the posterior end of the nasal tube is cut obliquely, turning the tube through 90° may unblock the end if it impacts against the posterior nasopharyngeal wall. The disimpacted maxilla may be held in position, locked to the mandible, by *dental* or *cranio-maxillary* fixation.

---

[8] René Le Fort, 1869–1951. Professor of Operative Medicine, Lille, France.
[9] Norman Rowe, Oral Surgeon, Roehampton, London.
[10] Sir Ivan Magill, formerly Anaesthetist, Westminster and Brompton Hospitals, London. Designed one of the first endotracheal tubes.

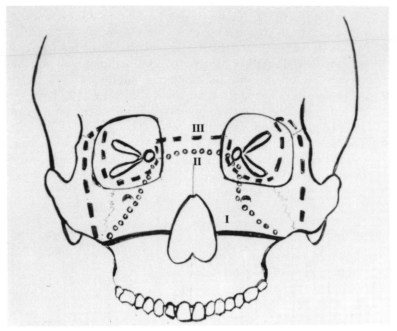

Fig. 93. *Planes of fracture of the maxilla.*

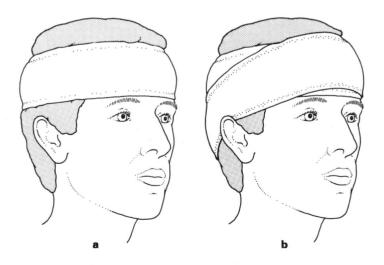

a   b

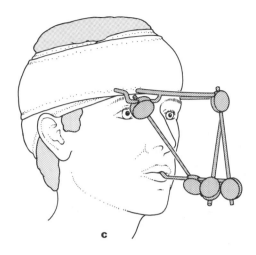

c

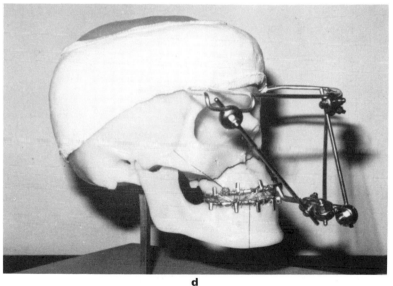

d

Fig. 94. *The plaster head cap. (a) First layer. (b) Second layer. (c) and (d) Third layer with rods and arch bars.*

Dental fixation

This is as described for fractures of the mandible.

Cranio-maxillary fixation

1. *Plaster head cap* (Fig. 94). A stockingette sleeve is placed over the head down to the neck with an area cut out for the face. The eyebrow ridges and the ears are marked on it with a skin pencil. A 7.5 cm plaster of Paris bandage is wound around the head 3 cm above the eyebrows. A second plaster bandage is applied obliquely at the level of the forehead hairline to the occiput. A metal bar is bound to the front of the head cap with a third plaster bandage. The bar is attached by universal joints to metal rods. These in turn are attached to dental cap splints on the maxillary teeth or to arch bars.

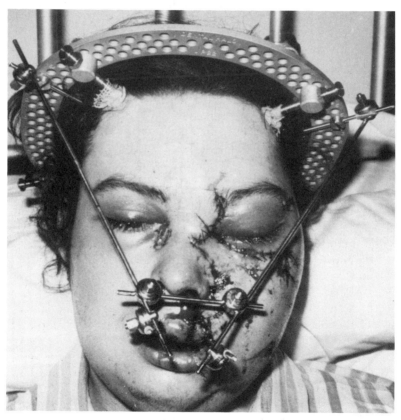

Fig. 95. *The halo frame.*

2. *Halo frame* (Fig. 95). Instead of a plaster head cap, a three-quarter halo frame is fixed to the head with self-tapping screws which penetrate the outer table of the skull. Rods are attached to the dental cap splints and the halo. Patients are unable to lie comfortably on their side with a halo frame in place.

3. *Temporal pins.* Two self-tapping screws into the temples are cemented together with a metal rod, to which the rods to the dental cap splint are then fixed. This fixation tends to be less rigid than either the plaster head cap or the halo frame, and is therefore unsuitable for multiple or unstable fractures.

NURSING CARE

- If dental fixation is used, nursing care is as for mandibular fractures.
- If cranio-maxillary fixation is used, the post-operative care is much less hazardous. Since the jaw can be moved freely the risk of airway obstruction is no greater than after any general anaesthetic.
- The general pre-operative preparation and counselling of the patient regarding his appearance post-operatively are the same as for mandibular fractures.
- Post-operatively the patient is sat up in bed as soon as possible, as described for malar fractures.
- A soft diet is given for 4 to 6 weeks until the fractures are stable and the fixation is removed.
- Mouth care and cleaning of the intra-oral splintage is the same as for mandibular fractures.
- If a plaster of Paris head cap is used, care is taken to ensure the plaster remains in the correct position, is comfortable and no plaster sores develop beneath the plaster.
- If a halo frame or temporal pins are used, the skin around the fixation points is kept clean by swabbing with sterile saline. The whole apparatus is kept clean by washing with soap and water.
- With any type of cranio-maxillary fixation, a male patient requires help with shaving until he becomes accustomed to manipulating the razor around and beneath the frame. Similarly, a female patient may require help in applying make-up.
- Discharge criteria and after-care are the same as for mandibular fractures.

MULTIPLE INJURIES OF THE FACE

Multiple injuries of the face frequently involve soft tissue damage and fractures of the nose, malar, orbits, maxilla and mandible. The nursing care of these patients requires very careful planning, taking into account the priorities of each of the separate injuries. The nursing care for each injury must be skilfully combined to provide a care plan which takes into account all the patient's needs.

FURTHER READING

Converse, J.M. (1974) *Surgical treatment of facial injuries*. Baltimore: Williams & Wilkins.

Rowe, N.L. & Killey, H.C. *Fractures of the facial skeleton*, 3rd edn. Edinburgh: Churchill Livingstone. (In prep.)

Zook, E.G. (1981) *The primary care of facial injuries*. London: Edward Arnold.

20 Aesthetic surgery of the face

The motivations of patients about to undergo aesthetic surgery often differ markedly from those undergoing most other types of surgery. The need to compete on equal (or better) terms with one's peers, the necessity to feel attractive to the opposite sex or partner, the desire to postpone the hallmarks of ageing, the urge to conquer a self-image of inadequacy are, in many patients' minds, compelling reasons to seek surgery. Though it may be easy to dismiss these needs as frivolous or undeserving of attention, many patient's anxieties are deep-seated and adequate surgery may transform an unhappy existence.

The criterion for success of aesthetic surgery is not restored biological function, but fulfilment of the patient's expectations. The nurse has a fundamental part to play in this; the right word at the right time may be crucial, while a disparaging or ambivalent attitude may cancel out the most successful of technical results.

NURSING CARE
- The surgeon and patient will already have discussed in detail the likely outcome of the operation. Do not increase or bolster those expectations, as it becomes easy for the patient to fantasise. Reassure the patient that any discomfort will be controllable, that many others have undergone similar operations with satisfactory outcomes, and that her reasons for seeking surgery are understood and supported.

RHYTIDECTOMY (FACE-LIFT)

Rhytidectomy (*rhytis* = Greek, a wrinkle) involves the redistribution and removal of excess facial skin through incisions in front of, below and behind the ear, extending to the hairline of the temple and the nape of the neck (Fig. 96). Since the dissection involves lifting most of the skin of the cheek and upper part of the neck off the subcutaneous fat, the area of tissue disturbed is considerable. The dissection is assisted by infiltrating the subcutaneous tissues

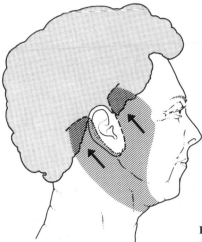

Fig. 96. *Incisions and skin undermining for a face-lift.*

with adrenaline 1:200 000 in 0.5% lignocaine before the incisions are made.

Complications

1. *Haematoma and bleeding.* Wound drainage does not alter the incidence of serious haematoma (3% to 7% in most series). However, pressure dressings and controlled hypotensive anaesthesia (see page 358) may prevent haematoma formation. Postoperative pain in the face is indicative of accumulating blood; if it is impossible to milk this out through the suture line, the patient is returned to theatre. Haematoma must not be ignored.

2. *Skin necrosis* may result from an untreated haematoma, excessive tension or too superficial a dissection. The area is kept clean with Eusol and dressed with Bactigras and gauze. Most heal with minimal scarring, though large losses may require skin grafting.

3. *Facial nerve damage* produces weakness of the facial muscles. If the damage has not divided the nerve, spontaneous improvement can be expected. However, if the nerve has been divided, repair and reconstruction will be undertaken.

PRE-OPERATIVE NURSING CARE

- The patient is admitted the day before the operation and the routine admission and pre-operative procedures carried out.
- Try to allay the patient's anxiety regarding her pre- and post-operative care, and make every effort to gain the patient's confidence in the tact and confidentiality of all the staff caring for her.
- Explain to the patient that after the operation her head and ears may be heavily bandaged, so she may not be able to hear very well.
- Explain that fine bore drainage tubes may be in situ on both sides of her face. During the immediate post-operative period she should not move around in bed without a nurse present to ensure the drains are not dislodged.
- Show her how to use the nurse call system and reassure her that she will have no difficulty in summoning a nurse when she wakes after the operation.
- Explain that she will quickly become accustomed to the dressings and will soon learn how to move without disturbing the drains.
- Tell the patient not to eat or drink anything after her operation until told she may do so.
- Hypotensive general anaesthesia is often used for this operation (see page 358). Explain to the patient that her posture will be adjusted using a varying number of pillows beneath her head and that she will be sat up as soon as possible to reduce the facial swelling. Ask her to maintain the position she finds herself in when she recovers from the anaesthetic.
- Tell her she will need to remain on bed rest until the day after the operation to avoid the risk of fainting as a result of the hypotensive anaesthesia used.

POST-OPERATIVE NURSING CARE

- On returning from theatre, the patient is supported by an increasing number of pillows, according to the blood pressure recordings, until she is sitting as upright as possible.
- Blood pressure is recorded every 15 minutes, then every 30 minutes, and the interval then gradually increased to every 4 hours as described for care following hypotensve anaesthesia (see page 359).

- Some surgeons prefer to leave the suture lines exposed; if so, they are kept clean using gauze swabs soaked in sterile saline.
- If dressings are used, ensure they remain comfortable and undisturbed.
- The most common complication following this operation is *haematoma formation*. Since so much of the skin of the face and neck has been undermined, any haematoma may lift the undermined skin off its bed of subcutaneous fat, resulting in skin ischaemia. This condition must be treated urgently if skin necrosis is to be avoided. Therefore very careful observation must be maintained to detect haematoma formation early.
- If dressings are in place, facial pain must be investigated by removal of the dressings to ensure that haematoma formation is not the cause.
- If a haematoma does occur, it requires urgent evacuation and haemostasis. This may require the administration of a general anaesthetic. Therefore the patient should not be given anything by mouth until about 4 hours after the operation, by which time any haematoma likely to occur will have formed.
- The rare complication of facial nerve damage may be difficult to detect in the first few post-operative days due to swelling of the face. During this period the patient's facial skin feels very tight and uncomfortable and she is reluctant to move her face in a normal manner. Continue to observe the patient carefully until normal bilateral facial movement has been seen.
- The patient is allowed up and about on the first post-operative day. She is advised not to bend head down for 7 to 10 days as this may increase oedema or provoke post-operative bleeding.
- Advise the patient to sleep with her head on a high pillow for 7 to 10 days to reduce the risk of oedema.
- For the first few days after surgery the patient is given a soft diet. Chewing is uncomfortable and may cause post-operative bleeding.
- Any drains in situ are removed when there has been no drainage for 12 to 24 hours, usually on the second or third post-operative day.
- Fine sutures are removed on the third or fourth post-operative day and larger supporting sutures within the hair on the seventh or eighth day.
- The patient is usually discharged from hospital on the fourth

or fifth post-operative day, returning for final suture removal as an out-patient.

● The patient's hair is washed carefully and set on the day after suture removal.

BLEPHAROPLASTY (EYELID REDUCTION)

Blepharoplasty aims to remove:
1. Excess skin due to loss of elasticity.
2. Protrusion of fat from the floor or the roof of the orbit beneath the eyelid skin.

A small quantity of adrenaline 1:200 000 in 0.5% lignocaine is infiltrated to aid haemostasis. Incisions are made in the upper lid crease line and in the lower lid immediately below the eyelashes. They are continued laterally into the 'laugh lines' at the outer canthus of the eye. Chloramphenicol eye ointment is instilled at the end of the operation and the eyes may be bandaged lightly for 24 hours. This operation may be performed under local anaesthesia or more commonly under hypotensive general anaesthesia (see page 358).

Complications

1. *Proptosis of the globe of the eye.* The eyeball protrudes forwards and becomes hard, and the tissues become pink and suffused. This indicates bleeding into the orbital tissue and may endanger the sight of the eye, though fortunately if blindness occurs it is usually transient. Treatment consists of suture removal, to permit the release of pressure, and intravenous administration of mannitol.

2. *Ectropion of the lids.* Oedema in the early post-operative period may lead to transitory ectropion. Persistent ectropion is caused by excessive removal of skin, haematoma or fixation of the lid to the orbital floor. Treatment is usually conservative, though insertion of a full-thickness graft may be needed for severe cases. 'Dry eye', which results from ectropion, produces a persistent gritty sensation. Polyvinyl alcohol eye drops 1.4% or methylcellulose drops act as artificial tears.

NURSING CARE FOR OPERATION UNDER LOCAL ANAESTHESIA

- When local anaesthesia is used, the patient is treated as an out-patient or a one day admission to hospital. In either case the eyes will not be bandaged.
- The patient is instructed how to clean the wounds and shown how to instill chloramphenicol eye ointment 1% as required.
- Explain to the patient that, in addition to the routine after-care arrangements, she must seek expert advice immediately if signs of any complications occur.

PRE-OPERATIVE NURSING CARE

- If the operation is to be performed under general anaesthesia, the patient is admitted to hospital the day before the operation.
- Explain the pre- and post-operative care to the patient and reassure her of the tact and confidentiality of all the staff caring for her.
- Explain that her eyes may be bandaged for the first 24 hours and how her temporary blindness will be managed by the nurses. Reassure her that she will sleep a lot during this time so the 24 hours will pass quickly.
- Show her how to use the nurse call system. If there is no call system available the patient should be provided with a hand bell placed within easy reached in a pre-arranged position for use post-operatively.
- Hypotensive general anaesthesia is often used for this operation (see page 358). Explain to the patient that her posture will be adjusted using a varying number of pillows beneath her head and that she will be sat up as soon as possible to reduce the swelling around her eyes. Ask her to maintain the position she finds herself in when she recovers from the anaesthetic.
- Tell her she will need to remain on bed rest until the day after the operation to avoid the risk of fainting as a result of the hypotensive anaesthesia used.

POST-OPERATIVE NURSING CARE

- On returning from theatre, the patient is supported by an increasing number of pillows, according to the blood pressure recordings, until she is sitting as upright as possible.
- Blood pressure is recorded every 15 minutes, then every 30

minutes and the interval then gradually increased to every 4 hours as described for care following hypotensive anaesthesia (see page 359).

- On removal of the bandages (or immediately after the operation if the wounds have been left exposed) the suture lines are cleaned using swabs soaked in sterile saline.
- If necessary, ice packs may be placed on the eyelids to reduce swelling.
- Even mild swelling of the eyelids may cause ectropion in the first few days following surgery. Therefore the eye is protected from corneal ulceration by instilling ointment every 4 hours. Since the suture lines are so near to the eye, an antibiotic eye ointment, such as chloramphenicol 1%, is commonly used to reduce the risk of infection. Explain to the patient that the ointment will cause blurring of the vision for about 20 minutes after instillation.
- Proptosis of the eye is the most serious complication following this operation. Careful observation for this must be maintained, especially during the first 24 hours. If proptosis occurs, it must be treated as an emergency as delay in treatment may result in permanent damage to the sight.
- The patient is allowed up and about from the first post-operative day. She is advised not to bend head down and to continue sleeping with a high pillow for 7 to 10 days to minimise oedema of the eyelids.
- Sutures are removed on the third or fourth day.
- The patient is usually discharged from hospital on the day the sutures are removed.
- If the patient normally wears spectacles, or chooses to wear dark glasses temporarily to hide the bruising and swelling, advise her not to knock the suture lines when taking them on and off. Check that the spectacles do not put any pressure on the delicate suture lines.
- In addition to the normal after-care arrangements, advise the patient to seek expert advice immediately if signs of any complications occur.
- The operations of face-lift and eyelid reduction are frequently performed together and therefore the nursing care for both conditions will apply. Reassurance of the nurse's presence will be particularly necessary if both the eyes and ears are to be

covered, resulting in a patient who is temporarily blind and cannot hear very well.

CORRECTIVE RHINOPLASTY

The skeleton of the nose can be altered through incisions in the mucous membrane of the nostrils. Altering the bridgeline requires removal of part of the antero-superior part of the nasal bones and midline septal cartilage. Reshaping the nasal tip involves refining the alar tip cartilages and the inferior part of the septum (Fig. 97).

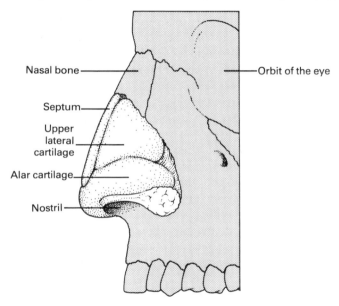

Nasal bone

Orbit of the eye

Septum

Upper lateral cartilage

Alar cartilage

Nostril

Fig. 97. *Anatomy of the nasal skeleton.*

A receding or underdeveloped chin may be corrected at the same operation either by cutting a wedge of mandible, sliding it forwards and wiring it into position (genioplasty) (Fig. 98), or by inserting a piece of silicone over the point of the mandible. Genioplasty is carried out through an incision in the mucosa of the sulcus between the lower alveolus and the lower lip or through a skin incision beneath the chin (see 'Micrognathia' in Glossary).

Subtotal submucous resection of the septum (SMR) is

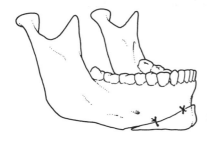

Fig. 98. *Sliding genioplasty to correct a receding chin.*

performed when the septal cartilage is buckled and obstructing the airway. If excessive amounts of septum are removed, the bridge-line sinks, producing a saddle-shaped deformity.

General anaesthesia is usually preferred. A dry operative field is achieved by:

1. *Hypotensive anaesthesia.* The patient's blood pressure is maintained below 70 mmHg systolic throughout the operation.

2. *Cocaine 4%* packed into the nose on cotton wool or orange sticks. Injection of the mucosa with adrenaline 1:200 000 in 0.5% lignocaine produces a similar effect, but cocaine and adrenaline should be used together only with extreme caution, since cocaine increases the effects of adrenaline on the heart and circulation.

To protect the nose from knocks, a plaster of Paris splint is usually applied at the end of the operation and retained for 7 to 14 days. Beneath this, pressure is applied to the skin using adhesive tape strips to reduce post-operative swelling. Intra-nasal packs, if used, are removed after 48 hours. Following submucous resection of the septum, packs are often retained for a further 24 hours.

Complications

1. *Haemorrhage.* This can usually be stopped by sitting the patient up and administering morphine. Persistent bleeding requires adrenaline-soaked or oxycel gauze packing or, rarely, postnasal packing with a Foley catheter.

2. *Infection* is uncommon. If an abscess develops, usually at the angle of the glabella, it is incised and drained.

3. *Proptosis* of the globe may rarely occur if a blood vessel in

the orbit ruptures. If the proptosis is progressive, the patient is returned to theatre at once for haemostasis.

PRE-OPERATIVE NURSING CARE

- The patient is admitted the day before the operation and routine admission procedures and pre-anaesthetic preparation are carried out.

- Reassure the patient that her request for surgery is understood and supported and make every effort to gain her confidence in the tact and confidentiality of all the staff caring for her.

- Explain the pre- and post-operative procedures to the patient. Warn her that her eyelids may be bruised and swollen for up to 7 days after surgery and explain that this will not leave any permanent damage.

- Explain that she will need to stay in bed for 24 hours after the operation to avoid the risk of fainting as a result of the hypotensive anaesthesia used.

- Tell the patient that after the operation her posture will be adjusted using a varying number of pillows, until she is sitting as upright as possible. Explain that this is to reduce swelling and any risk of bleeding, and ask her to maintain the posture she finds herself in on recovering from the anaesthetic.

- Explain that nasal packs may be in situ for 2 to 3 days and that even when the packs are removed she may not be able to breathe through her nose for up to 2 weeks.

- Advise her not to attempt to blow her nose for 7 to 10 days. Tell her that she may feel as if she has a head cold for up to 2 weeks after surgery. This is due to swelling inside the nose and will resolve spontaneously. Nasal decongestants (such as ephedrine 0.5%) are occasionally used.

- Explain that a plaster of Paris splint, held by adhesive tape, will be in place over the nose for about 10 days after surgery.

- Ask the patient if she is allergic to sticking plaster. If she is, patch tests using alternative types of adhesive tape, such as Micropore, should be carried out on the inner aspect of the arm to find the most suitable alternative. Any severe reaction will usually be apparent within 12 to 24 hours.

- The nasal hairs are clipped using fine-pointed, good quality scissors. The patient is kept as upright as possible to prevent the cut hairs falling into the nasal cavity and causing sneezing.

Smearing the scissor tips with liquid paraffin makes the loose hairs stick to the scissors, preventing them from being inhaled.

POST-OPERATIVE NURSING CARE

- Immediately after surgery the patient is supported by an increasing number of pillows, according to the blood pressure recordings, until she is sitting as upright as possible.
- Blood pressure is recorded every 15 minutes, then every 30 minutes and the interval then increased to every 4 hours as described for care following hypotensive anaesthesia (see page 359).
- Remind the patient not to touch or blow her nose.
- Ensure the nasal packs remain in the correct position.
- Observe the patient carefully for any signs of bleeding. While the patient is still sleepy from the anaesthetic, the only sign of bleeding may be repeated swallowing. If this is observed, careful examination with a torch may reveal blood trickling down the back of the throat. Ask the patient not to swallow, but to spit out any exudate so the severity of the bleeding can be assessed.
- If swelling of the eyelids is severe, ice packs may be applied, but care must be taken not to wet and soften the plaster splint.
- Swelling of the eyelids produces temporary ectropion, which may result in corneal ulceration. A bland eye ointment is therefore instilled 4 hourly to protect the eye.
- Proptosis of the eye is a rare but serious complication and therefore careful observation for this is carried out for the first 24 to 48 hours.
- Keep the upper lip and eyes clean by swabbing with normal saline.
- The patient is allowed up and about on the first post-operative day. Instruct her not to bend head down and to sleep with her head on a high pillow to reduce oedema and the risk of post-operative haemorrhage.
- A soft diet is given for the first few days after the operation, as chewing is uncomfortable and may disturb the fractured nasal bones, delaying their healing.
- Nasal packs are removed after 2 to 3 days. Remind the patient not to blow her nose or to attempt to clean the nostrils. If there is any discharge she is instructed to keep her upper lip

clean by gentle washing.

- If blood has leaked through the plaster of Paris splint, painting the plaster with white ink (such as Tipp-Ex) improves the patient's appearance. This simple procedure may boost the patient's morale at a time when she is feeling very uncomfortable and self-conscious of her appearance.

- The patient is discharged from hospital after the nasal packs have been removed, usually on the second or third day, provided no bleeding has occurred. If haemorrhage follows removal of the nasal packs, the patient remains in hospital until 24 hours after bleeding has ceased.

- The plaster of Paris splint is removed as an out-patient, usually after 7 to 14 days. The nose and face are cleaned very gently to remove all traces of blood and adhesive tape. The nostrils are cleaned using cotton buds soaked in saline.

- When cleaning of the face and nose is complete, the patient is asked to look into a mirror, but is reminded that the result of the operation cannot be fully judged for about 3 months as it takes time for the soft tissue swelling to settle.

- Considerable emotional support and encouragement is given to the patient, who, when first seeing her face after removal of the splint, may experience some difficulty in recognising herself.

HYPOTENSIVE GENERAL ANAESTHESIA

Under general anaesthesia, a state of hypotension is induced by intravenous administration of drugs such as trimetaphan (Arfonad), labetalol (Trandate) and sodium nitroprusside (Nipride). The degree of hypotension is controlled by the amount of drug administered. The patient is maintained in a state of 'controlled hypotension' throughout the surgical procedure.

As a hypotensive state is induced, the blood vessels in the peripheral circulation constrict in order to keep the central venous pressure at a level which will maintain an adequate blood supply to the vital organs. Therefore lowering the blood pressure reduces bleeding from surgical wounds in peripheral areas, such as the skin and soft tissues underlying it, and thereby shortens the operation time. Controlled hypotension is, therefore, particularly useful for surgery of the nose and face, where copious bleeding normally obscures the operating field.

When the blood pressure has been artificially lowered, the patient looks pale and unwell. After surgery the blood pressure is allowed to rise slowly over the first 6 to 12 hours, since a rapid rise may dislodge the blood clots sealing the cut ends of small blood vessels in the wound and predispose to haematoma formation and haemorrhage.

When the blood pressure falls in any other circumstances, the foot of the patient's bed is normally raised. This usually produces an increase in recordable blood pressure. Conversely an undesirable rise in blood pressure is controlled by raising the patient's head.

However, raising the foot of the bed will increase the blood pressure in the operation site, thus encouraging haemorrhage. Therefore raising the foot of the bed is contra-indicated following hypotensive anaesthesia unless the blood pressure is dangerously low, i.e. below 70 mmHg systolic.

POST-OPERATIVE NURSING CARE

- The pulse and blood pressure are recorded every 15 minutes, beginning immediately the patient leaves the theatre.
- A rise in pulse and a corresponding fall in blood pressure normally indicates post-operative haemorrhage, but when the blood pressure has been artificially reduced, such changes are more difficult to interpret. Therefore the wound is also observed frequently for any sign of bleeding.
- When the blood pressure is stable at 110 mmHg systolic, the patient's head is raised by adding one pillow. The blood pressure is measured again after 5 to 10 minutes. If there is a fall in blood pressure to below 100 mmHg, the pillow is removed.
- When the blood pressure again reaches 110 mmHg, the patient's head is raised higher by adding another pillow.
- More pillows are added at 15 minute intervals, or according to the blood pressure, until the patient is sitting as upright as possible.
- The patient's blood pressure is usually stable at the pre-operative level within 12 hours of recovery from the anaesthetic.
- As soon as the blood pressure is stable at the pre-operative

level with the patient sitting up in bed, the frequency of blood pressure recording is reduced to every 30 minutes, then hourly, 2-hourly and 4-hourly.

- Bed rest is maintained until the blood pressure has remained at the pre-operative level for 6 hours.
- When the patient first gets out of bed, explain that he may feel faint because of drug-induced postural hypotension.
- Stay with the patient when he first gets out of bed, until he is confident he is not going to faint.
- Blood pressure recordings are discontinued when the blood pressure has remained stable for 8 hours after the patient is fully ambulant.

FURTHER READING

Rees, T.D. (1980) *Aesthetic plastic surgery*. Philadelphia: W.B. Saunders.
Skoog, T. (1974) *Plastic surgery*. Stockholm: Almquist & Wiksell.

21   The operating theatre

The nursing disciplines in the Plastic Surgery theatre are soundly based on those of general surgery. The Plastic Surgery theatre nurse may be required to exercise knowledge of a wide range of other surgical specialities with which the Plastic Surgeon is associated, both in emergency and planned operations. Disease and injury are no respecters of surgical systems, so an orthopaedic, ophthalmic, neuro-, vascular and Plastic surgeon may all be called upon to bring their particular abilities to bear on one patient. The nurse should be equally at ease with all these specialities. For example, in reconstruction following cancer ablation, the nurse is required to be conversant with both the excision and the reconstruction, which may be carried out by two different surgical teams.

Because of the length of some operative procedures, it is preferable for a separate theatre to be used for Plastic Surgery. This also has the advantage that the theatre staff become especially adept at dealing with this type of surgery.

THE INSTRUMENTS

Operating instruments for Plastic Surgery tend to be more delicate than those for general surgery, require more careful handling and more meticulous maintenance. Since gentleness in tissue handling and precision in suture technique make the difference between a good scar and an indifferent one, it is essential that scissors and saws are sharp and forceps meet accurately at the tips.

All of the instruments required for an operation are set out on the nurse's trolley before the operation commences. It is useful to have several pre-packed 'sets' of instruments made up and sterilised, rather than having to collect together the many different instruments before every operation.

Sutures

Absorbable sutures. These materials, most commonly catgut and polyglycolic acid (Dexon), are removed by the body's defence system and excite a variable degree of inflammation. Chromatisation of catgut both prolongs its life in the tissues and reduces the amount of inflammatory response. Dexon excites a moderate chemical reaction which continues long after the suture material itself has been absorbed. Absorbable sutures are, therefore, not appropriate on the surface of the skin, but are useful in suturing deeper tissues or closing up dead-space at the bottom of a wound.

Non-absorbable sutures. Non-absorbable sutures, such as silk, nylon and polypropylene, are not removed by the body's defence system and excite little or no inflammatory reaction if properly inserted and removed within a few days. Most facial sutures can safely be removed after 4 days, abdominal after 7 to 10 days, and sutures on the back after 12 to 14 days, provided there is no tension on the skin. Any tension should be taken up by subcutaneous sutures. Delay in removing skin sutures and the presence of tension produces cross-hatches (Fig. 1, page 15) and redness of the wound.

Needles

For general use, sutures and needles are manufactured as one. These 'atraumatic sutures' have needles with no eye, the metal of the needle surrounding the end of the suture. Needles with a triangular or lance-shaped cross-section are for 'cutting'; they puncture and cut the tissue as they pass through, making the passage of the whole needle relatively easy. Round-bodied needles, despite a sharp point, have to push aside the tissue after the tip has entered; these are reserved for tissue which has little resistance, such as fat.

The needles of atraumatic sutures, especially the smaller sizes, tend to bend easily. This can be a serious disadvantage when difficult angles have to be negotiated in confined spaces. In these situations, many surgeons prefer the more robust, eyed needles which require threading.

For cleft palate work, the tiny Oldfield[1] needle and half curved and three-quarters curved needles are useful. The Reverdin[2]

[1] Michael Oldfield, Plastic Surgeon, Leeds.
[2] Jacques Reverdin, 1842–1928. Professor of Operative Medicine, Geneva, Switzerland.

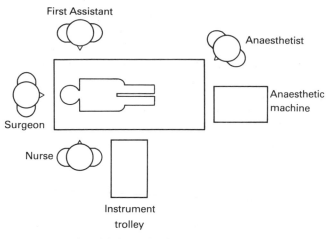

Fig. 99. *Table layout for cleft lip and palate operations.*

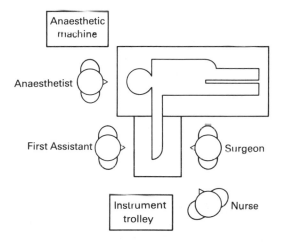

Fig. 100. *Table layout for operations on the hand.*

needle, which is on the end of a handle with a release catch to 'open the eye' is unnecessarily fiddly for cleft palate repair. The Holdsworth[3] needle, also on a handle but without the catch and more delicate, is preferred.

[3] William Holdsworth, Plastic Surgeon, Roehampton, London.

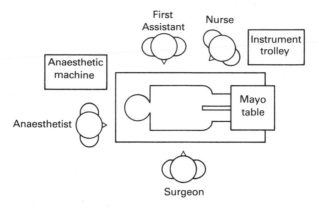

Fig. 101. *Table layout for operations on the chest and abdomen.*

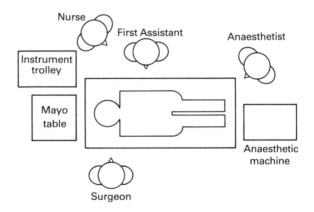

Fig. 102. *Table layout for operations on the nose, neck and head.*

ORGANISATION AROUND THE THEATRE TABLE

To participate fully in the operation, the nurse must be able to see precisely every stage of the operation and the tissues being manipulated. She therefore places herself so she can reach the instruments with ease and without turning away from the operating field. Some arrangements which fulfil these requirements are shown in Figs 99, 100, 101 and 102.

CARE OF THE PATIENT

Preventing pressure sores

To prevent pressure sores occurring on the operating table, care is taken to lay the unconscious patient on a well-padded mattress in order to distribute his weight evenly. The heels are massaged every half hour.

Post-operative recovery

A quiet transition from anaesthesia to sleep is desirable to avoid the patient going through a period of hypertension or straining on flaps. Such straining causes haematomas to collect beneath grafts or may recommence bleeding. Distressed babies need to be comforted, cossetted and given a drink.

To reduce post-operative oedema, the limbs involved in surgery are elevated above the level of the heart and kept in this position from the time the patient leaves the operating table. As soon as the patient who has had facial surgery is fully conscious, unless there are other contra-indications, he is sat up resting on pillows to reduce the facial tissue swelling.

COMMON THEATRE PROCEDURES

Split skin grafting

The blades. Partial-thickness (split skin) grafts (see page 33), though formerly taken with an unguarded blade, are now usually cut using:

1. A Watson[4] or Braithwaite[5] (or similar) knife. This has a disposable blade whose thickness of cut can be pre-set against a guard. The skin, the blade and two flat boards are first lubricated with liquid paraffin.

2. A Padgett[6] drum dermatome. The curved stainless steel drum and the skin are cleaned with alcohol and painted with

[4] John Watson, Plastic Surgeon, London Hospital, London.
[5] Fenton Braithwaite, Plastic Surgeon, Newcastle.
[6] Earl C. Padgett, 1893–1946. Surgeon, Kansas City, Missouri.

adhesive (such as Evo-Stik). The drum is applied to the donor area, to which it sticks. The blade is moved across the skin to cut the graft, which adheres to the drum. Grafts of uniform thickness and to fit an exact pattern can be cut by this method.

3. An electric or air-driven dermatome. The blade is oscillated mechanically at high speed, permitting grafts to be removed rapidly in strips 8 cm or less in width. Liquid paraffin is used to lubricate the dermatome and the skin.

The skin mesher (Fig. 9, page 34). In order to enlarge the area that a skin graft can be made to cover, multiple slits are made in the graft to produce a 'chicken-wire' pattern (Fig. 76, page 259). Commercial meshers are available which can expand a graft to two times, four times or eight times its original area. The appearance of the graft limits this method to use on unexposed surfaces, such as the trunk. (See also page 33.)

The technique for taking and applying a split skin graft is as follows:

1. The scrub nurse prepares sheets of paraffin gauze, spreading them out on a large wooden board.

2. The area from which skin is to be cropped and the area to be grafted are cleaned with Cetavlon and thiomersal 0.1% and towelled.

3. The skin of the donor site is painted with liquid paraffin on a cotton gauze swab.

4. The skin grafting knife blade and two flat wooden boards are similarly coated with liquid paraffin.

5. The assistant standing opposite the surgeon holds one wooden board in his left hand firmly against the donor skin at the point of commencement of the cut. With his right hand he stretches the adjacent skin taut.

6. A clean sweep of the skin-grafting knife by the surgeon removes a sheet of skin (Fig. 103a).

7. The scrub nurse takes the skin and spreads it, using 2 pairs of non-toothed forceps, shiny (dermis) side up, onto a sheet of paraffin gauze.

8. The paraffin gauze around the skin graft is cut with scissors to conform exactly to the graft so that no excess gauze remains.

9. The skin graft and paraffin gauze may be cut into postage stamp sizes (Fig. 103b).

10. The spread skin is covered with a saline-soaked gauze swab to prevent it drying out until ready for use.

11. The donor skin area is dressed with one layer of paraffin gauze, several layers of cotton gauze and cotton wool and, if a limb, a crepe bandage. Alternatively, the donor area may be dressed with Opsite, preferably applied circumferentially so that it adheres to itself if used on a limb.

12. The sheet of spread skin graft is laid shiny side down onto the area to be grafted (recipient site) (Fig. 103c). The graft may be immobilised by sutures at the periphery or by firm elasticated bandaging.

13. If laid on as postage stamps, a second large sheet of paraffin gauze is laid over the smaller ones.

14. The paraffin gauze is covered with cotton gauze and bandaged to immobilise it.

15. The nurse now changes her gloves, keeping the trolley sterile.

16. Any unused skin on paraffin gauze is covered with a cotton gauze swab well rung out in saline. It is then rolled up with the saline-soaked gauze innermost.

17. Each roll is placed in a *separate* universal sterile container marked with the patient's name and stored in the refrigerator. Skin will remain viable in this way for up to about 14 days, when it should be discarded.

Epithelial inlay

When a skin graft is to be applied to a hollow or gutter, such as the buccal sulcus of the mouth or the orbit of the eye, the graft may first be draped by its epithelial side down on to a mould which has been previously contoured to fit the hollow. A useful mould is stent, which softens in warm water and hardens again at room temperature. Contact can therefore be maintained between the bed and the graft by pressure of the mould. The stent can be removed after a week, leaving the graft in place on its bed.

Chemical peel

Phenol-croton oil, applied to the skin by a swab or orange stick, causes destruction of the upper epidermis and keratin layer. It is

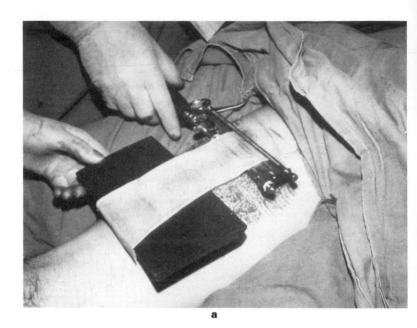

a

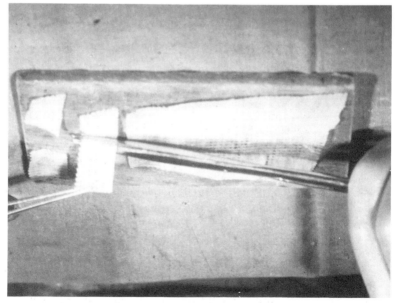

b

c

Fig. 103. *Technique of skin grafting. (a) Partial-thickness skin graft removed as a sheet, (b) laid on tulle gras and cut, and (c) applied to the wound bed.*

used to improve the appearance of wrinkles. A suitable mixture comprises 3 ml of 50% phenol, 2 drops of croton oil, 8 drops of liquid soap and 2 ml of distilled water.

A waterproof adhesive dressing is applied to the skin and removed under sedation after 48 hours. The skin is dusted with thymol iodide powder for the next 4 to 5 days. The crust is then softened with 5% boracic acid ointment and washed with water. Repeated daily treatment with ointment and washing results in the crust falling away. A facial cream may be applied. The patient is advised not to expose the treated areas to strong sunlight for 6 months.

Cryotherapy

Liquid nitrogen (boiling point − 196°C), carbon dioxide (boiling point − 79°C) or nitrous oxide (boiling point − 70°C) applied to skin or mucosa produces ice inside and outside the cells, causing cell death. These icing agents can, therefore, be used to remove benign skin lesions. Pain is usually minimal and the procedure may be carried out under local anaesthetic or, less commonly, with no anaesthetic. Blistering occurs within a few hours and healing follows with minimal inflammation.

Loss of skin pigmentation and paraesthesiae occasionally occur.

Curettage

A sharp spoon is used to destroy or remove small skin lesions, such as keratoses, verrucae and tophi.

Comedo expression

A small spoon with a hole in its centre is pressed on the skin over the comedo (black-head). The comedo is squeezed out through the hole.

Dermabrasion

A wire or carborundum brush is rotated rapidly on a cylinder by means of a dental drill or similar engine. The superficial layers of the dermis are pared away by the brush until bleeding occurs. This technique is used for treating acne and smallpox pits, for smoothing scars and removing superficial tattoos. The wound is best left undressed as all types of dressing tend to adhere. It may be gently cleaned with saline. Within 48 hours, an eschar forms as the serum dries; this can be aided by using a hair blow-drier. The eschar separates spontaneously after 10 to 14 days, leaving exposed pink epithelium, which eventually fades. Hypo- or hyper-pigmentation may persist in the treated area, particularly in dark skins. Patients are advised to keep out of strong sunlight for 6 months.

Intralesional therapy

Corticosteroids such as triamcinalone are used to reduce hypertrophic and keloid scars. They may be injected using a syringe and needle or a needleless high pressure jet gun. These jet guns (such as Panjet, Dermojet and Porton gun) eject the steroid under sufficient pressure to penetrate the skin and enable multiple areas to be treated quickly.

Laser therapy

The laser (Light Amplification by Stimulated Emission of Radiation) is light energy concentrated into a fine pencil beam. When shone on the skin it produces coagulation of blood vessels and is therefore currently being used experimentally to treat capillary haemangioma. Extreme care is taken that the beam does not strike the eye; eye shields must be worn by the staff and the patient.

Preparation of (pro)flavine wool

Flavine emulsion is heated to lukewarm. Cotton wool is thoroughly mixed into the emulsion, then well wrung out to remove excess emulsion until the wool feels dry. It is then placed in a warm cupboard to remove the remaining moisture, and autoclaved for use.

FURTHER READING

Barron, J.N. & Saad, M.N. (Eds) (1980) *Operative, plastic and reconstructive surgery*. Edinburgh: Churchill Livingstone.

Ellison Nash, D.F. (1980) *The principles and practice of surgery for nurses* and allied professions, 7th edn. London: Edward Arnold.

Kyle, J. (Ed.) (1977) *Pye's surgical handicraft*, 12th edn. Bristol: John Wright.

Watson, J. & McCormack, R. (Eds) (1979) *Operative surgery – fundamental international techniques*, 3rd edn. London: Butterworth.

22 Non-biological implants

The rejection by the body of 'foreign' substances implanted into tissues has excluded a large number of otherwise satisfactory materials from being used in repairing contour defects. Other suitable substances produce an unacceptable fibrous reaction or are not sufficiently robust to withstand the movement required of them. Also many of the materials implanted need to conform not only in size and shape to the area being replaced, but also in consistency and texture. These factors have reduced the number of substances used in Plastic Surgery to a handful, although a wide range of materials such as rubber, paraffin, various metals and foam have been used and discarded.

Only the more commonly implanted materials are discussed here.

SILICONES

Silicones are a family of compounds which range from liquids through gelatinous forms to foams and solids of varying hardness. Only 'medical grade' silicones have been biologically tested and used in implant surgery.

Solid silicone

Solid silicone is available in the form of pre-shaped prostheses or as a block which can be carved at the operating table. It has a wide range of uses. These include metacarpophalangeal joint replacement and reconstruction of the floor of the orbit following a blow-out fracture. Struts of solid silicone may be inserted into the nose to correct a saddle deformity of the bridgeline, into the chin to augment a recessed mandible, or behind scalp skin to reconstruct an ear. The underdeveloped cheek prominences of the child with Treacher Collins syndrome (see page 94) may be built up by solid silicone implanted on the malar bones. A rod of silicone may be slid into a surgically formed pouch in a reconstructed penis to stiffen it prior to intercourse. Hypernasal speech due to a large gap between the posterior wall of the pharynx and the back of the palate may be improved by implanting a block of silicone behind the posterior pharyngeal muscles (see Fig. 32, page 85).

Solid silicone implants are smooth and therefore tend to be displaced downwards under the action of gravity. Some surgeons, therefore, prefer to use implants which have a patch of Dacron attached to them, the implant being fixed by the growth of fibrous tissue into the patch.

Care has to be taken that undue pressure is not exerted on surrounding tissue. If this should occur, the overlying skin will ulcerate, exposing the prosthesis. This invariably leads to infection, which necessitates removal of the material. There is, therefore, a strict limit on the size of prosthesis which can be implanted.

Silicone Elastomer rubber

Silicone in a semi-liquid state can be changed into a rubbery compound by the addition of stannous octoate catalyst. This property can be used in repairing contour defects such as pectus excavatum (see page 114). The silicone elastomer and catalyst are autoclaved separately and then mixed. The proportions used give the surgeon enough time to insert the compound under the skin and mould it before it sets.

Alternatively, a three-dimensional mould of the defect may be made, from which a ready shaped prosthesis of silicone can be prepared. The prosthesis, already in its rubbery form, is then inserted through an appropriate incision.

Silicone fluid injection

The subcutaneous injection of liquid silicone to build up contour defects, though not a difficult technique, has rightly been slow to acquire widespread use. Its early use to augment breasts led to a number of reports of chronic inflammation and granulomata, which were almost impossible to eradicate because of the widespread diffusion of silicone throughout the breast tissue.

Silicone fluid injection is mainly useful for small areas of loss of subcutaneous fat on the face and for hemi-facial atrophy (Romberg's disease, see page 94). Using a strictly aseptic technique, 2 to 3 ml of silicone is injected beneath the skin using a Luer-lock syringe with an 18 to 20 gauge needle. The area is then gently massaged to disperse the injection. The injection hole is sealed with collodion. The procedure can be repeated at weekly intervals, gradually building up the contour.

Silicone gel

Silicone gel contained within an envelope or outer covering of thin silicone sheeting is used for augmentation of the breasts because it has a consistency similar to breast tissue. Various shapes, ranging from tear-drop to oval, as well as different sizes, are commercially available. If a Dacron patch is attached to the silicone prosthesis, some degree of fixation occurs to the chest wall. Alternatively, the prosthesis is allowed to 'free-float'.

In about 10 to 15% of patients, a fibrous capsule forms around the prosthesis, causing the breast to feel firm and become spherical in shape. This may be due to the gel leaking out through the thin envelope into the breast tissue.

Prostheses consisting of a silicone envelope without a gel interior are also available and are supplied with a filler valve. Once the prosthesis has been positioned on the chest wall beneath the breast, the valve tube is brought out through the wound and the envelope filled with sterile normal saline (0.9%) or dextran to the required size. This type is useful in cases of breast asymmetry when the requisite volume can only be determined with the prosthesis in place (Fig. 44, page 120).

Although silicone does not react with other materials, it tends to attract dust particles. It is, therefore, important to rinse the prosthesis in sterile saline before implantation and to handle it only through a gauze swab.

TEXTILES

Dacron

Dacron is a terylene fibre, usually presented as a cloth or sheet, used in vascular surgery for aortic and aorto-iliac prostheses and in Plastic Surgery when fibrous ingrowth is required to fix an otherwise unrestrained prosthesis (for example the Niebauer[1]

---

[1] Dr John Niebauer, Surgeon, San Francisco, USA.

finger joint prosthesis, which is made of silicone covered with Dacron mesh).

Teflon

Teflon, also presented as a cloth or sheet, is derived from tetrafluoroethylene. This, too, can be used as an arterial prosthesis. In Plastic Surgery, a sheet of Teflon may be used to repair a blow-out fracture of the floor of the orbit (see page 328). A derivative of Teflon is *Proplast*, available as a black (Teflon and carbon) or white (Teflon and alumina) porous block, which can be carved and into which fibrous tissue will grow. It has been used to repair cheek and nose contour defects. The block is carved with a scalpel, rinsed in water and then autoclaved.

PLASTICS

Polypropylene

Polypropylene is pre-fabricated in an injection mould to the required shape. The Nicolle[2] metacarpophalangeal joint prosthesis uses polypropylene for the stems and stainless steel for the articulating part of the joint.

Polyvinyl alcohol

Polyvinyl alcohol, in the form of an Ivalon sponge, was used in the past to augment the breast. However, it has now been superseded by silicone implants.

Polyethylene

Polyethylene, marketed as *Marlex*, is used as a woven sheet to reinforce abdominal hernias. In a solid form, it is used in the St Georg finger joint prosthesis.

---

[2] F.V. Nicolle, Plastic Surgeon, Hammersmith Hospital, London.

ELEMENTS AND METALS

Carbon fibre is currently under evaluation as a replacement for tendons and ligaments. *Stainless steel*, and other inert metals such as cobalt, chrome and molybdenum, are used in a number of metacarpophalangeal joint prostheses. *Vitallium* plates have been used to close holes in the skull following trauma or surgery. *Tantalum* mesh has been used for reconstruction of the mandible.

COMPLICATIONS

All the implants discussed above produce little or no immunological response (which would result in rejection). Nevertheless they all have disadvantages when compared with autogenous (self) biological tissue. Where use can be made of the patient's own tissue without creating an unacceptable defect or deformity at the donor site, this remains the method of choice.

Infection

Acute suppurative infection around an implanted prosthesis almost always necessitates its removal. Infection may be introduced when the implant is inserted, by septic handling of the overlying wound, by ulceration of the skin over the prosthesis, or via the bloodstream (bacteraemia).

Low-grade chronic infection, from which organisms are only rarely cultured, may occur around mobile prostheses, particularly those adjacent to bone, such as finger joint prostheses. It may progress to ulceration and acute inflammation. Rest may cause the infection to subside.

Fibrous capsule formation

The body responds to implants by surrounding them with a layer of scar collagen. This problem has already been mentioned in connection with silicone gel breast augmentation (see page 121), but applies also to other implants to a greater or lesser degree. This may be used to the patient's advantage; for example a concavity may be filled out by collagen forming around an implant.

Prosthetic failure

Fracture of a prosthetic finger joint or failure of the valve of the inflatable breast prostheses, though unacceptably common in the past, is now, with newer designs, a rare occurrence. Some prostheses, however, may be expected to fail since, being non-biological tissue, they lack the ability to heal when put under stress. A failure rate of under 5% is acceptable.

PRE-OPERATIVE PREPARATION

Scrupulous preparation of the implant and of the skin of the patient is essential. If the prosthesis is not supplied sterile, the manufacturer's directions for sterilisation are followed meticulously. Just before insertion into the patient, the implant is washed in saline to remove all adherent matter.

FURTHER READING

Converse, J.M. (Ed.) (1977) *Reconstructive plastic surgery: principles and procedures in correction, reconstruction and transplantation*, 2nd edn. Philadelphia: W.B. Saunders.

Appendix

NORMAL VALUES

Blood

Bicarbonate	22–30 mmol/l	pH	7.35–7.45
Creatinine	44–120 μmol/l	Potassium	3.5–5.0 mmol/l
Gases		Protein (total)	60–80 g/l
Po_2	10.5–14.0 kPa	Albumin	35–50 g/l
Pco_2	4.7–6.0 kPa	Globulin	25–45 g/l
Glucose	3.5–5.5 mmol/l		
Osmolality	275–295 mosmol/kg	Sodium	135–145 mmol/l
Packed cell volume (haematocrit):		Urea	2.3–6.7 mmol/l
Males	40–54%		
Females	36–47%		
Children (mean)	38%		

Urine

Acetone	Nil	Volume	
Creatinine		Adult	35–60 ml/h
clearance	80–125 ml/min	Child	
Potassium	30–90 mmol/24 h	0–1 year	8–20 ml/h
Protein	Nil	1–10	20–30 ml/h
Sodium	80–220 mmol/24 h	10–15	25–35 ml/h
Specific			
gravity	1.005–1.035		
Sugar	Nil		
Urea	170–580 mmol/24 h		

Table of expected normal values at various ages

Age	Weight kg	Packed cell volume %	Hb g/l	Blood volume ml	Minimum urine output ml/h	Oral fluid requirement ml/h
Birth	3.5	60	212	260	10	30
6/12m	7	36	123	520	10	30
1	10	38	116	750	10	30
2	12.5	38	117	940	15	30
3	15	38	121	1120	15	30
4	17	39	126	1270	15	30
5	19	39	127	1420	15	50
6	22	40	127	1650	20	50
7	24	40	128	1800	20	50
8	26	40	129	1950	20	50
9	30	40	130	2250	20	50
10	32	40	130	2400	25	70
12	40	41	134	3000	25	70
14	50	42	139	3750	30	70
16	55	42	140	4200	35	100
Adult: M	70	47	152	5250	35	100
F		42	140			

RATE OF INTRAVENOUS TRANSFUSION

Time for 1 l of fluid to be transfused	Approximate number of drops/min
12 h	25
8 h	36
6 h	50
4 h	70
2 h	135

BURNS NUTRITION

Table of energy requirements (kcal); nitrogen requirements (g) are given in brackets

Weight kg	Percentage body surface burned			
	20%	40%	60%	80%
Adults				
40	2200 (16.0)	3600 (25.6)	5000 (35.2)	6400 (44.8)
60	2600 (19.2)	4000 (28.8)	5400 (38.4)	6800 (48.0)
70	2800 (20.8)	4200 (30.4)	5600 (40.0)	7000 (49.6)
90	3200 (24.0)	4600 (33.6)	6000 (43.2)	7400 (52.8)
100	3400 (25.6)	4800 (35.2)	6200 (44.8)	7600 (54.4)
Children				
5	1000 (5.6)	1000 (5.6)	1000 (5.6)	1000 (5.6)
10	1300 (8.0)	1300 (8.0)	1300 (8.0)	1300 (8.0)
15	1600 (10.4)	1950 (12.0)	1950 (12.0)	1950 (12.0)
20	1900 (12.8)	2600 (16.0)	3300 (19.2)	4000 (22.4)
30	2500 (17.6)	3200 (20.8)	3900 (24.0)	4600 (27.2)

Data are taken from Sutherland, A.B. & Batchelor, A.D.R. (1968) *Annals of the New York Academy of Sciences, 150, 700.*

Weights and measures of foods

Food	Measure	Weight	Volume	Energy kcal
Milk	1 glass	7 oz	200 g	130
Cheese, Cheddar	1 inch cube	$\frac{3}{4}$ oz	21 g	80
Bacon	1 rasher	1 oz	28 g	125
Sausage	1 large	2 oz	56 g	170
Potato	1 large boiled	6 oz	170 g	135
Egg	1 fresh	2 oz	56 g	85
Bread	1 thick slice	2 oz	56 g	130
Butter	For 1 slice of bread	$\frac{1}{4}$ oz	7 g	52
Cornflakes	1 helping	1 oz	28 g	100
Tea	1 cup	$\frac{1}{8}$ oz	5 g	0
Coffee, instant	1 cup	$\frac{1}{10}$ oz	2 g	2
Beer	1 pint	20 fl oz	570 ml	175
Wine	1 glass	$2\frac{1}{2}$ fl oz	70 ml	47

1 kilocalorie (often written 'Calorie') is the amount of heat needed to raise the temperature of one litre of water by one degree centigrade; it therefore is a measure of heat energy.

CONVERSION FACTORS

Weight

1 g	=	1000 mg	=	0.035 oz	
1 kg	=	1000 g	=	2.2 lb	= 0.16 st
1 oz	=	28.35 g		
1 lb	=	16 oz	=	453.6 g
1 st	=	14 lb	=	6.35 kg

Volume

1 l	=	1000 ml	=	1.76 pt
1 pt	=	20 fl oz	=	568 ml
1 gal	=	8 pt	=	4.55 l

Length

1 cm	=	10 mm	=	0.39 in
1 m	=	100 cm	=	39.4 in
1 in	=	2.54 cm		
1 ft	=	12 in	=	0.3048 m

Temperatures

To convert °C to °F, multiply by 9/5 and add 32.
To convert °F to °C, subtract 32 and multiply by 5/9.

Energy

1 kcal	=	4.18 kJ
1 kJ	=	0.24 kcal

INSTRUMENTS FOR PLASTIC SURGERY

Basic general plastic set

1 Barron's handle
3 spongeholders
10 Bachaus towel clips
1 sinus forceps
3 no. 3 BP handles
2 McIndoe dissecting forceps, plain
1 Gillies dissecting forceps, toothed
1 Adson dissecting forceps, toothed (5 in)
1 Lanes dissecting forceps, toothed
1 McIndoe scissors
1 Aufright scissors, fine straight
1 Aufright scissors, fine curved
1 Aufright scissors, heavy straight
1 scissors, small fine straight
1 Strabismus scissors, small fine curved
1 Mayo scissors, straight (7 in), for dressings
2 Gillies skin hooks
2 Kilners cats paw skin retractors
2 Josephs skin hooks, 10 mm double
1 scissors, small curve on flat
1 Mitchell trimmer
1 Desmarres retractor
1 Kilner retractor
1 Howarth elevator
1 6 in rule
1 12 in rule
1 mapping pen
1 Tilleys nasal packing forceps
1 diathermy cable
1 Adson diathermy forceps
1 american pattern suction tube
1 sucker tube
10 mosquito forceps, curved
1 Neiverts needleholder
1 cartridge syringe
1 diathermy quiver
1 chip syringe
1 BP tray
1 bottle ink
1 sponge
1 gallipot
2 Kilner skin hooks

Skin graft extras

3 skin boards
1 Watson skin graft knife and blade
1 specimen pot (for skin storage)

Hand surgery extras

2 Kilners cats paw skin retractors
2 small retractors, double hook
2 single hooks
2 Adson forceps, plain (5 in)
1 Volkman scoop
5 mosquito artery forceps
1 scissors, small curved
1 scissors, small straight
1 needleholder, small
1 McDonald dissector
4 spongeholders
8 towel clips
2 no. 3 BP handles
1 Weislander retractor, light model (5½ in)
1 Neiverts needleholder (5 in)
2 receivers, small stainless steel
2 gallipots, stainless steel
1 bowl, stainless steel

Cleft palate extras

1 Kilner Dotts mouth gag including 3 blades
2 no. 5 or no. 7 BP handles
1 Waughs dissecting forceps, toothed
1 Waughs forceps non-toothed
3 McIndoe cleft palate raspatories (1 small, 1 medium, 1 large)
2 cleft palate raspatories (1 right, 1 left)
1 Mitchells trimmer
1 Kilner suture carrier
1 Gillies combined needleholder and scissors
1 divider
2 cleft palate raspatories, upward curved
2 cleft palate raspatories, downward curved
2 Kilners modification of Lanes mouth gag
1 Trelats needle
1 ligature hook
1 Reads chisel (3 mm)
1 cleft palate raspatory, small
1 Barsky pharyngeal elevator
1 elevator, double-ended
2 Dennis Browne raspatories (1 small, 1 large)

Mammoplasty extras
1 scissors, heavy angled upward
2 Doyens breast clamps
10 Spencer Wells artery forceps (6 in)
1 Gillies caliper, large
10 Allis tissue forceps
1 measure glass
1 sinus forceps
1 no. 4 BP handle
1 compass including 2 end pieces.

Rhinoplasty set
1 Aufright nasal retractor
1 set of 8 Thudicums nasal specula (assorted sizes)
3 St Clair Thompson nasal specula, self retaining
1 Spencer Wells forceps, straight
1 scissors, curved on flat, including short blades
2 alar cartilage scissors, small (1 pointed)
1 cartilage scissors, straight serrated
2 Ballengers swivel knives
1 Hartmans conchotome
2 Lucs nasal turbinectomy forceps (1 small, 1 medium)
2 Walsham nasal septum forceps (1 right, 1 left)
1 Aschs septum forcep
1 set of McIndoe nasal chisels (5, 7, 9, 11, 13 and 15 mm)
1 set of Duray osteotomes (5, 7, 9, 11, 13 and 15 mm)
1 Heaths mallet, lightweight
2 Josephs nasal saws (1 right, 1 left)
3 Maltz nasal rasps, straight (1 fine, 2 heavy)
1 Maltz nasal rasp, curved
1 Josephs nasal raspatory
1 set of Josephs double skin hook retractors
1 Tilleys dressing forceps
1 Peets rasp
1 Barron handle
1 Negus aspirating dissector
1 curette, double-ended
2 nasal saws, angled (1 right, 1 left)
2 Kilner alae nasal retractors (1 small, 1 large)
1 Freer nasal septum forceps, narrow
1 wire brush

SMR set
1 no. 3 scalpel handle
1 McDonalds dissector
2 Killians elevators (1 right, 1 left)
1 Jansen Middleton bone nibbler
1 Symes elevator, double-ended
1 Freers elevator, blunt
1 Ballengers swivel knife
1 Tilleys nasal forceps
1 mallet
1 Freers elevator, curved to left
2 Dunhill artery forceps

Bone graft set
5 osteotomes, straight
4 osteotomes, curved
4 gouges
1 mallet
2 rugines (1 straight, 1 curved)
2 wood boards, thick
2 bone cutters (1 small, 1 large)
2 bone nibblers, (1 small, 1 large)
1 Fergusson bone-holding forceps (lion)
1 sequestrum forceps, angled
1 Travers retractor, large
2 deavers, small
2 Langenbeck retractors, medium
2 Rake retractors

Basic oral surgery set
7 extraction forceps, upper (nos. 1, 29S 76, 147, 95, 94 and 67)
5 extraction forceps, lower (nos. 74N, 137H, 73, 73S and 144)
2 No. 3 BP handles
1 Fickling elevator
1 Howarth Hill elevator
1 Wards fan elevator
2 Cryers elevators
3 Warwick James elevators
1 Cumine scaler
3 Colemans elevators (1 right, 1 left, 1 straight)
1 nasal rasp
1 Wards double ended cheek retractor
1 Kay Austin cheek retractor
1 cheek retractor, plain
1 Fickling forceps, toothed
1 Fickling forceps, non-toothed
1 laryngeal mirror
1 Mitchell trimmer

1 McIndoe dissecting forceps, non-toothed
1 Gillies dissecting forceps, toothed
1 scissors, small straight
2 skin hooks
1 needleholder
1 bone nibbler, double action
2 osseous chisels (2 sizes)
1 no. 3 dental chisel
1 no. 5 dental chisel
1 no. 3 or no. 5 dental osteotome
1 no. 5 or no. 6 dental chisel, curved
2 dental probes (4A and 14)
1 pterygoid chisel
2 Obweger's chisels
1 mallet
1 spike
3 mosquito forceps, large straight
4 mosquito forceps, curved
1 dental syringe
8 towel clips on a pin
2 airways (No. 2 and No. 3)
2 spongeholders, small
1 Yankhauer sucker
1 Magills sucker
1 set of mouth props
1 receiver, large
1 gallipot, large
2 gallipots, small
1 gallipot, foil
1 stitch scissors

Wiring tray
6 Dunhill artery forceps
5 Spencer Wells forceps (7 in)
2 probes (4A Brialt and no. 11)
12 wire twisting forceps
1 wire cutter, small
1 wire cutting scissors, gold-handled
10 eyelet wires (nos. 24, 26 and 28)
3 reels of wire (nos. 24, 26 and 28)

Mandibular osteotomy set
Basic oral surgery set with the following removed:
1 pterygoid chisel
2 Obweger's chisels

Add the following:
2 wire cutters including selection of wires
1 screwdriver
12 wire twisting forceps
4 mosquito forceps, curved

2 malleable retractors
1 Bristow's elevator
1 Harrison bone hook
1 rugine, straight
1 rugine, curved
1 Kocher artery forceps
2 Langenbeck retractors
2 Kilner cats paw retractors
2 Brock retractors

Trauma tray

1 Kocher artery forceps
1 no. 3 BP handle
1 Adson forceps, toothed
1 Rowe's boat hook
2 Spencer Wells forceps
2 Allis tissue forceps
2 rugines (1 curved, 1 straight)
2 cats paw retractors
2 Langenbeck's retractors
2 Brook's retractors
1 Lane's elevator
1 Hall Friday chisel
3 bone awls
1 Langenbeck bone hook
1 Bristow's elevator
1 zygomatic arch awl
2 Gillies' skin hooks
1 Obweger's awl
1 screwdriver
2 Cairn's malleable retractors
1 mapping pen and bottle
1 cheek retractor
1 film clip

Tracheostomy set

5 spongeholders
4 towel clips
2 no. 3 scalpel handles
1 no. 4 scalpel handle
2 dissecting forceps, toothed (5 in) (1 Gillies, 1 Treves)
2 dissecting forceps, plain (5 in)
1 Waughs dissecting forceps, toothed (7 in)
1 Waughs dissecting forceps, plain (7 in)
1 McIndoe scissors
1 Mayo scissors (6½ in)
1 stitch scissors
5 Dunhill artery forceps

5 mosquito artery forceps, curved
2 mosquito artery forceps, straight
2 Allis tissue forceps
2 double hook retractors, blunt
1 single hook, blunt
1 mastoid retractor, self retaining
2 needleholders, small
1 tongue depressor
1 tracheal dilator
2 Langenbeck retractors, small
1 Yankhauer sucker
1 self-clearing sucker
1 catheter mount including Nosworthy connection
2 gallipots, stainless steel
2 receivers, small stainless steel

1 bowl, stainless steel
1 diathermy cable
1 diathermy forceps

Suture of simple skin lacerations

1 mapping pen and ink
1 scalpel handle and No. 15 blade
2 skin hooks
6 mosquito artery forceps
1 Adson dissecting forceps, toothed
1 Adson dissecting forceps, non-toothed
1 scissors, fine
1 needle holder (e.g. Nievert)
Fine sutures (e.g. 5/0 silk or 6/0 nylon)

Glossary

Active movement. Movement at a joint produced by the patient's *own* muscles and tendons around that joint.

Adamantinoma. A tumour of the mandible which only occasionally metastasises to the neck lymph nodes, but recurs locally in the mandible unless widely excised.

Aerobe. An organism which requires oxygen for survival.

Ala of the nose. That part of the nose which joins the dome of the nose-tip to the cheek. The soft tissues are supported by the alar cartilages. (See Fig. 97, page 354.)

Alveolus. The gum bearing the teeth.

Anabolism. Synthesis of substances into more complex compounds.

Anaerobe. An organism which lives only in the absence of oxygen.

Antibiotic. A substance produced by or derived from micro-organisms which inhibits the growth of or destroys other micro-organisms.

Antibody. A serum protein (globulin) made by lymphatic tissue in response to the presence of an antigen and often resulting in destruction of the antigen.

Antigen. A foreign substance, usually a protein, which, when introduced into the body, causes the formation of antibodies. (See also 'Immunity'.)

Antiseptic. A chemical substance, usually made synthetically, which inhibits growth of micro-organisms.

Autogenous. Derived from the same individual; his own.

Bactericidal. Causing death of bacteria.

Bacteriostatic. Causing inhibition of growth of bacteria.

Canthus. See Fig. 104.

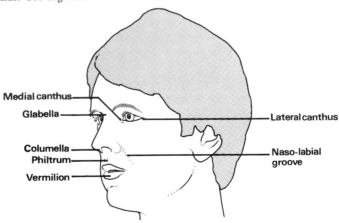

Fig. 104. *Anatomical landmarks of the face.*

Catabolism. The breakdown of body tissue. Opposite of *anabolism*.

Cellulitis. A spreading inflammation in subcutaneous tissue, characterised by a red flush and often due to streptococci.

Colloid. A state of matter in which large molecules (such as starch or proteins) are suspended in a fluid; they do not settle under the influence of gravity.

Columella. See Fig. 104.

Dermis. The inner vascular and sensitive layer of the skin.

Dialysate. Substances which pass through the semi-permeable membrane during dialysis.

Dialysis. The separation of electrolytes and proteins in solution by placing different concentrations of them on either side of a semi-permeable membrane. Electrolytes cross the membrane rapidly, while the proteins cross slowly or not at all.

Distal. Farthest from the midline of the body or root of the limb.

Ectropion. An out-turning of the eyelid so that the eyelid margin does not make contact with the eyeball. The condition may occur as the result of injury, removal of too much eyelid skin at surgery or, in the elderly, from loss of tissue elasticity. It leads to *epiphora* and conjunctivitis.

Electrolytes. Ions (such as sodium or potassium) which, when in solution, will conduct electricity.

Entropion. An in-turning of the eyelid margins which produces irritation and corneal ulceration.

Epidermis. The outer, non-vascular layer of the skin.

Epiphora. Spillage of lacrimal secretions over the eyelid margin. May be due to blockage of the tear ducts or to ectropion.

Fistula. An abnormal communication between two body cavities, such as the intestine and bladder, or a cavity and the body surface. A *sinus* is an abnormal blind-ending track which opens on to the surface or into a cavity. A fistula or sinus may fail to close due to:

1. Presence of a foreign body or dead tissue such as sequestrum.

2. Dense scarring or nearby muscle activity preventing contraction of the wound.

3. Ingrowth of epithelium lining the track.

4. Discharge of urine or faeces, or inadequate drainage.

5. Tuberculosis or actinomycosis.

Haemoglobin. The molecule which carries oxygen in the red blood cells; the molecule contains a protein (globin) and iron.

Haematocrit. See *packed cell volume.*

Hyperbaric oxygen. When a patient is placed in a chamber in which the atmospheric pressure is raised (hyperbaric), his tissues take up oxygen at increased rates. When a skin flap is temporarily deprived of oxygen, treatment with hyperbaric oxygen may allow time for the circulation to improve. It also has been used in the treatment of gas-gangrene (since the causative organism, *Clostridium*, cannot survive in the presence of oxygen) and to increase the sensitivity of tumours to the effects of radiotherapy.

Immunity. A reaction of the body to the effects of invasion by a foreign substance such as smallpox or mumps virus, or foreign tissue.

It is thought that a cell in the yolk sac migrates into the developing embryo, multiplies and produces 'immune centres'. These differentiate into two systems – lymphoid cell-based and humoral-based.

Lymphoid system. The thymus gland in the chest of the child produces T lymphocytes. In adulthood these are produced in bone marrow and lymph nodes. When foreign antigens enter the body, T lymphocytes move towards them to destroy them.

Humoral system. Bone marrow (B) cells produce large protein molecules – immunoglobulins. These are antibodies which react with the foreign antigens

resulting in an inflammatory response and usually, in destruction of the antigen.
These immune mechanisms are weakened by diabetes mellitus, malignancy, uraemia, malnutrition and corticosteroid drugs.

Immunization. 1. *Active immunization.* The injection of a dead or non-virulent strain of an organism, or of a toxin (vaccine) causes the body to develop antibodies (see *immunity*) against it. If an infection with a virulent strain of the same organism is later contracted, the antibodies previously produced will reduce its effects. In order to maintain the production of antibodies, active immunization must be repeated at intervals. Active immunisation does not give immediate protection against the organism, since it takes time (and often more than one injection) for antibodies to be produced.

Examples: Tetanus toxoid, BCG (bacille Calmette-Guerin)

2. *Passive Immunization.* Antibodies prepared either in an animal (antiserum) or another human (immunoglobulin) are injected into the patient. Immediate protection is given but the effect is short-lived since the injected antibodies are destroyed.

Examples: human antitetanus immunoglobulin (Humotet), antirabies immunoglobulin.

Serum reactions (such as urticaria or bronchospasm) may occur, particularly with antibodies prepared in animals, and may be life threatening. Serum reaction is prevented by:

(a) Giving a small dose of the immunoglobulin 30 minuutes before injecting the full dose (for example giving 0.2 ml of Humotet before the remaining 0.8 ml), in order to detect a hypersensitive patient.

(b) Giving chlorpheniramine 10 mg i.m. ten minutes before immunizing.

In the established case:

(a) Give 0.2 to 0.5 ml of adrenaline 1:1000 subcutaneously slowly over 1 minute.

(b) If convulsing, give 50 mg of thiopentone 2.5% intravenously.

(c) For laryngeal oedema and stridor, puncture the cricothyroid membrane in the neck with a large bore (aspirating) needle and administer oxygen.

(d) For pulmonary oedema, give 100 mg of hydrocortisone succinate intravenously.

(e) For cardiac arrest, perform external cardiac massage.

Malignant hyperthermia. A rare complication of anaesthesia which may be fatal. During or within an hour or two of the operation, the temperature rises, the pulse and respiration become rapid or irregular and the muscles go into spasm. The patient may become cyanosed and sweaty. Urgent treatment is necessary and consists of sponging with ice-cold cloths, and rectal washouts with ice-cold water to keep the temperature at 36°C. Oxygen is administered. Further cooling may be achieved with cold intravenous 0.9% sodium chloride. Dantrolene (1 mg/kg) is given intravenously.

Micrognathia. Underdevelopment of the mandible, due to a failure of mandibular growth resulting from, for example, infection or fracture in childhood. When it persists into adult life, it can be masked by:

1. Grafting iliac crest bone onto the outside of the mandible.

2. Incising a furrow in the sulcus in front of the lower front teeth, lining it with a skin graft and inserting a dental mould (for grosser degrees of micrognathia).

3. Cutting the ramus of each mandible horizontally and sliding forwards the lower part to bring forward the chin (genioplasty). The position is held by dental cap splints until the bone has united.

4. Inserting a silicone prosthesis under the skin of the point of the chin. Apart from 3., these procedures do not, of course, alter the dental malalignment.

Myoglobin. The protein (globin) in muscle which stores oxygen.

Nitrogen balance. The difference between the amount of nitrogen (protein and amino-acids) taken into the body by all routes and the amount lost (mainly in the urine as urea).

Osmolarity. The osmotic concentration of a solution. The amount of water in any particular compartment of the body is determined by the number of particles (of electrolytes or proteins) attracting water there. This attraction is the osmolarity of the fluid concerned. Osmotic diuretics such as mannitol, given intravenously, attract water into the circulation out of body tissues. Water in the circulation is then conveyed to the kidneys where it is excreted.

Packed cell volume. The ratio of red blood cells to whole blood.

Passive movement. Movement at a joint controlled by the attendant, for example the physiotherapist, and not by the patient.

Phagocyte. A cell which is capable of ingesting micro-organisms and foreign particles.

Philtrum. See Fig. 104.

Prognathism. Overgrowth of the mandible causing protrusion of the lower jaw and malocclusion of the teeth. This may be corrected by excising a block of bone from the mandible, wiring the two parts and fixing the teeth in the correct alignment with dental cap splints.

Proximal. Nearer to the midline of the body or root of a limb. Opposite to *distal*.

Pyrogen. A substance capable of producing a fever.

Radiotherapy. The irradiation of cells with highly charged particles. This prevents multiplication or causes alterations in their genetic structure. It offers a good cure rate for many skin tumours and may be the treatment of choice for patients unfit for surgery. It is not used for lesions of the eyelids, nose tip or pinna, as closeness to the eye or necrosis of cartilage prevent acceptable results.

The reduction in blood supply caused by irradiation makes subsequent surgery in the event of tumour recurrence more difficult; it is often difficult to skin graft irradiated tissue and flaps are prone to suture dehiscence and infection.

Serum. The fluid remaining after blood has clotted. It is essentially plasma without the clotting factors.

Sinus. See *fistula*

Tattooing. An electrically driven reciprocating needle implants pigment into the dermis. The pigments used include carbon (blue-black), mercuric sulphide (red), cobalt aluminate (light blue), chromic oxide (green), cadmium sulphide (yellow), iron oxide (brown) and titanium oxide (white). These must be sterilised. The amateur uses soot or indian ink. The surgeon uses pigments to simulate a desired skin colour, a skin feature (such as an areola) or to camouflage a skin blemish (such as a capillary haemangioma).

Complications include:

1. Inoculation of hepatitis virus, syphilis and tuberculosis.
2. Allergy to the pigment.
3. Cellulitis.

Thermography. A means of recording changes in the skin temperature by detecting infra red emission from the surface. Areas of skin at the same temperature (isotherms) are represented by the same tone of grey (or if a colour code is used, by the same colour) on the monitor screen, so that tone or colour changes signify temperature differences. Thermography has been used to detect areas of denervated skin (which are cool) and to determine the depth of burns.

Tourniquet. Most operations on the hand and forearm require an operative field which is not obscured by bleeding. This is achieved by applying a tourniquet to the upper arm over a padding of orthopaedic wool. The hand and arm are exsanguinated by an Esmarch rubber bandage. The tourniquet is inflated to 200 mmHg and the time is noted. To avoid permanent damage to tissues from prolonged lack of a blood supply, the surgeon should be informed by the scrub nurse when the tourniquet has been in place for 1 hour and then at 15 minute intervals thereafter.

Ulcer. A discontinuity in an epithelial surface. Causes include:

1. *Non-specific.* Wounds, physical and chemical agents, dental irritation.

2. *Specific.* Tuberculosis, syphilis.

3. *Trophic* (*trophe* = Greek, nutrition). Impairment of nutrition for example in ischaemia or anaesthesia (Raynaud's disease, diabetes mellitus, spina bifida, leprosy, nerve injury).

4. *Gravitational* (see Chapter 11).

5. *Malignant.* For example squamous or basal cell carcinoma.

Treatment includes:

1. Treatment of the underlying cause.

2. Eusol dressings.

3. 1% zinc sulphate applications, which promote the formation of granulation tissue.

4. Removal of 'proud flesh' by excision, curettage or silver nitrate.

5. Chronic ulcers may respond to infra red, short wave or ultraviolet light therapy.

6. Amnion laid into the ulcer to promote healing. The amnion is cleaned with sterile gauze, washed in hypochlorite, rinsed in saline and cut to size. It is applied as a skin graft. The rough side (chorion) stimulates granulation tissue; the smooth side promotes epithelialisation. Amnion may be stored at 4°C in saline.

Vermilion. The red mucosa of the lip (Fig. 104).

Viscosity. The ability of a fluid to flow. Low viscosity fluids flow more readily than high viscosity fluids. Normal plasma viscosity is 1.50 to 1.72 centipoise.

Index